JOURNAL FOR THE STUDY OF THE OLD TESTAMENT SUPPLEMENT SERIES

367

Sheffield Academic Press
A Continuum imprint

Signs of Jonah

Reading and Rereading
in Ancient Yehud

Ehud Ben Zvi

Journal for the Study of the Old Testament
Supplement Series 367

To Perla, Amos, Naamah and Micha

Copyright © 2003 Sheffield Academic Press
A Continuum imprint

Published by Sheffield Academic Press Ltd
The Tower Building, 11 York Road, London SE1 7NX
370 Lexington Avenue, New York NY 10017-6550

www.continuumbooks.com

British Library Cataloguing-in-Publication Data
A catalogue record for this book is available from the British Library

Typeset by Sheffield Academic Press
Printed on acid-free paper in Great Britain by Bookcraft Ltd, Midsomer Norton, Bath

ISBN   0-8264-6268-5

CONTENTS

ABBREVIATIONS

AB	Anchor Bible
ABRL	Anchor Bible Reference Library
AJSRev	*Association for Jewish Studies Review*
ASOR	American Schools of Oriental Research
AusBR	*Australian Biblical Review*
AUSS	*Andrews University Seminary Studies*
BBR	*Bulletin for Biblical Research*
BEATAJ	*Beiträge zur Erforschung des Altes Testament und des antiken Judentum*
Bib	*Biblica*
BibInt	*Biblical Interpretation*
BN	*Biblische Notizen*
BR	*Biblical Research*
BZ	*Biblische Zeitschrift*
BZAW	Beheifte zur ZAW
CB	Coniectanea biblica
CBQ	*Catholic Biblical Quarterly*
CCARJ	*Central Conference of American Rabbis Journal*
CurrTM	*Currents in Theology and Mission*
DBAT	Dielheimer Blätter zum Alten Testamen und seiner Rezeption in der Alten Kirche
DBI	J.H. Hayes (ed.), *Dictionary of Biblical Interpretation* (Nashville: Abingdon Press, 1999)
DJD	*Discoveries in the Judaean Desert*
EstBib	*Estudios bíblicos*
FOTL	The Forms of the Old Testament Literature
FRLANT	Forschungen zur Religion und Literatur des Alten und Neuen Testaments
GTJ	*Grace Theological Journal*
HAR	*Hebrew Annual Review*
HBT	*Horizons in Biblical Theology*
HS	*Hebrew Studies*
IB	*Interpreter's Bible*
ITC	International Theological Commentary
JBL	*Journal of Biblical Literature*
JBQ	*Jewish Bible Quarterly*
JETS	*Journal of the Evangelical Theological Society*

JHS	*Journal of Hebrew Scriptures*
JJS	*Journal of Jewish Studies*
JNES	*Journal of Near Eastern Studies*
JNSL	*Journal of Northwest Semitic Langugages*
JPS	Jewish Publication Society
JQR	*Jewish Quarterly Review*
JSOT	*Journal for the Study of the Old Testament*
JSOTSup	*Journal for the Study of the Old Testament*, Supplement Series
Jud	*Judaism*
LA	*Liber Anuus. Studium Biblicum Franciscanum*
NIB	New Interpreter's Bible
NJPSV	New Jewish Publication Society Version = 'Tanakh' version
NRSV	New Revised Standard Version
OBO	Orbis biblicus et orientalis
OTE	*Old Testament Essays*
OTG	Old Testament Guides
OTL	Old Testament Library
OTP	James Charlesworth (ed.), *Old Testament Pseudepigrapha*
OTS	Oudtestamentischen Studiën
PNW-SBL	Pacific Northwest Society of Biblical Literature
RB	*Revue Biblique*
REB	Revised English Bible
REJ	*Revue des études juives*
RHPR	*Revue d'histoire et de philosophie religieuses*
SBLDS	Society of Biblical Literature Dissertation Series
SBLSP	*Society of Biblical Literature Seminar Papers*
SBT	Studies in Biblical Theology
SEÅ	*Svensk exegetisk årsbok*
SJOT	*Scandinavian Journal of the Old Testament*
STAR	Studies in Theology and Religion
Tbei	*Theologische Beiträge*
TLOT	*Theological Lexicon of the Old Testament*
TynBul	*Tyndale Bulletin*
TZ	*Theologische Zeitschrift*
UBS	United Bible Societies
UMI	University of Michigan
VT	*Vetus Testamentum*
VTSup	Supplements to Vetus Testamentum
WBC	World Biblical Commentary
ZAW	*Zeitschrift für die alttestamentliche Wissenschaft*

Note: The list above does not include references to journal, series or societies whose names are not abbreviated in this volume (e.g. *Maarav*, Orita, *Beit Miqra*, Soundings, Brit Olam, Canadian Society of Biblical Studies).

Chapter 1

INTRODUCTION

The Book of Jonah[1] (hereafter, 'the book of Jonah') has fascinated millions of people through generations. The book and its imagery have influenced such diverse fields as art, literature, liturgy and theology. The book has been used for innumerable purposes, from sermons to political debates to the writing of edifying children's literature. Its imagery is among the best known of all biblical imagery.

To be sure, Jonah has some of the charm associated with simple but fantastic narratives characterized by an abundance of folkloristic motifs.[2] Part of the appeal of the book and its continuous influence through generations is due to the presence of such folkloristic motifs, because they are memorable. Simple narratives also tend to be easy to remember.[3] In addition, the book of Jonah is a strange book within the Twelve, and even within the Hebrew Bible as a whole.[4] Just as the use of folkloristic motifs

---

1.   By the term 'Book of Jonah' I refer to the book in its present form. Hypothetical forerunners, whether in the form of written sources or orally transmitted stories, do not qualify as the particular social product we call 'the book of Jonah'. Incidentally, redactional hypotheses about Jonah have not received as much attention and support as in the case of other prophetic books. For a survey of proposed—and unverifiable—redactional histories of Jonah, and for a new proposal, see J. Nogalski, *Redactional Processes in the Book of the Twelve* (BZAW, 218; Berlin: W. de Gruyter, 1993), pp. 255-69.

2.   See, for instance, P. Trible, 'Studies in the Book of Jonah' (PhD dissertation, Columbia University, 1963, UMI order no. 65-7479), pp. 146-51; *idem*, 'The Book of Jonah', in L.E. Keck, D.L. Petersen *et al.* (eds.), *The New Interpreter's Bible* (Nashville, TN: Abingdon Press, 1996), pp. 467-68.

3.   Yet its disarming simplicity conceals a large number of vexing questions and a large degree of equivocality and plain polysemy, as the following chapters will demonstrate again and again.

4.   As E. Bickerman stressed when he included it among its 'four strange books'. See E. Bickerman, *Four Strange Books in the Bible: Jonah, Daniel, Kohelet, Esther*

carries rhetorical effects that contribute to its memorability, so does 'strangeness' within a repertoire. Strangeness calls attention to its carrier and causes the book to stand out within the accepted repertoire of the readership.[5]

Prophetic books were used to educate or better socialize the communities that accepted them as authoritative texts. They encouraged particular sets of theological outlooks, norms, constructions of the past, and discouraged others. Memorable imagery and a good plot served these socializing purposes. Jonah, more than many other prophetic books, has been associated with a great variety of basic communal meta-narratives, such as those involving sin and repentance, divine judgment and compassion, death and resurrection, rejection and acceptance of the divine will, God's power over all creation, universalism and nationalistic particularism.[6]

Thus, the fact that Jonah is an excellent and memorable story served well to channel and socialize the people's imagination in communities of readers. Rather than each person running with her or his imagination in disparate ways, the reading (and reading to others)[7] of Jonah created a frame within which shared, interpersonal imagination is possible. So, for instance, images of sea monsters turned into that of 'the fish', images of mythical great cities of sinners into Nineveh, and wandering thoughts about turning away from the normative behaviour in the community, which were often associated with the divine will, were suddenly embodied in Jonah. Imagination was not only socially channelled, but also chan-

(New York: Schocken Books, 1967). On these matters, see Chapter 6.

5.   Of course, this is a limited strangeness. There are socially agreed (and construed) limits that, if trespassed, cause the book to be excluded completely rather than stand up within an accepted repertoire. For instance, had it advocated the cult of Ashera or Baal, it would have been rejected by the mentioned postmonarchic communities. In fact, it is most likely that it would not have been written at all.

6.   See Chapter 9. It is worth stressing that some of these meta-narratives existed in, and were central to, the society within which and for which the book was written. In fact, most of the basic meta-narratives of this society are reflected in the book. The only salient exception, namely, that associated with the centrality of Jerusalem/Zion and related matters is only a false exception. See Chapter 8.

7.   The book was not always read, but often read *to* those unable to read for themselves, that is the vast majority of the population in ancient times, and for that matter at almost all times in history. On these issues see E. Ben Zvi, 'Introduction: Writings, Speeches, and the Prophetic Books-Setting an Agenda', in E. Ben Zvi and M.H. Floyd (eds.), *Writings and Speech in Israelite and Ancient Near Eastern Prophecy* (Symposium, 10; Atlanta: Society of Biblical Literature, 2000), pp. 1-29.

nelled to something. The (interpersonal) activities of reading, rereading and reading to others the book of Jonah contributed to the shaping of partially shared imagination that became intertwined with, and led to what was presented as the message of a prophetic book accepted by the community as authoritative and legitimate. Thus, imagination was channelled to serve an ideological or theological goal; namely, to bring the community's attention to the book and through it to central and authoritative meta-narratives, such as those mentioned above.

The creation of a (partially shared) space of imagination among the readership community, and the reaffirmation of the basic meta-narratives held by the group contributed to an ongoing positive self-identification of its members, to the creation of borders around it,[8] and contributed to the constant shaping of its worldview and world of knowledge.[9]

This book is about the reception of the book of Jonah. But a historian writes it. I am mainly interested in the book of Jonah as a historical source for the study of ancient Israel. To be sure, by this I do not mean to resurrect the by now almost defunct and plainly wrong enterprise of using the basic narrative of Jonah, taken at its literal value, as a source for the study of such matters as the history of the Assyrian empire[10] or ancient marine biology.

Unlike other historians who deal with prophetic books, I do not propose to focus on the historical author/s or editor/s of the book of Jonah, nor on their intentions. Instead I propose to focus first on the reception of the text,

8.   These borders separate those who read or 'correctly' read the book—and similar books—from those who do not. Of course, within this world, only those who read the book correctly have access to the true Word of God (i.e. the message of the authoritative prophetic book).

9.   It is worth stressing that these social processes were dynamic, not static. Changes in the community of readers affected their readings and their imagination, but still the latter remained attached to the book of Jonah (and to other authoritative or sacred literature). Similarly, the same community may have approached the book in different ways, for different purposes and in number of possible settings. These changes also affect the way in which the book shapes the imagination of the community. The same holds true for all other prophetic books (see my contribution, 'The Prophetic Book: A Key Form of Prophetic Literature', in M.A. Sweeney and E. Ben Zvi [eds.], *The Changing Face of Form Criticism for the Twenty-First Century* [Grand Rapids: Eerdmans, forthcoming]).

10.   'Almost defunct' implies that here and there one may still find someone promoting such positions. For one such case see M.R. Lehmann, 'הרקע להתנהגותו של יונה נביא על־פי מקורות מקראיים', *Beit Miqkra* 35 (1999), pp. 348-50.

that is, to focus on the *readers* and their *readings*. The reasons for this focus on the recipient side involve not only the speculative character of reconstructions of the writers' intentions, but also the fact that the readers of the book had access to the written text, rather than to the intentions of the writer. The *book*, not the writer, was read, reread, studied and read to others. As such, *it* reflects and shapes society.

To be sure, most historical readers of Jonah, including its primary readers, have endeavoured and claimed to 'understand' it. But the emphasis on the readership is justified, even if one assumes, as it is most likely, that the ancient readers on which this study focuses thought that 'to understand' was basically to meet the interactive/communicative expectations of an authoritative communicator.[11]

Since the book was considered to provide legitimate knowledge about YHWH and YHWH's ways, and as such was included in the accepted repertoire of prophetic books, the communicator must have been construed as 'authoritative'. Had this not been the case, there would have been no reason to continue studying, copying, reading and reading to others this text. But the authoritative communicator was certainly not the actual historical author of the book (or a composite figure of authors and editors). The authoritative communicator was the implied author that the readers construed through their readings and rereadings of the text (see below). Readings were (and are, in general) by necessity socially and historically dependent.[12] These ancient readers approached a text with a particular

11. Cf. G. Rusch, 'Comprehension vs. Understanding of Literature', in S. Tötösy de Zepetnek and I. Sywenky (eds.), *The Systemic and Empirical Approach to Literature and Culture as Theory and Application* (Siegen: Siegen University Press, 1997), pp. 107-19 (115).

12. As demonstrated by the large number of readings of Jonah that have been attested. See, among others, R.H. Bowers, *The Legend of Jonah* (The Hague: Martinus Nijhoff, 1971); Bickerman, *Four Strange Books*, pp. 3-49; J. Limburg, *Jonah* (OTL; Louisville, KY: Westminster/John Knox Press, 1993), pp. 99-123; Y. Sherwood, 'Rocking the Boat: Jonah and New Historicism', *Bib Int* 5 (1997), pp. 364-402; *idem*, 'Cross-Currents in the Book of Jonah: Some Jewish and Cultural Midrashim on a Traditional Text', *Bib Int* 6 (1998), pp. 49-79; *idem*, *A Biblical Text and its Afterlives: The Survival of Jonah in Western Culture* (Cambridge: Cambridge University Press, 2000); U. Steffen, *Die Jona-Geschichte: Ihre Auslegung und Darstellung im Judentum, Christentum und Islam* (Neukirchen–Vluyn: Neukirchener Verlag, 1994); and see Chapter 9 in this volume. Different understandings of the book of Jonah shape the implied author in different ways. For a short survey of the history of interpretation of Jonah see J. Magonet, 'Book of Jonah', in J.H. Hayes (ed.), *Dictionary of Biblical*

world of knowledge. The latter included, in addition to the obvious linguistic abilities to decode the words of the text, ideological or theological
viewpoints, a construction of the past, an understanding of the present,
hopes and fears for the future, a literary/theological awareness that set
their book within the framework of the general cultural repertoire, as well
as literary sensibilities. Thus the nature of the communicator with whom
the actual ancient readers and rereaders of the book of Jonah interacted
was dependent on their particular worldview and world of knowledge.

Although in Chapter 9 I deal with many historical communities, the
focus of this work is certainly on the ancient communities of readers for
whom and within whom the book was written.[13] What did the book of
Jonah tell them? And, more importantly, what does the book of Jonah tell
us about them?

This particular choice is not meant to convey a sense of hierarchy. The
ancient communities I will be focusing on are as important and as worthy
of study as any other community of readers. My focus reflects my
professional guild; it is not about hierarchy but about occupation. Since I
am a historian of ancient Israel, it is only natural that my focus is on the
primary readership/s for which the book of Jonah was written. Historians
of other periods and social groups are better equipped to study other
readerships. My only contribution to such endeavours is the minimal
theoretical frame developed in Chapter 9.[14]

Methodologically, I will focus on textually inscribed markers that can
be reasonably assumed to have led the intended readership to prefer
certain reading strategies over others, to ponder on certain matters but not
others; and above all on the likely readings and rereadings of this intended
readership. The reason for this choice is simple: it is very unlikely that the
original or *historical* readership/s for whom the book of Jonah was written

---

Interpretation (Nashville: Abingdon Press, 1999), pp. 620-22.

13. From the fact that readers read a book from within a particular world of
knowledge and social location necessarily follows that any study of the way in which
the book has been read (or reread) *has* to focus on a particular community of readers—
or rereaders—and accordingly be explicit about the identity of that community. As
explicitly mentioned here, this book focuses on the original rereadership/s for which
the book of Jonah was composed. There are many other (re)readerships of the book of
Jonah. Centuries, cultural and geographical distances and other factors separate them.

14. Other readerships approached the book in a way that was governed by
substantially different but still—from their perspective—authoritative interpretative
keys. My only contribution to such matters is Chapter 9 of this volume, which focuses
on heuristic matters rather than on a register of interpretative approaches.

were much different from its *intended* readership.[15] A large variation
between the two would have rendered the book unintelligible for its target
readership, and as such it would not have been read, reread, studied and,
eventually, would not have been preserved.[16]

Reading, rereading and studying books that claim, and were considered,
authoritative by a certain society are social activities. They necessitated a
process of production of books that included writing, editing and copying.
They also required a system of storage and retrieval of texts. All these
activities demanded resources. Moreover, they required the existence of
some educational system to produce bearers of high literacy who were
able to read and study these texts, and at least a few who were able to
write or edit them. Such a system required the allocation of resources. A
historical analysis of the book of Jonah (or of any other prophetic book for
that matter) should take into account these socio-economic considerations.
The group of bearers of high literacy or literati within which the book of
Jonah was written and for whom it was written were an integral part of
their society and the 'system' governing their society, and so were their
social-literary activities. These considerations bring to the forefront the
interrelation between the literati and the socio-political elite (or inter-
related elites) that allocated resources in their times. From a systemic
perspective the question is not so much why the latter were supportive of
the works of the former, but in which way the works of the literati
contributed to the stability of the society.[17] The latter include both social
and ideological aspects. In both cases, the question of the interrelatedness
between the literati and the vast majority of the population turns out to be
a central matter. I have dealt elsewhere with matters of social realia and

15. Cf. D. Kraemer, 'The Intended Reader as a Key to Interpreting the Bavli',
Prooftexts 13 (1993), pp. 125-40.

16. Needless to say, all these activities also involved resources that were unlikely to
be committed for a book without any 'market'. To be sure, books may have a social
market as sacred icons, and in fact prophetic and other biblical books served in such a
role already in antiquity. Moreover, books were unintelligible to the vast majority of
the population, namely, anyone who was not a bearer of high literacy. Only after they
are read for generations and accepted in society as sacred, they may become such
icons. Yet it is unlikely that any society would accept for long such books if *no one*
could read (and 'decode') them.

17. Stability should not be misunderstood as inflexibility, opposition to change or
to the possibility of alternative responses. In fact, inflexibility most often leads to
instability. Flexibility and adaptability tend to contribute substantially to the ability of a
society to reproduce itself through generations, that is, to its stability.

the formation of prophetic literature, of symbiosis between literacy and orality, and with some questions involving aural and oral communication in ancient Israel.[18] It suffices here to state that these issues inform much of the discussion in this study.

Following the immense majority of scholars, I date the book of Jonah to the postmonarchic period.[19] Although I think that it is more likely that it

18. See, E. Ben Zvi, 'Introduction: Writings, Speeches'.

19. See, for instance, J.S. Ackerman, 'Jonah', in R. Alter and F. Kermode (eds.), *The Literary Guide to the Bible* (Cambridge: Belknap Press, 1987), pp. 235-43; L.C. Allen, *The Books of Joel, Obadiah, Jonah, and Micah* (Grand Rapids, MN: Eerdmans, 1976), pp. 185-88; K. Almbladh, *Studies in the book of Jonah* (Studia Semitica Upsaliensia 7; Uppsala: Uppsala University, 1986), esp. pp. 41-46; A.J. Band, 'Swallowing Jonah: The Eclipse of Parody', *Prooftexts* 10 (1990), pp. 177-95, esp. pp. 179, 184, 192-94; E. Bickerman, *Four Strange Books*, p. 29; A. Brenner, 'לשנו של ספר יונה כמדד לקביעת זמן חיבורו', *Beit Miqra* 24 (1979), pp. 396-405; R.E. Clements, 'The Purpose of the Book of Jonah', in J.A. Emerton *et al.* (eds.), *Congress Volume Edinburgh 1974* (VTSup, 28; Leiden: E.J. Brill, 1975), pp. 16-28; B. Dan, 'לשון ספר יונה בספרות מחקר עיון והערכה נוספים', *Beit Miqra* 41 (1996), pp. 344-68; J. Day, 'Problems in the Interpretation of the Book of Jonah', in A. S. van der Woude (ed.), *In Quest for the Past: Studies on Israelite Religion, Literature and Prophets. Papers Read at the Joint British–Dutch Old Testament Conference, Held at Elspeet, 1988* (OTS, 26; Leiden: E.J. Brill, 1990), pp. 32-47 (34-36); T.E. Fretheim, *The Message of Jonah* (Minneapolis, MN: Augsburg, 1977), pp. 34-37; F.W. Golka, 'Jonah', in G.A.F. Knight and F.W. Golka, *Revelation of God: The Song of Songs and Jonah* (ITC; Grand Rapids, MI: Eerdmans, 1988), pp. 65-136 (70-72); A. Hurvitz, 'The History of a Legal Formula כל אשר חפץ עשה (Psalms cxv 3, cxxxv 6', *VT* 32 (1982), pp. 257-67 (263); A. LaCoque and P.-E. Lacoque, *Jonah: A Psycho-Religious Approach to the Prophet* (Columbia, SC: University of South Carolina Press, 1990), esp. pp. 26-48; G.M. Landes, 'A Case for the Sixth-Century BCE Dating for the Book of Jonah', in P.H. Williams Jr and T. Hiebert (eds.), *Realia Dei: Essays in Archaeology and Biblical Interpretation in Honor of Edward F. Campbell, Jr. at his Retirement* (Atlanta: Scholars Press, 1999), pp. 100-116; Limburg, *Jonah*, pp. 28-31; J. Magonet, 'Book of Jonah', p. 621; Nogalski, *Redactional Processes*, pp. 255-62, 270-73—includes a good survey of redactional theories; D.F. Payne, 'Jonah from the Perspective of its Audience', *JSOT* 13 (1979), pp. 3-12; E. Qimron, 'לשנו של ספר יונה כמדד לקביעת זמן חיבורו', *Beit Miqra* 25 (1980), pp. 181-82; A. Rofé, *The Prophetical Stories* (Jerusalem: Magnes Press, 1988), pp. 152-59; R.B. Salters, *Jonah and Lamentations* (OTG; Sheffield: Sheffield Academic Press, 1994), pp. 23-27; J.M. Sasson, *Jonah* (AB, 24B; New York: Doubleday, 1990), pp. 20-28, esp. pp. 26-27, and note his remark that 'for centuries may separate the invention and oral circulation of stories about errant holy men from the artfully narrated and theologically sophisticated book we now call "Jonah" ' (p. 28)—the latter, of course, is the object of this study of the book of Jonah; U. Simon, יונה עם מבוא ופירוש (מקרא לישראל); Tel Aviv: Am Oved, 1992), pp. 31-33;

was written and first read and reread in Persian Yehud rather than in Ptolemaic Judah—or neo-Babylonian Judah for that matter[20]—the conclusions advanced here are not dependent on any particular date within the postmonarchic period.

Further, I will not attempt to provide a narrow date for the book of Jonah. More importantly for this study, I will not attempt to locate the intended and primary readerships in any narrow range of years within the postmonarchic period. Not only are attempts at precise dating fraught with insurmountable problems,[21] but in any case such a precise date would not contribute to the present discussion. It is unlikely that the world of the Jerusalemite literati, within which these primary readerships lie, underwent essential changes during these years.[22]

idem, Jonah (JPS Bible Commentary; Philadelphia: Jewish Publication Society of America, 1999), pp. xli-xlii; S. Schumann, 'Jona und die Weishet: Das prophetische Wort in einer zwedeutigen Wirklichkeit', *TZ* 45 (1989), pp. 73-80; M.A. Sweeney, *The Twelve Prophets* (2 vols.; Collegeville, MN; Liturgical Press, 2000), I, pp. 306-307; P. Trible, *Studies*, pp. 104-16, includes a good survey on the matter; H.W. Wolff, *Obadiah and Jonah: A Commentary* (Minneapolis, MN: Augsburg, 1986 [German, 1977]), pp. 76-78. The fact that all these scholars, despite their at times very substantial differences, agree that it is more likely that Jonah was written after 587 BCE than before is highly significant.

To be sure, full unanimity is beyond reach, on this and almost on any matter in biblical studies. For the proposal that the book of Jonah was written in the monarchic period see Y. Kaufmann, תולדות האמונה הישראלית (4 vols.; Tel Aviv: Mosad Bialik, 1938–56), II, pp. 279-87; B. Porten, 'Baalshamem and the Date of the Book of Jonah', in M. Carrez *et al.* (eds.), *De la Tôrah au Messie: Etudes d'exégèse et d'herméneutique bibliques offertes à Henri Cazelles pour ses 25 années d'enseignement à l'Institut Catholique de Paris, octobre 1979* (Paris: Desclée, 1981), pp. 237-44. For a critique of these works see, for instance, U. Simon, *Jonah*, p. xli, and Nogalski, *Redactional Processes*, pp. 255-56 n. 17, respectively. For the position that the book could have written any time between c. 750–250 BCE, see, for instance, D. Stuart, *Hosea–Jonah* (WBC, 31; Waco, TX: Word Books, 1987), pp. 432-33.

20. My position here is based on socio-economic considerations associated with the production of authoritative books in and for a small community. See E. Ben Zvi, 'The Urban Center of Jerusalem and the Development of the Literature of the Hebrew Bible', in W.G. Aufrecht, N.A. Mirau and S.W. Gauley (eds.), *Aspects of Urbanism in Antiquity* (JSOTSup, 244; Sheffield: Sheffield Academic Press, 1997), pp. 194-209.

21. 'We conclude, then, that the book of Jonah was written during the Second Temple period but we have no way to determine whether it should be dated as early as the late sixth century or the fifth or even the fourth century BCE…' (Simon, *Jonah*, p. xli).

22. The substantial range of observations about their world that I advance in Ben

By far the most important divide is between the monarchic and the postmonarchic period.[23] To state the obvious, there were major political, social and demographic differences between the two polities. The latter was much smaller, poorer, and centered around the Temple and its teachings than the former. Moreover, postmonarchic communities understood the events around 586 BCE as a major tragedy, and as a watershed in their past. Issues associated with the fall of monarchic Judah and its temple and with the possibility of a future restoration and elevation of Israel to its proper place in the divine economy loomed large in the postmonarchic communities. They captivated their imaginations and became central nodes in their theological thinking.[24]

Readers of this introduction have most likely already noticed references not only to reading but also to rereading. These references will be ubiquitous in this work. The concept of rereading is of major importance,

Zvi, 'Introduction: Writings, Speeches', apply to the period in general.

23. The discontinuity here is of a completely different order that the one between Yehud in fifth and Yehud in the fourth century.

24. One has to admit that had the worldview regarding 'foreigners' reflected in Ezra–Nehemiah been dominant in Yehud during the second half of the postmonarchic period, one could argue that two significantly different pre-Ezra and post-Ezra periods can be or should be discerned. But there is no evidence to support that such a worldview governed the Yehudite polity and its discourse for any substantial period. Leaving aside the question of the historicity of these books, references to 'acceptable' mixed marriages are abundant in the discourse of the period. See Deut. 21.10-14, the stories of Zipporah, Aseneth, Tamar, Ruth, the multiple places in Chronicles in which exogamy is explicitly mentioned (e.g. 1 Chron. 2.34-35 and cf. Knoppers's work on the Judahite line in Chronicles that certainly demonstrates exogamy repeatedly; see G.N. Knoppers, 'Intermarriage, Social Complexity, and Ethnic Diversity in the Genealogy of Judah', *JBL* 120 [2001], pp. 15-30; *idem*, ' "Great among his Brothers" but Who is He? Heterogeneity in the Composition of Judah', *JHS* 3–4 (2000); available at www.purl.org/jhs and www.jhsonline.org). On these matters, see K.S. Winslow, 'Ethnicity and Exogamy in the Bible' (paper presented at the 2000 annual meeting of the PNW-SBL, held in Spokane, WA). For an instructive, general reconstruction of the period and its discourse in volume II of R. Albertz, *A History of the Israelite Religion in the Old Testament Period* (2 vols.; Louisville, KY: Westminster/John Knox Press, 1994 [German, 1992]). It should also be mentioned that had an Ezra-like worldview regarding 'foreigners' been dominant in Persian Yehud, that 'fact' would be of little direct relevance to the understanding of the text of Jonah in its historical context. The position that the main purpose of the book of Jonah in its primary setting was to address the relations between Israel and 'the nations' should be rejected. On these matters see, among others, R.E. Clements, 'Purpose', esp. pp. 17-20. See also Chapter 7 of this volume.

because there are significant differences in the way people *reread* texts as opposed to their *first* reading of the same text, and all but the very first reading of a prophetic text were rereadings.[25] Rereaders, and particularly those who meditate upon the text, are aware of the entire text even as they reread its first line. They may make connections between different units not only according to their sequence in the book, but in multidirectional and crosslinked paths. They are also likely to find signposts that remind them of particular issues dealt with in the book as a whole. Moreover, texts that are suitable for continuous rereading show at least some degree of double meaning, ambiguity and literary sophistication. The continuous rereading of YHWH's word—within a community that accepts the text as such—involves a particular mode of reading, namely, careful reading, studying and meditating upon (cf. Josh. 1.8; Hos. 14.10; Sir. 38.34–39.3). This approach to the act of reading and rereading is consistent with, and in fact requires, some polyvalence.[26] As it is shown in this volume, the book of Jonah is an excellent example in this regard. The writers of these books were clearly aware that they would be read and reread. And in any case, the 'market' tended to prefer and actively keep 'in use' books that were well suited for rereading.

Thus the text of the book of Jonah allowed and encouraged its intended rereaders to read the book in multiple ways, and from a variety of perspectives. Of course, this being the case, each of these rereadings can only be a 'partial' rereading. This study, and particularly Chapters 2 through to 5, demonstrates that these (at times contradictory) 'partial' rereadings inform and balance each other. As a result one may trace a well interwoven ideological tapestry that better reflected and shaped the theological or ideological discourses of the literati of the time than any reading if taken alone.[27] To be sure, a system in which multiple claims balance and inform each

25. On the importance of rereading, see, for instance, E. Ben Zvi, *Micah* (FOTL, 21B; Grand Rapids: Eerdmans, 2000), pp. 5-6 and passim; *idem, A Historical-Critical Study of the Book of Obadiah* (BZAW, 242; Berlin: W. de Gruyter, 1996), pp. 4-5, and passim.

26. See E. Ben Zvi, *Micah*, pp. 5-6 and passim. Cf. *idem, Obadiah*, pp. 3-5 and passim.

27. The process of creating such an ideological or theological tapestry through multiple readings of one book is somewhat comparable to the larger tapestry created by the reading and studying of different authoritative texts within a very limited circle of Jerusalemite literati, which is even responsible for their writing in their present form in the first place. On the latter issues, see my previous works, E. Ben Zvi, 'Urban Center', pp. 194-209; *idem*, 'Introduction: Writings, Speeches'.

other implies that none of these claims *taken separately from the others* was seen as universally valid, but rather as relative and contingent (see also Chapter 7). Not surprisingly, then, the multiplicity of meanings was not, and could not be, without limitations. Within a sea of multivocality, the few 'islands' of univocality are salient. This study points out some of these areas as they appear in Jonah (see, for instance, Chapters 2 and 7)

It has been almost universally recognized that the book of Jonah is different from the other prophetic books. In Chapter 6, I point out that atypical features serve in many ways to characterize the book of Jonah as a *meta-prophetic* book, and will have drawn the attention of the intended readership to such recognition.

The authorship and the primary readership of a book tend to be reflected in the book itself, and particularly if the book deals with issues that stand at the center of their self-understanding. As shown in Chapter 7, the burlesque tone of the book masks a critical discourse of the literati about themselves, their works and their own claims of knowledge. If there is some mockery in the book, to some extent it is self-mockery, or more precisely, it is transformed into a discourse that sets the producers of the texts and readings and their world in perspective by hinting at and reflecting crucial questions of self-understanding.

The world of knowledge and ideological horizons of the literati naturally permeate their works. Jonah is no exception. Chapter 8 deals with the pervasive presence of central concepts in the discourses of the Yehudite elite and literati (e.g. Jerusalem, Zion, Israel)[28] in the book of Jonah.

Any student of the history of interpretation of Jonah is aware of the bewildering variety of readings of the book of Jonah developed by different interpretative communities. Chapter 9 represents an attempt to develop a heuristic theoretical framework for the study of this variety of readings. This is the only chapter that deals with readers and rereaders within communities of interpretation other than postmonarchic Israel/Yehud.

This study, then, is not a verse-by-verse commentary, and nor does it follow the usual pattern of monographs on a particular biblical book or

---

28. On these concepts, I wrote elsewhere. See E. Ben Zvi, 'Inclusion in and Exclusion from Israel as Conveyed by the Use of the Term "Israel" in Postmonarchic Biblical Texts', in S.W. Holloway and L.K. Handy (eds.), *The Pitcher is Broken: Memorial Essays for Gosta. W. Ahlstrom* (JSOTSup, 190; Sheffield: JSOT Press, 1995), pp. 95-149, and *idem*, 'What Is New in Yehud? Some Considerations', in Rainer Albertz and Bob Becking (eds.), *Yahwism after the Exile* (STAR, 5; Assen: Van Gorcum, 2003), pp. 32-48.

theme associated with them. Further, it is not designed to be a comprehensive analysis of the book of Jonah. Rather here is a collection of 'explorations' on the book of Jonah carried out within the approach described above. The goal is to show through examples how this methodological approach sheds light on the study of the book of Jonah, and on the historical communities within which and for which the book was written.

Most of these explorations were first presented as papers at scholarly conferences since 1998.[29] I have attempted to keep some of their separate character to allow them to be read and understood by themselves. Yet they are interconnected in multiple ways, and I have indicated such connections at relevant points.

Before we begin our explorations on ancient readings and rereadings of Jonah a note concerning style is in order. Readers of this book will easily notice that I have avoided the use of the masculine pronoun for YHWH. Such a choice carries a price in terms of elegance of style and it should be explained in a work that deals with *history* and concepts of deity held in *ancient times*. The following is a concise summary of that explanation. The literati, whose characterizations of YHWH were reflected and shaped by the texts that eventually became included in the Hebrew Bible, imagined this deity as one who has not, and could not have, a female partner. YHWH was understood as the only figure that populated the realm of 'high god'.[30] Since YHWH was the sole member of the genus 'high god', the latter was imagined as one in which no intraspecies sexual (or gender) differentiation existed. As a result, YHWH had to be imagined by these

---

29. 'A Story of Jonahs', delivered at the Annual Meeting of the Pacific Northwest AAR/SBL, Portland, OR, May 1998; 'Nineveh's Fates and the Book of Jonah', delivered at the Annual Meeting of the Society of Biblical Literature in Orlando, FL, November 1998; 'Differentiation and Characterization of the Book of Jonah vis-à-vis the Other Prophetic Books', delivered at the Annual Meeting of the Pacific Northwest AAR/SBL, Tacoma, WA, May 1999; 'Infinite but Limited Diversity: A Heuristic, Theoretical Frame for Analyzing Different Interpretations of the Book of Jonah', delivered at the Annual Meeting of the Catholic Biblical Association, Notre Dame University, IN, August 1999; 'Producing and Reading the Book of Jonah in Antiquity: Some Reflections on How the World of the Readers/Producers May Be Reflected in the World of the Book', delivered at the Annual Meeting of the Pacific Northwest AAR/SBL, Spokane, WA, April 2000; 'Jonah, the Runaway Servant/Slave?', delivered at the Annual Meeting of the Canadian Society of Biblical Studies in Edmonton, May 2000. My sincere thanks are due to participants at these meetings for their feedback.

30. Other, less important heavenly beings were thought to inhabit the divine realm; see, for instance, Exod. 15.11; Ps. 97.7.

literati as a deity that fulfills the roles that within the discourse of 'the others' were assigned to both gods and goddesses. Surely, as one would expect from an ancient Near Eastern, the asymmetrical relation between deity and people was metaphorically associated with images of other typical such relationships found in their actual social world, such as 'king–subject', 'husband–wife', 'father (not 'parent')–son', 'master–servant', 'shepherd–flock', and its derivatives. These metaphors are all variants of a general approach to asymmetrical relationships in terms of 'patron–client'. Since society was patriarchal, males were almost always associated with the powerful side in these relationships, and so was, metaphorically, YHWH. Yet these common associations do not make YHWH fully male, anymore than they make this deity fully human—a position that, of course, these literati would have strongly rejected.[31]

This introduction is not complete without an expression of my deep gratitude to Philip Davies. He read written versions of these lectures, commented on them, advanced very helpful suggestions for their transformation into chapters in this work, and even edited the final manuscript. Of course, any errors that remain are my responsibility.

31. Since YHWH within this discourse is not really 'male' even when described by means of male analogies, there remains the potential to use female analogies to describe YHWH. Although rare, for the reasons mentioned above, such female analogies were produced in ancient Israel; see, for instance, Isa. 42.14. Cf. M.I. Gruber, 'The Motherhood of God in Second Isaiah', in *The Motherhood of God and Other Studies* (Atlanta, GA: Scholars Press, 1992), pp. 3-15 and bibliography there.

Chapter 2

NINEVEH'S FATES

1. *Introduction*

The story of Jonah clearly maintains that Nineveh was saved from destruction despite its previous behaviour. The city was not overthrown either because of its repentance (see Jon. 3, and esp. v. 10) or because of YHWH's compassionate character (see Jon. 4, and esp. vv. 2, 11),[1] or from the perspective of the book as a whole, by a combination of both. The plot of the book of Jonah collapses without the salvation of Nineveh.

The same holds true for the characterization of its two main personages, YHWH and Jonah, which is conveyed largely through their sharp differences

---

1.   It is almost universally accepted that Jon. 4.11 poses a rhetorical question. This interpretation is followed here. For the alternative position that Jon. 4.11 is to be understood as a direct, positive statement and, accordingly that YHWH says, 'I shall not take pity upon Nineveh, the great city…'; see A. Cooper, 'In Praise of Divine Caprice: The Significance of the Book of Jonah', in P.R. Davies and D.J.A. Clines (eds.), *Among the Prophets* (JSOTSup, 144; Sheffield: Sheffield Academic Press, 1993), pp. 144-63. For critiques of this position, see, for instance, G.M. Landes, 'Textual "Information Gaps" and "Dissonances" in the Interpretation of the Book of Jonah', in R. Chazan, W.W. Hallo and L.H. Schiffman (eds.), *Ki Baruch Hu: Ancient Near Eastern, Biblical, and Judaic Studies in Honor of Baruch A. Levine* (Winona Lake, IN: Eisenbrauns, 1999), pp. 273-93 (291-92), P. Trible, *Rhetorical Criticism: Context Method and the Book of Jonah* (Guides to Biblical Scholarship; Minneapolis, MN: Fortress Press, 1994), p. 215 n. 48, and see also E. Levine, *The Aramaic Version of Jonah* (New York: Sepher-Hermon Press, 3rd edn, 1981), p. 98.

It is worth stressing that readings of Jon. 4.11 as a rhetorical question do not create any grammatical or syntactical difficulty. Moreover, they are coherent with the well-known and widely attested principle of 'from minor (v. 10) to major premise (v. 11)'— in Hebrew קל וחומר. Although it eventually became a famous rabbinic principle, it was well attested in the ancient Near East long before the composition of Jonah or any piece of biblical literature for that matter. See Sasson, *Jonah*, pp. 307-308 and bibliography there; see also Limburg, *Jonah*, p. 97.

in attitude towards the salvation of Nineveh. This is precisely the matter that sets up the final confrontation between the two (Chapter 4), to which the story leads up and which represents the climax of the book as a whole.

The salvation of Nineveh is also a necessary plot for the communication of the high value of repentance (Chapter 3) that plays a central role in the narrative itself, and in the elaboration of central theological issues. In sum, the salvation of Nineveh is a *necessary* motif in the story and an explicit fact in the world of the book. The intended readership is surely asked to take it seriously, and so most likely did the readership for whom the book was written.

Yet texts are read, reread and composed by human beings, and human beings do not exist in a vacuum. It is a truism to say that readers approach and understand texts from a perspective informed by their world of knowledge.[2] This being so, it is worth stressing that the historical audience for which this book was composed lived in the postmonarchic, and likely Persian period[3] and, accordingly, knew well that Nineveh was eventually destroyed.[4]

Nineveh was associated in the discourse of this audience not only with the image of an enemy of Israel (a point usually made in research[5]), but also with absolute destruction. Within the ancient eastern Mediterranean world, Nineveh served as a most poignant example of a great city, a capital of a powerful empire, that was not only utterly destroyed but also

2. See Introduction to this volume.

3. See Introduction and bibliography mentioned there.

4. Cf., among others, D.F. Payne, 'Jonah from the Perspective of its Audience', *JSOT* 13 (1979), pp. 3-12.

5. E.g. T.E. Fretheim, 'Jonah and Theodicy', *ZAW* 90 (1978), pp. 227-37 (227); Allen, *Joel, Obadiah, Jonah and Micah*, p. 203; Wolff, *Obadiah and Jonah*, pp. 99-100; D. Marcus, *From Balaam to Jonah: Anti-prophetic Satire in the Hebrew Bible* (BJS, 301; Atlanta: Scholars Press, 1995), pp. 93-94; Limburg, *Jonah*, pp. 41-42; Y. Gitay, 'Jonah: The Prophet of Antirhetoric', in A.B. Beck *et al.* (eds.), *Fortunate the Eyes That See: Essays in Honor of D.N. Freedman* (Grand Rapids, MI: Eerdmans, 1995), pp. 197-206 (200); Sweeney, *Twelve Prophets*, p. 305; and eventually cf. LaCocque and Lacoque, *Jonah*, p. xxiv; N. Rosen, 'Jonah: Justice for Jonah, or a Bible Bartleby', in D. Rosenberg (ed.), *Congregation: Contemporary Writers Read the Jewish Bible* (New York: Harcourt Brace Jovanovich, 1987), pp. 222-31. On the interpretative tendency shown in the last two works, see Chapter 9 in this volume. See also, 'Nineveh: that name would raise a mingled fear and anticipation in the heart of any prophet commanded to go there. The capital of Assyria, *the very symbol of utter moral degradation...*' (emphasis mine; quotation from E.M. Good, *Irony in the Old Testament* [Sheffield: Almond Press, 2nd edn, 1981 (1965)], p. 42).

never rebuilt.[6] This image accounts, in part, for common explanations of its terrible fate in terms of its 'abhorrent' behaviour, or of its supposed last king, Sardanapallus, in classical Greek literature. The cultural premise was, of course, that only some appalling act or behavior could cause such a fate.[7]

It follows that, from the vantage point of a Persian-period rereadership of the book of Jonah, Babylon could have evoked negative associations similar to those evoked by a reference to Nineveh, namely, the image of an enemy of Israel and a bloody destroyer. Moreover, it was Babylon, not Assyria, who destroyed Jerusalem, the first Temple and the Judahite monarchic polity. The choice of Nineveh over Babylon for the tale, and above all—within the research approach advanced here—the way in which it shapes the meaning of the text for the intended and primary readerships, is significant. The main difference between the two cities in this regard seems to be that Babylon could not have evoked the image of a great city that has been 'removed' from the world forever,[8] as Sodom and Gomorrah. Nineveh *did* evoke that image.[9] The oblique references to the story of the destruction of Sodom and Gomorrah in the book of Jonah seem to support this.[10]

---

6.   It bears note that Ibn Ezra refers to 'sages of Israel in Greece' who equate Nineveh and Troy. The functional equivalence between the two is based on the idea that both were main, quasi-mythical capitals of great nations that were utterly destroyed. See J.-V. Niclós, 'Comentario al profeta Jonás de Abraham Ibn Ezra y la liturgia del perdón', *EstBib* 53 (1999), pp. 483-515 (495, 509; see lines 23-24 in the Hebrew text).

7.   For a summary of the 'classical' evidence, see T.M. Bolin, ' "Should I Not Also Pity Nineveh?" Divine Freedom in the book of Jonah', *JSOT* 67 (1995), pp. 109-20 (111-15). These references to Sardanapallus and his characterization are interesting from the point of view of ancient constructions of the past (and ancient historiography), and above all, about the 'facts' about the past that ancient societies may agree upon, even if they have little historical value. The issue, however, stands beyond the scope of this volume.

8.   It is worth noting that the author of Tobit, and probably the intended readership of the book, did not know the precise location of Nineveh. Tobit is described as marching eastward from Nineveh and reaching the Tigris, but Nineveh was east of the Tigris. See C.A. Moore, *Tobit* (AB, 40A; New York: Doubleday, 1996), pp. 10, 198. The book of Tobit was probably written sometime between 300 and 175 BCE (see Moore, *Tobit,* pp. 40-42). The book uses folkloristic motifs and irony in ways that are reminiscent of Jonah.

9.   Within this perspective, Babylon may be considered as a potential equivalent to Rome (or its equivalent Esau) in later literature.

10.   It is most likely that the story of the judgment of Sodom and Gomorrah and of

Moreover, the social location of the author of the book of Jonah—one of the literati from the postmonarchic and most likely Achaemenid period—should be taken into consideration. It is very likely that this author was aware of this implication. More importantly, it is almost impossible to maintain that the *implied* author construed by the communities of re-readers in Achaemenid Yehud was not aware that Nineveh was destroyed (cf. Tob. 14.4, 8).[11]

the related conversation of YHWH and Abraham (Gen. 18–19) informed the composition and rereadings of the book of Jonah within the circle of literati for whom the book was written. One may point to the probable relation between Gen. 18.20 and Jon. 1.2 (see Sasson, *Jonah*, p. 75), and to the reversal of expectations, as Abraham cannot save the sinning city from destruction despite his efforts and stature, whereas Jonah, a more than reluctant prophet who does not argue for the sinning city, is instrumental in its salvation. The LXX seems to reflect a tradition of interpretation that associates the text of Jonah with that of Gen. 18.20 (see Sasson, *Jonah*, p. 87 n. 12). To be sure, there is much more at stake in the theological relation between the narrative of Sodom and Gomorrah and the book of Jonah than the negative characterization of the persona of Jonah by means of an implied comparison with Abraham. There is no hint in the former that YHWH will relent from punishment even if the inhabitants of these cities will repent, and certainly not if they do not repent at all, that is, because YHWH will spare God's creatures (cf. Jon. 4). See B.A. Levine, 'The Place of Jonah in the History of Biblical ideas', in S.L. Cook and S.C. Winter (eds.), *On the Way to Nineveh: Studies in Honor of George M. Landes* (ASOR Books, 4; Scholars Press: Atlanta, 1999), pp. 201-17 (211-15). The book of Jonah points at this traditional text, but in order to reshape radically the theological views communicated in the Sodom and Gomorrah pericope. See also below.

11.   Cooper proposes an understanding of the book of Jonah that includes an awareness of the total destruction of Nineveh, but he does so on the basis of a reading of the book of Jonah that considers it as an integral part of the 'Book of the Twelve' (Cooper, 'In Praise', pp. 144-63). My own position regarding the issue of the 'Book of the Twelve' is well expressed in E. Ben Zvi, 'Twelve Prophetic Books or "The Twelve"', in J.W. Watts and P.R. House (eds.), *Forming Prophetic Literature: Essays on Isaiah and the Twelve in Honor of John D.W. Watts* (JSOTSup, 235; Sheffield: Sheffield Academic Press, 1996), pp. 125-56. For my present purposes it suffices to state the obvious: these literati did not have to read the Twelve in any particular unified way to know that Nineveh was destroyed. In fact, they did not have to read it at all to know about Nineveh's fate. On Cooper's position regarding Jon. 4.11 see above.

Bolin has proposed an understanding of the book of Jonah that is based on 'Jonah need not to be read with a Near Eastern context informing its conception of Nineveh, but rather a Hellenistic one'. This conception of Nineveh includes, of course, among others its being opulent, lawless and its being destroyed. See Bolin, ' "Should I Not" '; quotation from p. 109.

These readers and rereaders of the book of Jonah also construed YHWH not only as signified by the character YHWH in the book of Jonah,[12] but also as the divine being who exists outside the text of this (or any) book. From the perspective of these postmonarchic rereaders YHWH, the transcendental deity, surely knew about the destruction of Nineveh,[13] and it is likely that at least some of them thought that YHWH already knew of the eventual fate of Nineveh at the putative time of YHWH's interaction with Jonah, the son of Amittay.[14]

In sum, rereadings of the book of Jonah within these postmonarchic communities would activate the memory of two opposed fates of Nineveh. One of them was strongly interwoven into the plot of the book, and the other was deeply ingrained in their world of knowledge. *Neither* of these two fates can be dismissed as irrelevant without losing much of the integrity of the reception of this book in these rereaderships, and concomitantly, much of the theological/ideological message that these communities could have 'drawn' from the book. In fact, as it will be demonstrated below, *it is the awareness of both fates* that strongly contributes to the theological/ideological meanings developed within those communities through their reading and rereading.

2. *The Double Ending Situation and Targets of Criticism*

a. *Presenting the Issues*

The book of Jonah has often been considered a satire, or at least a work that bears satirical features.[15] Even if one were to object to such a clear-cut

---

12. Provided that they accepted the claims advanced by the book. But if this had not been the case, the book of Jonah would not have been accepted by mentioned community/ies of literati and accordingly would not have been transmitted.

13. Cf. my review of K.M.Craig, *A Poetics of Jonah: Art in the Service of Ideology* (Columbia: University of South Carolina Press, 1993); *Canadian Journal of Comparative Literature* 22 (1995), pp. 371-74.

14. YHWH is often characterized as one who knows the fate of nations in the distant future (e.g. Deut. 31.16-21; Isa. 2.1-4). On some relevant general issues regarding the interpretation of the text, cf. my review of Craig, *Poetics of Jonah*. This, of course, does not mean that all literati had to construe YHWH as one who knew the future of Nineveh at the time of Jonah. See Chapter 3.

15. See, among others, Good, *Irony*, pp. 39-55; J.C. Holbert, ' "Deliverance Belongs to YAHWEH!" Satire in the book of Jonah', *JSOT* 21 (1981), pp. 59-81; J.J.S. Ackerman, 'Satire and Symbolism in the Song of Jonah', in B. Halpern and J.D. Levenson (eds.), *Traditions in Transformation: Turning Points in Biblical Faith*

characterization of the book,[16] it is almost universally agreed that the book suggested to its intended rereadership one or more central targets of strong criticism. It is most likely that an ancient readership would have imagined the implied author to agree with the position advanced by YHWH in the book,[17] who therefore was not a target. This leaves, of course, the character Jonah. But he was certainly not the ultimate target of criticism. Beyond and through him, the implied author was construed as pointing at real targets in society. The latter are usually construed as (a) those who stand for the positions advocated by this character in the book, or (b) the positions themselves, or most likely (c) a combination both.[18]

This being so, attention has usually focused on the precise identification of the main theological position or positions that are criticized or perhaps even ridiculed. This endeavor has not generated any simple and un-equivocal result. This is due, in part, to the complexity of the book. For example, there is a certain tension—at least on the surface—between the theological positions advanced by YHWH and rejected by Jonah in Chapter 3

(Winona Lake, IN: Eisenbrauns, 1981); *idem*, 'Jonah'. LaCoque and Lacocque, *Jonah*; I.J.J. Spangenberg, 'Jonah and Qohelet: Satire Versus Irony', *OTE* 9 (1996), pp. 495-511; and Marcus, *From Balaam to Jonah*, esp. pp. 93-148 and bibliography mentioned there.

16. The issue involves the matter of definition of what a satire is. According to Sasson, for instance, a main question is whether 'the narrator *intentionally* derides Jonah when wishing to ridicule other targets' (*Jonah*, p. 332, emphasis in the original). For a survey of scholarly positions concerning the satirical status of the book of Jonah, see Sasson, *Jonah*, pp. 331-34.

The position advanced here regarding a complex multivalent set of targets balancing each other suggests that although satirical elements are present and serve important rhetorical purposes, the book as whole is anything but a simple satire. On these matters see also Chapter 7.

These issues raise the question of the genre of the book. For short surveys of research—and bibliography—on the general question of the 'genre' of the book of Jonah, see Sasson, *Jonah*, pp. 331-40; Salters, *Jonah*, pp. 41-50. My own position is that its genre is 'prophetic book', and, within that general genre, that it belongs to 'meta-prophetic books'. See, Ben Zvi, 'Prophetic Book' and Chapter 6 of this volume.

17. Cf. Y. Amit, ' "The Glory of Israel Does Not Deceive or Change his Mind": On the Reliability of Narrator and Speakers in Biblical Narrative', *Prooftexts* 12 (1992), pp. 201-12.

18. These combinations are frequently phrased in strong theological language, for example, 'the folly of those of who do not embrace a God of love' (Trible, *Studies*, p. 261). On these matters, see also Chapter 7 in this volume.

and those advanced and rejected by the same characters in Chapter 4.[19] The following positions, however, are often considered among the targets of the satire: (a) that YHWH's characterization as 'a gracious God, and merciful, slow to anger and abounding in steadfast love, and ready to relent from punishing' (Jon. 4.2; NRSV) is accurate but a liability, (b) that the efficacy of repentance is regrettable, (c) that whatever a faithful prophet has proclaimed must come to pass, and (d) that the living prophet is someone who must have a significant role in the development of the events.[20]

Some of these issues will be discussed in Chapter 7 of this volume, but here we need only to recognize that the understanding of these positions as central targets of the satire is directly related to, and dependent on a particular reading and rereading of the book of Jonah. They all revolve around a simple premise: Nineveh was eventually saved from destruction, just as the plot within the book maintains.

As mentioned above, the rereaders knew all too well that eventually Nineveh was not only destroyed, but, unlike all other exceedingly great capital cities in their horizon of knowledge, blotted out of existence forever.[21] What would be the message shaped among the primary com-

19. In theological terms the first one may be referred to as a 'theology of repentance' and the other as a 'theology of pity' (see Trible, *Rhetorical Criticism*, p. 223), and accordingly as describing a 'God of Repentance' and a 'God of Love'. The point is that the first one seems to be willing to punish the city unless they repent, whereas the latter is willing to relent even if they do not repent; though 'pity' or 'love' are often presented as the grounds on which YHWH accepts human repentance. In any case, the text of Jonah asks the readers of the book to interweave the two motifs rather than accept one and completely reject the other.

20. The theological/ideological stand according to which prophets and their actions and words neither have nor should have a defining role in the development of events underlies much of the literature of the postmonarchic period. On these issues I wrote elsewhere (see E. Ben Zvi, 'Prophets and Prophecy in the Compositional and Redactional Notes in I–II Kings', *ZAW* 105 [1993], pp. 331-51).

21. See Jon. 3.3, and for the expression there B. Waltke and M. O'Connor, *An Introduction to Biblical Hebrew Syntax* (Winona Lake, IN: Eisenbrauns, 1990), §14.5b, p. 268, and cf. Jonah 1.2; 3.2; 4.11. Of course, the readership knew of two other cities that were destroyed and disappeared forever: Sodom and Gomorrah. Although these two cities were not as large as Nineveh, were paradigmatic of (justified) total destruction in their discourse (see, for instance, Isa. 1.9; 13.19; Jer. 49.18; 50.40; Lam. 4.6; Amos 4.11; Zeph. 2.9). It is certainly not an accident that the choice of words in the book of Jonah evoked the images of Sodom and Gomorrah episode in the rereading community/ies. Cf. Jonah 1.2 with Gen. 18.20. (In addition, the use of a

munity of rereaders if they approached the text in a way informed by this awareness of the final fate of Nineveh?

b. *Jonah and the God of Love Alone*
To begin with, when these ancient readers and rereaders approached the text from this perspective, they could not have held any characterization of YHWH as *only* 'a gracious God, merciful, slow to anger and abounding in steadfast love, and ready to relent from punishing'. They would certainly agree that these attributes are associated with YHWH (Exod. 34.6-7; NRSV; cf. Num. 14.18), but a characterization of the deity based *only* on these attributes would be clearly misleading.[22] This being the case, such a characterization has no potential to be a liability, because it does not actually represent YHWH.

The character of Jonah is then ridiculed twice. First, because he opposes YHWH's mercy, and, second, because he is convinced that these attributes of mercy are the defining, or perhaps even only predicates of YHWH. For a readership that focuses only on the fate of Nineveh in the explicit literary plot of the book, the target of the satire are those who are upset, or even infuriated, by YHWH's mercy and their theological positions. But a rereading of the book that is strongly informed by the eventual fate of Nineveh ridicules a construction of YHWH as deity in which mercy is the final and most essential attribute. From this perspective, Jonah was absolutely wrong in imagining YHWH as a deity who cannot be expected to carry out a massive destruction of human (and animal) life (contrast Jon. 4.10-11).[23] The text advances a satire within a satire, or rather two satires informing and balancing each other.

---

verbal form from the root הפך was probably meant to evoke the image of that narrative, see Deut. 29.22; Isa. 13.19; Jer. 49.18; 50.40; and cf. already Ibn Ezra on 4.11, Radak on 3.4—there are additional reasons for the use of verbal form from הפך in Jon. 3.4; see below).

On the relation between Jonah and the Sodom and Gomorrah narrative, see, among others, Sasson, *Jonah*, pp. 75, 87, 133, 235-36; and see above.

22. This suggests that the text advocates—and reflects—a theological approach in which various, and even competing, claims advanced in diverse authoritative texts and expressions should be placed in their 'proper' perspective, and that this can be achieved by approaching each of them from a perspective that is informed by the other.

23. Or in taking at face value and categorically YHWH's own words in these verses. On these matters see especially Chapter 7.

c. *Repentance*

Similarly, within a reading of the book that focuses only on the fate of Nineveh in its explicit literary plot, the targets of the satire include (theological or ideological) positions that regret the efficacy of repentance—and those who uphold them. It is worth noting that such efficacy is qualified in the text from more than one perspective. The Ninevites are described as being unsure of the efficacy of repentance (Jon. 3.9). Indeed, their position in this respect is presented in positive terms. YHWH's reference to the explicit concern of the deity about a great city of 'one hundred thousand persons who do not know their right hand from their left' (Jon. 4.11) clearly advances the case that the repentance of the Ninevites—which is not mentioned at all at the heightened conclusion of the book—was not the main reason (or any reason at all) for YHWH's action.[24] Thus, the target of the satire even within this type of reading could not have been a position that advocates the (absolute?) efficacy of repentance, but rather the regret that repentance might contribute to the manifestation in worldly affairs of YHWH's will to relent from punishing. But if this is one of targets of the satire developed by a reading that focuses only on the explicit fate of Nineveh in the book's plot, then a rereading of the text in the light of the eventual fate of Nineveh in worldly terms blunts the message. In fact, from this perspective, it is even possible to consider the text as a satire against those who are concerned over the potential results of a nonexistent 'overbearing' efficacy of repentance.

d. *What a Faithful Prophet Prophesies…*

If one of the targets of the satire is the concept that whatever a faithful prophet has proclaimed must come to pass, then this holds true for a reading of the book that is not informed by the eventual fate of Nineveh. But one that is informed by its historical fate satirizes that satire. The 'fact' is that Nineveh was destroyed as the prophet Jonah proclaimed.[25]

---

24. This stands in tension with Jon. 3.10. On these matters see also Chapter 8.

25. As it is well known, Jonah's proclamation ונינוה נהפכת in Jon. 3.4 creates another level of textual ambiguity (see below), because the text may be understood as 'Nineveh is to be overturned' (i.e. destroyed) or 'Nineveh is to turn over' (i.e. to reform itself, as it actually does in the narrative). See Sasson, *Jonah*, pp. 234-37, 267-68, 295, 345-46, and the bibliography mentioned there. Cf. Abrabanel.

The word נהפכת (be overthrown) most likely served also to bring up in the readership reminiscences of the Sodom and Gomorrah episode (see above). Reading and rereading the text of Jonah with the latter narrative in mind both sharpens the

Accordingly, a different group must stand as the target of this satire within a satire, namely, those who were proven wrong by historical events.[26] This group consists of (a) those who believe that the proclamation of a faithful prophet may *not* come true (i.e. those ridiculed by a satirical reading of the book that does not pay attention to the historical fate of Nineveh; and notice the inversion of the targets), but also (b) those who, like the character Jonah, focus literally on deadlines for divine judgment rather than on the assertion of divine judgment itself.[27] The latter are imagined as waiting impatiently for an immediate divine action or, in despair, begging for their deaths (Jon. 4.5-8). Because of their haste and lack of 'true' understanding of the divinely appointed times, they cannot bear that which, from their perspectives, seems an unreasonable delay in the divine actions.[28]

The text shows an additional level of intertwined multiplicity, beyond that of these satirical rereadings informing and balancing each other.

image of destroyed Nineveh (within a reading that stresses the eventual fate of the city) and that of the 'turning around' (or repentance) of the city that sets its fate diametrically opposed to that of Sodom and Gomorrah, within a reading that focuses on the plot narrative.

26. These events were understood as expressions or manifestations of YHWH's will by these readerships.

27. Of course, there is the matter of the 'forty days' (Jon. 3.4). Although Jonah, the character, may have taken it literally or meaning a very short period (another satirical element), the term may be understood in symbolic terms, and notice the common use of the number 'forty'. Such an understanding of the 'forty days' is clearly at work in Tobit 14 and *Ant.* 9.214 (see C. T. Begg, 'Josephus and Nahum Revisited', *REJ* 154 [1995], pp. 5-22 [15 n. 49]). On the 'forty days' and its ability to suit more than one reading, see below.

28. Cf. Tobit's words in Tob. 14.4: 'I believe the word of God that Nahum spoke about Nineveh, that all these things will take place and overtake Assyria and Nineveh. *Indeed, everything that was spoken by the prophets of Israel, whom God sent, will occur. None of all their words will fail, but all will come true at their appointed times*' (NRSV, emphasis added). Significantly, Codex Vaticanus, Alexandrinus and Venetus have 'Jonah' instead of 'Nahum'. This reading is preferred among others by E. Bickerman. See his *Four Strange Books*, p. 37; and *idem*, 'Les deux erreurs du prophète Jonas', in *Studies in Jewish and Christian History Part One* (Leiden: E.J. Brill, 1976), pp. 33-71 (60) (originally published in *RHPR* 45 [1965], pp. 232-64). See also T. Bolin, *Freedom Beyond Forgiveness: The book of Jonah Re-examined* (JSOTSup, 236; Sheffield: Sheffield Academic Press, 1997), p. 40 n. 97 and bibliography. The reading 'Jonah' may be the original, for it is easier to understand why 'Jonah' would become 'Nahum' than vice versa. For the opposite position see, among others, Moore, *Tobit*, p. 290.

Jonah's words in 3.4 carry a double meaning. Although it seems to have escaped the character Jonah, it was not missed by the narrator, the implied author, or the intended rereadership. Most importantly, it is very unlikely that the *actual* ancient literati who read, reread and studied this book missed this double reading. Jonah's ונינוה נהפכת (usually translated, 'Nineveh will be overthrown') may be seen as fulfilled in one of two sets of circumstances or in both of them, from a larger multivocal perspective. The first set of circumstances is represented by the 'turning-over', which is the repentance of the Ninevites described in Jonah 3.[29] If this is so, the target of the satire will be the character Jonah and those who, although they proclaim or repeat faithfully the wording of a divine message, lack the ability to understand it. The second set of circumstances is the later and eventual destruction of Nineveh. If this is the case, then we return to the situation discussed above.[30]

One may add to those mentioned above another way to approach the double fate of Nineveh, along with its implications for the construction of possible primary or original rereadings of the book. The worldview/s

---

29. The 'forty days' also play a role in the shaping of this polyvalent message. Jonah seems to have understood it as a very short period of time within which—or perhaps, but less likely, at the end of which—Nineveh will be overturned. From the perspective informed mainly by the fact that the city was eventually destroyed, his mistake was to take 'forty days' too literally, rather than in a symbolic way that allows it to be translated into a substantial number of years (see above and the references to Tob. 14 and *Ant.* 9.214; see C. Begg, 'Josephus and Nahum Revisited', *REJ* 154 [1995], pp. 5-22 [15 n. 49]). But readings that focus on the fate of the city within the plot of the book—that is, as a city that successfully turned itself away from evil, see Jon. 3 in particular—the limit introduced by the 'forty days' creates a period in which repentance is still possible (see, for instance, Sweeney, *Twelve Prophets*, p. 325). To be sure, within the narrative the Ninevites do not require so much time, they immediately repent. Cf. Sasson, *Jonah*, pp. 233-34. In other words, the expression 'forty days' is well suited for, and supports both readings. (The argument here holds even if one doubts the originality of the MT reading 'forty' and tends to prefer that of the LXX/OL 'three'. The latter is also a symbolic number, but most scholars prefer the MT here). See Levine, *Aramaic Version*, p. 85; Trible, *Studies*, pp. 89-90; Wolff, *Obadiah and Jonah*, pp. 144, 149-50; Sasson, *Jonah*, pp. 233-34 and bibliography cited there. For an interesting mediaeval, allegoric reading of the 'forty days', see H. Shy, *Tanhum HaYerushalmi's Commentary on the Minor Prophets: A Critical Edition with an Introduction* (Jerusalem: Magnes Press, 1991), p. 136.

30. Cf. Sasson, *Jonah*, pp. 234-37, 267-68, 295, 345-46, and the bibliography mentioned there; B. Halpern and R.E. Friedman, 'Composition and Paronomasia in Jonah', *HAR* 4 (1980), pp. 79-92 (87, 89).

of the literati of Achaemenid Yehud was informed by, and reflected in, their repertoire of authoritative literature. If so, they could have also approached—and because of their continuous rereading, most likely did approach—the matter in a way informed by the theological viewpoint that repentance and good deeds may provide relief from an immediate (and deserved) punishment, but such a relief only postpones the inevitable manifestation of the announced divine judgment.[31] But, of course, this viewpoint is only one of many that the same literati could have taken, and in fact, they were likely to have taken different approaches at different times and for different purposes.[32]

It is most significant that all the possibilities covered above are consistent with rereadings by, and the world of knowledge of, a postmonarchic community, such as the one for which the book of Jonah was written. Moreover, all these possibilities point to theological/ideological issues that were central to the discourse of these communities, such as the value of repentance, of yet unfulfilled, or 'delayed', prophetic divine announcements regarding divine actions, and the related question of the 'proper' understanding of, and the social control over, the understanding of YHWH's word, as well as questions about the role of active prophets, as opposed to scribes and rereaders of prophetic literature.[33]

e. *Characterization and Role of the 'Living Prophet'*
The issue mentioned above brings us to the fourth possible target of the plot satire mentioned above. *No matter* which fate befalls Nineveh, from the perspective of this postmonarchic rereadership, Jonah, that is the 'living prophet' and reciter of godly words (see Jonah 2), is unable fully to understand the content of the divine message, whereas the community of rereaders is able to.

Also, according to *both* rereadings the image of a prophet who thought that he should play a significant role in the divine economy is ridiculed. After all, if Nineveh is saved from destruction it is because of YHWH's will and not to Jonah's performance. In fact, Jonah complains about his secondary, even essentially irrelevant role.[34] If alternatively, the rereaders

31. See, for instance, 2 Kgs 20.12-19 (//Isa 39.1-8), and esp. 22.15-20.

32. According to the horizon of pertinence of the reading of the text. On these matters, see Ben Zvi, 'Introduction: Writings, Speeches, and the Prophetic Books'.

33. On these issues I have written elsewhere; see, for instance, E. Ben Zvi, *A Historical-Critical Study of the Book of Zephaniah* (BZAW, 198; Berlin: W. de Gruyter, 1991), pp. 348-51. See also Chapter 7.

34. See Jon. 4.1-3, and cf. T. Eagleton, 'J. L. Austin and the Book of Jonah', in

focus on the eventual destruction of Nineveh, then the city was still razed because of YHWH's will, and Jonah's actions are, at the very best, of only secondary value.

f. *Two Comments*
According to Marcus, 'a satirist will try to write so that his [*sic*] work can be taken on two levels (the real and the apparent), and by doing so will thus give no hint of his real purpose'.[35] If the implied author of the book of Jonah can be described as a satirist, then this satirist developed a work that can be taken at multiple levels, each informing and interacting with the other.

Some scholars have claimed that the book of Jonah is a parody on other prophetic texts.[36] The 'peculiarities' of the book of Jonah that set it apart from the other prophetic books (i.e. the 'Latter Prophets')[37] may undermine the strength of this characterization of the book. The claim that the characterization of the prophet Jonah involves a parody of prophets such as Isaiah, Amos, Jeremiah and others is also doubtful, because Jonah clearly does not talk like them. Yet, there is an element of parody in the book of Jonah. If it is reread from a perspective strongly informed by the knowledge of the final fate of Nineveh, it suggests itself as partial parody of a rereading that focuses only on the basic narrative in the book, and concludes that with a Nineveh that survives, that is saved from destruction.

3. *The Double Ending and Multiplicity of Theological Messages*

a. *Multiple Theological Voices Informing Each Other*
Prophetic books contain multiple instances in which seemingly competing claims are presented to the intended readership. To be sure, the same happens in other books (e.g. Chronicles). In these cases, the book as a

R. Schwartz (ed.), *The Book and the Text: The Bible and Literary Theory* (Cambridge, MA: Blackwell, 1990), pp. 231-36, esp. pp. 232-33.

35. Marcus, *From Balaam to Jonah*, p. 147.

36. E.g. M. Orth, 'Genre in Jonah: The Effects of Parody in the Book of Jonah', in W.W. Hallo *et al.* (eds.), *The Bible in the Light of Cuneiform Literature: Scripture in Context III* (Lewiston, NY: Edwin Mellen Press, 1990), pp. 257-81; cf. J.A. Miles, 'Laughing at the Bible: Jonah as Parody', *JQR* 65 (1975), pp. 168-81 (reprinted in Y.T. Radday and A. Brenner [eds.], *On Humour and the Comic in the Hebrew Bible* [JSOTSup, 92; Sheffield: Almond Press, 1990], pp. 203-15).

37. E.g. the narrative character of the book of Jonah as a whole has no parallel in any other prophetic book. On atypical features and their possible communicative function see Chapter 6.

whole advocates and reflects a theological approach in which various and even competing claims are placed in their 'proper' perspective. The latter can be achieved by approaching each claim from a perspective that is informed by the other. These considerations are true, for instance, regarding the fate of the nations in Micah 4–5,[38] or the so-called principle of reward and punishment in Chronicles.[39] They are also true regarding the centrality of the repentance of Nineveh in Jonah as motive or reason for YHWH's actions in the plot of the book of Jonah (cf. Chapters 3 and 4). The book of Jonah, unlike other prophetic books, carries an additional level of meanings because of its double ending.

The double ending, along with the ensuing multiple 'satirical' rereading informing and to some extent ridiculing each other, results in a plurality of theological voices. Each of these voices is distinct, but all are integral to the message of the book to its intended rereadership. Within such a readership none of these voices can silence the others: they inform each other and interact at different levels. At one level are voices that stand by the ending advanced by the plot,[40] and at another level all these readings and rereadings meet the other readings and rereadings shaped by the sharp awareness that YHWH *did* destroy Nineveh—which was common and salient knowledge within the discourse shared by the community/ies of readers and rereaders. The result of the interaction is a more sophisticated theological discourse.

To be sure, the theological discourse of the period is often represented by sets of multiple, partial meanings that interact with each other and reflect an image of the rich discursive world they continuously shape.[41] The double ending in Jonah provides, however, an overall, heightened level of polyvalence that is not present elsewhere in prophetic literature. It is now time to look at that world of theological discourse and its con-

38. See Ben Zvi, *Micah*, pp. 123-24 and passim.

39. See E. Ben Zvi, 'A Sense of Proportion: An Aspect of the Theology of the Chronicler', *SJOT* 9 (1995), pp. 37-51. On these issues see also Chapter 7.

40. Rereadings informed by the salvation of Nineveh show multiple readings informing each other in such matters as those regarding the centrality of the repentance of Nineveh, the message of the prophet's proclamation, and the obvious open-ended situation created by Jonah's silence at the conclusion.

41. It bears mentioning that most prophetic books show multiple possible outlines (or 'structures'), each reflecting a possible reading. Atypical also in this regard, the book of Jonah shows a relatively tight structure. For the structure of Jonah, see, for instance, Simon, *Jonah*, pp. xxiv-xxx; Trible, 'Jonah', and her detailed discussion in Trible, *Rhetorical Criticism*. On these matters see also Chapter 6 here.

tribution to the study of the probable ancient readings and rereadings of Jonah.

b. *Central Cases and the General Discourse of the Period*
The reconstruction of readings advanced above is supported by the fact that the positions reflected by their interactions occur elsewhere, and relatively often, in the discourse of the period. For instance, the book communicates to its intended readership that repentance has much significance (cf. Jer. 18.7-8; 2 Chron. 33.13). To be sure, there are good social, cultural and psychological reasons to reject any preaching, doctrine; theology or ideology that claims that repentance is meaningless or worthless. Yet the book also communicates that repentance is *not everything*, because YHWH is *not* conceived of as necessarily bound to relinquish judgment whenever someone repents from evildoing (cf., among others, Amos 5.15; Joel 2.14; Jon. 3.9; Zeph. 2.3; and see Jon. 4.11, and see also, among others, Jer. 11.11, 14; Ezek. 8.18; cf. Jer. 4.28).[42] In its double ending the book communicates that YHWH is to be understood as 'a gracious God, merciful, slow to anger and abounding in steadfast love, and ready to relent from punishing' (cf. Joel 2.13; Pss. 86.15; 103.8-10; 145.8-9; Neh. 9.17b), but *also* as a God of justice who executes judgment as:

> a God merciful and gracious, slow to anger, and abounding in steadfast love and faithfulness, keeping steadfast love for the thousandth generation, forgiving iniquity and transgression and sin, yet by no means clearing the guilty, but visiting the iniquity of the parents upon the children and the children's children, to the third and the fourth generation' (Exod. 34.6-7; NRSV; cf. Num. 14.18).

YHWH is construed as the deity who saves Nineveh from judgment; YHWH is construed as the deity who executes judgment against that sinful city. YHWH does both, and is defined by both, within the discourse of the community.

Similarly, one the one hand, the word of YHWH may be seen as fulfilled by the new circumstances that are created due to its proclamation (cf. Isa.

---

42. The hyperbolic character of the repentance in the story of Jonah also connotes a sense of 'uniqueness' to the event that makes it somewhat similar to the appointment of the great fish or the mysterious plant. The more unique (miraculous?) the event is, the less directly related to expectations of human motivated behaviour it is. Any reading of the book that is strongly informed by the destruction of Nineveh would certainly emphasize the temporary character of even such a unique event in 'history'.

55.6-11).[43] On the other hand, YHWH's word will be fulfilled as pro-claimed (cf., among others, Num. 23.19; 1 Sam. 15.29; Tob. 14.4).[44] Indeed, if the latter were not the case, the element of hope communicated by YHWH's promises of a better future would be seriously undermined. It is worth noting that the 'destroyed Nineveh' rereading not only reassures the readership that YHWH's promises and justice will be fulfilled, but also conveys a sense of 'proper attitude' towards the delay of their fulfillment, something akin to 'although it tarries, I will wait daily for its coming'[45] (cf. Zeph. 3.8, among others).

Similarly, Nineveh, and likely by extension 'the nations', are con-structed as willing to listen to YHWH's word (cf. the non-Israelite sailors), to repent, and accordingly not only able to avoid YHWH's judgment, but even able to develop a positive communication with YHWH, though there is a role for the Israelite here. But, on the other hand, Nineveh is destroyed for its own sins. This double approach towards Nineveh and the nations other than Israel is comparable, for instance, to that present in the images of the future developed in Micah 4–5. But this is not the only case.

It should be stressed that all the mentioned multiple and *complementary* (not alternative) theological voices evoked within historically likely rereadings of the book of Jonah by the communities of literati for which the book was composed resonate in much of biblical literature. The multivocality of Jonah is not accidental.[46]

c. *Beyond Multivocality (and beyond the Obvious)*

There are also limits to the multivocality arising from the double ending of the book of Jonah. Some of these are obvious. One may mention, for instance, the identification of YHWH and God, YHWH's control of the physical world and similar propositions. Others are less obvious. Accord-ing to either ending, one of the targets of the critique is those who are knowledgeable about authoritative texts and traditions, and are even able to quote them (see Jonah's 'psalm' in Chapter 2 and his rendering of the attributes of YHWH in Jon. 4.2). There is no multivocality in this regard. (The issue will be discussed further in Chapter 7.)

43. See Rofé, *Prophetical Stories*, pp. 169-70.

44. Cf. Rofé, *Prophetical Stories*, pp. 166-70.

45. The language of the last expression is, of course, an adaptation of the 'Twelfth Principle' of Rambam, which expresses a comparable position regarding the coming of the Messiah.

46. For other reasons for multivocality see below.

Similarly, there is no multivocality in the critique of positions that wish to grant the prophet something more than a secondary role in the administration and manifestation of the divine economy. Jonah is upset at being a pawn in the chain of events initiated and controlled by YHWH that leads to the salvation of Nineveh, and, in a manner unknown to Jonah, also to its eventual destruction. His reaction, his being upset, is presented negatively, as a target of criticism, within this discourse. Similar theological/ideological positions are expressed elsewhere in the Hebrew Bible.[47]

This being so, and despite the unequivocal character of the criticism of the prophet expressed by the plot, the narrator and above all the most reliable character in the book, YHWH, I cannot agree with the conclusions of Marcus's excellent study of Jonah:

> It is our contention that it is this negative portrayal of the prophet, *not any ideological message*, which is the principal 'message' of the book. What we have here is nothing less than a satire on the prophet himself. It is the behaviour of the prophet with which the book is dealing. Jonah is satirized for behaviour thought to be unbecoming to a prophet.[48]

My objection is based on a recognition of the multiplicity of meanings conveyed by the book to its intended and primary rereaderships, and on considerations about the contingent value of the words of YHWH and on their self-reflection on their own status and role to be discussed in Chapter 7 of this volume.

d. *In Sum…*

In sum, the double ending of the book reflects the universe of ideas within which the book was composed, read and reread. It expresses and shapes some theological views in terms of a plurality of voices and rereadings. In many cases, these voices present theological/ideological views that not only stand in tension, but also complement one another. 'Both/and' mediates the potential absolute claims of each other. In other cases, however, the different rereadings and its corresponding multiple voices converge, as in the case of the quasi-irrelevance of the prophet in comparison to YHWH, and on the negative characterization of those who hold to godly, authoritative texts and expressions but miss their context (see Jon. 4.2).

---

47. See Ben Zvi, 'Prophets'.
48. Marcus, *From Balaam to Jonah*, p. 158, emphasis mine.

4. *Multivocality and Social World*

a. *Multivocality and Rereadings*

The degree of multivocality present in Jonah and in prophetic literature in general facilitated the continuous rereading of the book within ancient communities of rereaders, and contributed to the transmission and preservation of the book, and eventually to its 'authoritative' value.[49] This is due in part to the fact that texts with a degree of ambiguity are more likely to be continuously reread than unequivocal texts.[50] Without such an activity, it is unlikely that the texts would have taken up their role as conveyers of divine knowledge within the community, and that they would have been copied again and again and eventually preserved as 'authoritative', theological/ideological texts.

b. *Multivocality and Shaping the Image of the Communicator: Social Considerations*

The 'canonization' of such a text is also influenced by the suitability to several social processes in postmonarchic Israel that results from its ability to carry some degree of multivocality. If the book of Jonah (or any prophetic book) was understood as communicating knowledge, then the rereaders were actually invited to interact with a 'communicator'. As mentioned above, this communicator was not independent of the particular worldview, world of knowledge and particular vantage point of the community of rereaders, because this communicator was actually their construction of the implied author.[51] The more the text became 'authoritative', the more likely it was that socially accepted 'authorities' would take control of the interpretation of the text so as to ensure a communally accepted 'correct' reading or set of readings. In other words, one is to expect that the higher the stakes are on the construction of the figure of the 'author', the more likely it is that the authorities will take over the task of constructing this author and, indirectly, that they will take over a role akin to that of the 'author' (i.e. 'the communicator').

To be sure, under these circumstances the 'author' is likely to look

---

49. See Introduction to this volume. I have written on these matters elsewhere (see Ben Zvi, *Obadiah*, passim; *Micah*, passim; and 'Introduction').

50. See Ben Zvi, *Obadiah*, pp. 4-5 and bibliography mentioned there.

51. Of course, within the discourse of those communities the implied author was not identified as such, rather the implied author was constructed as 'the actual author'.

congenial to the constructing 'authorities'.[52] Theological/ideological texts
that carry multivocality allow, and at times require the social participation
of the 'authorities' in the negotiation of theological/ideological knowledge
held to be true.[53] Moreover, multivocality allows not only different
'authorities' but also even the same 'authorities' under different circumstances or in particular contexts to 'appropriate' the same text and con-
struct different (but still interwoven, see below) 'communicators', and
accordingly different (but interwoven) messages to be communicated
among themselves and to the general population.

'Authorities' involved in the process of shaping (and controlling) the
meaning or meanings of high-literacy texts (such as the book of Jonah)
were competent to read such written texts, and as such were most likely
located among the few bearers of high literacy within which and for which
a book such as the book of Jonah was written and within which they were
read and reread.

In addition, the mentioned multivocality of the text also allows 'different' authorities or potentially alternative authorities within the circle of
literati to uphold the authority of the same text, because of the room left by
their respective constructions of the communicator and its message/s. Thus
indirectly, the multivocality that has been identified as a central feature of
the book of Jonah furthers a sense of cohesiveness of the social group by
these sharing of authoritative texts. This sense of cohesiveness contributed
to the stability of the community, and indirectly to the preservation of its
'authoritative texts'.

c. *Multivocality and the Existing Theological Discourse*
Finally, it should not be forgotten that the degree of textual multivocality
in Jonah is consistent with, and representative of the essentially multivocal
(or balanced, or perspectivized) theological/ideological discourse of the
'writing authorities/literati' of the postmonarchic period (see above).[54]

---

52. Cf. Rusch, 'Comprehension'. Needless to say, these considerations apply not
only to ancient Near Eastern circumstances, but the issue is beyond the scope of the
present work on the book of Jonah.

53. Needless to say, the immense majority of the population of Yehud, who had no
direct access to the book of Jonah because they did not know how to read, required the
intermediation of interpretative authorities able to read and interpret the text to them.

54. It should be stressed that multivocality characterizes only *some* aspects of that
universe, but certainly not all. In some regards, this universe is clearly univocal. See
above.

These considerations hold even if particular readings of Jonah (or other biblical texts, for that matter) placed more emphasis on one of the possible partial readings of the book. The book as a whole was meant to be read, reread and studied generation after generation, and most likely read to others in a number of possible settings. Such a continuous dealing with the book along with the unavoidable awareness of the momentarily dispreferred readings contributes to the construction of an overall, multilayered theological message, which suits well the general discourse of the period. The same process shapes the Yehudite literati's construction of the communicator or implied author of the book as one who conveys all these messages to the Yehudites.[55]

---

55. As the book becomes part of the prophetic corpus, this authorial voice begins to be blurred with the divine voice, for prophetic books are YHWH's word. Notice for instance, how the prayer of Habakkuk (Hab. 3) becomes an integral part of prophecy (משא) revealed (חזה) to a prophet . Thus, the written report of the words of a prophet (i.e. a human) to God becomes a revelation or divinely originated vision. The same process led to the consideration of the book of Psalms, for instance, as scripture. See also Chapters 6 and 7.

Chapter 3

JONAH 1.2, DIVINE FOREKNOWLEDGE AND THE FATES OF NINEVEH

In the previous chapter, I demonstrated that the awareness of the fate of
Nineveh in postmonarchic times led to a set of multilayered readings
informing each other. This chapter focuses on another set of multiple readings anchored into the actual text of the book, in the wording of YHWH's
first and second call to Jonah. This set of readings deals with a number of
central issues in the theological discourse/s of ancient Israel and closely
interacts with the two main sets of interlocking readings discussed in the
previous chapter.

The implied author places the expression קרא על (translated in the
NRSV as 'cry out against it') in the mouth of YHWH (Jon. 1.2). קרא על may
be read as equivalent to קרא אל in Jon. 3.2 (translated in the NRSV as
'proclaim to it'), as the similarities between the texts suggest. This understanding is already attested in the LXX and the Targum,[1] and is followed by
many scholars today.[2] It is based on the tendency towards exchange of
על and אל, and their overlap in meaning in some other contexts.[3] Moreover, if the reader (and implied author) grants that the two prepositions are
interchangeable here, then the choice of the preposition על instead of
אל in Jon. 1.2 can be easily understood in terms of a stylistic preference
for alliteration, and the same holds true for the choice of אל in 3.2.[4] In

---

1. See Levine, *Aramaic Version*, pp. 55-56, 83.
2. E.g., Almbladh, *Studies*, p. 17.
3. See B.K. Waltke and M. O'Connor, *Biblical Hebrew Syntax*, §11.2.13b, p. 216.
על may carry a meaning usually associated with אל; see, for instance, 2 Kgs 23.29 and
Neh. 6.17; for instances of interchangeability between אל and על, either carrying a
meaning usually associated with אל or על, see 1 Sam. 25.17 and Isa. 53.1 (cf. Isa.
49.22; Jer. 51.35), and see also Joüon-Muraoka, §133b. The possibility that קרא אל in
3.2 stands for an original or meant קרא על is, however, remote given the extensive use
of the expression קרא אל in the Hebrew Bible (tens of times), and the use of קרא אל
in Jonah itself.
4. See Almbladh, *Studies*, p. 17; Y. Peleg, 'עוד ארבעים יום נינוה נהפכת'

addition, the use of קרא אל in 3.2 is consistent with a quite common
technique of providing textually inscribed veiled hints at future developments in the story, in particular to the next קרא אל in the text, namely,
ויקראו אל־אלהים (they [the Ninevites and their beasts] must call on
[/appeal to] God) in Jon. 3.8.[5]

All this taken into account, still the fact remains that the text reads
קרא על—and not only על. The expression קרא על carries at the very least
the potential to connote a sense of a coming disaster for the object of the
proclamation (cf. 1 Kgs 13.2, 4; Lam. 1.15).[6] In fact, some scholars
maintain that קרא על denotes such a negative message.[7]

On the one hand, the similarity between the two passages in Jonah, the
tendency towards exchange of על and אל in other contexts, and the
testimony of some of the ancient versions suggest one reading; on the
other hand, the expression קרא על carries at the very least the potential to
evoke a different one. It seems that this is another case in Jonah of an
'open' text, that is, of a text that may be read and reread in more than one
way, that is, one in which potential readings within the discourse of the
community eventually become readings and begin to interact with
previous readings. This openness creates a multilayered network of
meanings as it becomes interwoven by necessity in the set of readings
shaped around the two fates of Nineveh discussed in the previous chapter.

Some of these readings bear particular notice. For instance, the reading
of קרא על as implying that the 'decree' has already been issued against
Nineveh (cf. 1 Kgs 13.2, 4) raises questions about the degree of truth-
fulness of YHWH's message to Jonah in 1.2 within an interpretative frame
informed mainly by the narrative of the book and the salvation of Nineveh.
Does the choice of קרא על over קרא אל suggest a characterization of
YHWH as one who crafted the speech so as to mislead Jonah by hinting

---

(בספר יונה—שתי קריאות ג' יונה) (4 'יונה ג')', *Beit Miqra* 44 (1999), pp. 226-43 (227). Or a
tendency towards stylistic variety, see A. Brenner, 'לשונו של ספר יונה', *Beit Miqra* 24
(1979), pp. 396-405.

5.   Although in different contexts, קרא אל carries positive connotations elsewhere in Jonah (e.g. Jon. 1.6, 16; 3.8). Cf. Halpern and Friedman, 'Composition and
Paronomasia', esp. p. 88 n. 17.

6.   Although קרא על means 'proclaim concerning'—most likely not 'against'—in
Neh. 6.7. In any case, even if קרא על carries here a possible undertone of 'proclaim
concerning', the connotation of 'proclaim against' does not disappear. The readings
and rereadings informed by this connotation and by the, at least potential, interchangeability between על and אל are our main concern in this chapter. See below.

7.   See, for instance, Sasson, *Jonah*, pp. 72-75; Simon, *Jonah*, p. 4.

that the divine will bring calamity against Nineveh? Did Jonah know better than to fall for the 'rhetorical trick' intended to mislead him and so rejected the proposal?[8] To be sure, any negative characterization of YHWH was unlikely in these communities of readers. But one has to keep in mind that the rereadership certainly knew that the narrative as a whole deals with YHWH's attempt to educate Jonah, as the conclusion of the book clearly suggests. Within such educative endeavor 'tricking' Jonah to help him to understand is not necessarily unthinkable. After all, YHWH surely made Jonah believe that he was about to die when he was hurled into the raging sea. Further, within the theological discourses of the period YHWH is described as willing to mislead people if the latter are construed as deserving such a treatment.[9]

Alternatively, some of these ancient literati could have construed YHWH as a deity who does not know at the time of the first call to Jonah that Nineveh will not be destroyed on this occasion. This holds true in particular within readings that stressed the necessary—though, to be sure, not sufficient by itself—repentance of Nineveh. If the focus is on the repentance of the city, did they think that YHWH knew that the city would repent, and accordingly, did they construe the future of the Ninevites as closed, that is, they had no choice but to repent? Was the great city conceived of as similar to the great fish in the sense that both creations were meant only to help YHWH to educate the prophet and had no choice of action whatsoever?

To be sure, some biblical texts conveyed and shaped an image of YHWH as one who knows the fate of nations even in the distant future (e.g. Deut. 31.16-21; Isa. 2.1-4; and notice all the promises to Israel; see also the explicit reference to foreknowledge in Jer. 18.12). But others seem to imply some lack of divine foreknowledge in relation to human affairs. Theological texts that emphasize human choice or human repentance in the discourse/s of the period are difficult to accommodate with closed futures (e.g. 2 Chron. 12.5-8). The same holds true for the concept of divine repentance and even explicit divine thoughts about former mistakes (cf. Gen. 6.7; 1 Sam. 15.11).[10]

---

8. These questions are valid even if קְרָא עַל only connoted a sense of decreed calamity; after all, YHWH could have said קְרָא אֶל in Jon. 1.2.

9. See, for instance, Ezek. 20.25-26; cf. 1 Kgs 22.20-23.

10. Cf. T.E. Fretheim, 'The Repentance of God. A Key to Evaluating Old Testament God-Talk', *HBT* 10 (1988), pp. 47-70; *idem*, 'Divine Foreknowledge, Divine Constancy, and the Rejections of Saul's Kingship (1 Sam 15)', *CBQ* 47 (1985),

If YHWH is imagined as not knowing whether punishment will be executed or not at the time narrated in Jon. 1.2, such characterization might be affected by the change of language in Jon. 3.2. Was YHWH construed as intentionally removing the strong negative connotation and choosing a more neutral one? Since the text does not suggest any reason for a decisive change of mind regarding Nineveh in the time span from 1.2 to 3.2, it is difficult within this type of readings to assume that the change was intentional, but if so, the implied author is characterizing YHWH as using a language that within the world of the text conveys an important shift of connotations but is not intended to. Similarly, Jonah is described as announcing the doom of the city, but in a way unbeknownst to him announcing—at least according to one possible reading—its turning away from injustice, its repentance. The divine is thus imagined as a human-like character that may speak without fully recognizing the connotations of what she or he is actually saying.[11]

Of course, readings that tend to diminish the importance of Nineveh's repentance and to emphasize the theology of Jonah 4 and its characterization of YHWH were more likely to assume that YHWH knew of YHWH's attributes, and knew from the very beginning that Nineveh will not be destroyed, just as Jonah of the plot is described as imagining YHWH.[12]

Therefore, if at least the negative connotation of קרא על was accepted by some of these ancient readers who were well versed in their repertoire of authoritative texts and very knowledgeable of Hebrew and its subtleties,

pp. 595-602; J.T. Willis, 'The "Repentance" of God in the Books of Samuel, Jeremiah and Jonah', *HBT* 16 (1994), pp. 156-75; R.W.L. Moberly, ' "God Is Not Human That He Should Repent" (Numbers 23:19 and 1 Samuel 15:29)', in T. Linafelt and T.K. Beal (eds.), *God in the Fray: A Tribute to Walter Brueggemann* (Philadelphia: Fortress Press, 1998), pp. 112-23.

11. It is worth stressing that the mentioned shift resides at the connoted level. קרא אל is neutral and does not preclude a proclamation of disaster. But still the shift from קרא על to קרא אל is not necessarily meaningless from the perspective of an entire book read and studied again and again in ancient times.

12. The final note in Jon. 4.11 does not condition YHWH's refrain from punishing Nineveh on the latter's repentance. In other words, the reported self-presentation of YHWH here is different from that in, for instance, Jer. 18.1-12. Jonah's words in 4.2b also do not presuppose the necessity of Nineveh's repentance for YHWH's relenting. In fact, Jonah and YHWH—within a reading that is not strongly informed by the fall and destruction of Nineveh—are characterized as essentially agreeing on the attributes of the latter; they differ, however, on how they evaluate them. See Chapter 4 of this volume.

then it was possible for them to understand the text as stating that YHWH either suggested or told Jonah that his role will be to pronounce disaster only, not to effect any repentance, and that Nineveh will face disaster.[13]

Of course, such a characterization of Jonah's role also suits well readings of the book that stress the eventual destruction of Nineveh.[14] Moreover, קרא על in 1 Kgs 13.2, 4—which is perhaps the case closest to the use of the expression in Jon. 1.2—explicitly points out that the disaster announced by the prophet does *not* have to fall on its object soon after the proclamation is made, but rather that it may take centuries. If so, YHWH's choice of words in Jon. 1.2 is congruent with the actual ending of the story—for those who factored in the destruction of Nineveh.[15] Within this reading, the divine is construed as one who speaks precise and truthful words. Jonah—that is, a human being—may either misinterpret them or not fully understand them. This image of Jonah is consistent with his characterization as a prophet who proclaims without fully recognizing the meaning of his words in Jon. 3.4.[16]

In sum, the precise choice of words in Jon. 1.2 and 3.2 leads to a multiplicity of readings. Each of these readings informs and complements the others. None of them alone can be considered the only valid reading in antiquity. To be sure, readers could have read and did read קרא על in terms of Jon. 3.2. If 3.2 is taken as the interpretative key for 1.2, then the two are fully consistent with, and well suited to advance a reading of the book strongly informed by ch. 3 and the repentance of the Ninevites (cf. 3.2; 3.8). From this perspective, the potential negative implication of קרא על not only channels the readers' attention to the fate of Nineveh and to its own 'disambiguation' in 3.2, but also serves as a signpost to rereaders that are well aware of the plot as they begin to reread their book. The literary shift from קרא על to קרא אל serves then as a hint at one of the larger messages of the book, the change from decreed destruction to the hope of survival, from an absolute and irrevocable 'against her' to a multivalent 'against her' that is also or may turn out to be in the larger frame 'concerning her'.[17]

A reading of קרא על as pointing to incoming disaster raises theological

---

13. Jerome and Josephus understood Jonah's role in these terms. For short discussion and bibliography, see Sasson, *Jonah*, p. 87.

14. See Chapter 2 of this volume.

15. On the 'forty days' see Chapter 2 of this volume.

16. See Chapter 2 of this volume.

17. Or even 'for her sake', 'on her behalf'.

questions that have direct bearings on the message of the book and on theological constructions of YHWH within the literati. Such a reading interacts and supports some readings of the text informed by the eventual destruction of Nineveh. In addition, it enhances the image of Jonah as a prophet who fails to grasp the subtleness of the divine message in general and of the proper stance regarding a judgment that tarries.

Chapter 4

A TALE OF TWO JONAHS AND TWO ACCOUNTS

1. *On Jonah the Son of Amittay*

One of the two main characters in the book of Jonah is Jonah, the son of Amittay. The fact that the name Jonah appears 18 times in this brief book points to the clear emphasis on the persona of Jonah, as it is developed in the text. His name, Jonah, resounds again and again in the mind of the re-readers of the book. Even for prophetic narratives, this rate of occurrence of the name of a main protagonist is quite remarkable.[1] Yet it is important to keep matters in proportion. The name of the other main protagonist in the book of Jonah, YHWH, appears 26 times (including יהוה־אלהים [translated in the NRSV as 'the LORD God'] in Jon. 4.6). Moreover, to these instances one has to add the substantial number of times in which the deity is referred to as אלהים (God) or האלהים (the God) (e.g. Jon. 1.6; 3.5, 8, 9, 10; 4.7, 8, 9).[2] It is most likely that within the original communities of literati, the text was read again and again, studied, meditated upon and copied, in the main, so as to gain some knowledge about the deity and its attributes, rather than to obtain knowledge about Jonah, a certain individual

---

1.   It is worth stressing that, for instance, the narratives in 2 Kgs 19–20 are significantly longer, but still the name Isaiah appears there only 13 times. In fact, the rate of occurrence of the name Jonah is comparable to that of Elisha in 2 Kgs 2. This text is about one-third shorter than the book of Jonah, but it contains 13 occurrences of the name Elisha. The centrality of Elisha in 2 Kgs 2 is beyond dispute.

2.   On the distribution of the divine names in Jonah, as well as a critical summary of previous scholarship on the matter, see Trible, *Studies*, pp. 82-87; cf. J.D. Magonet, *Form and Meaning: Studies in Literary Techniques in the Book of Jonah* (Sheffield: Almond Press, 1983), pp. 33-38; *idem*, 'The Names of God in Biblical Narratives', in Jon Davies, Graham Harvey and Wilfred G.E. Watson (eds.), *Words Remembered, Texts Renewed: Essays in Honour of John F.A. Sawyer* (JSOTSup, 196; Sheffield: Sheffield Academic Press, 1995), pp. 80-96; Limburg, *Jonah*, pp. 45-46; Day, 'Problems', pp. 43-44.

from the past (cf. Ezek. 33.32).[3] Notwithstanding this observation, the focus of this chapter is on Jonah and the probable ways in which the features and memories that his name evoked or recalled in the original audiences affected their rereadings of the text.

The name 'Jonah the son of Amittay' suits well the story for a number of reasons. First, the name Jonah evokes the image of a 'dove'. Within the world of the Hebrew Bible, the image of a dove has been associated, among others, with 'moaning sounds' (see Isa. 38.14; 59.11; Ezek. 7.16; Nah. 2.8), lack of understanding (see Hos. 7.11); flight (e.g. Ps. 55.7); powerlessness before a mighty and merciful god (cf. Hos. 11.11); good tidings followed by the disappearance of the messenger (Gen. 8.11-12), sacrifices, but particularly with the sacrifice of the poor (Lev. 5.7, 11), and also with the image of someone who is beloved (Song. 1.15; 2.14; 4.1; 5.2, 12; 6.9). Significantly, each of these images is consistent with a possible understanding of the figure of Jonah, for he may be understood as one who utters 'moaning cries' (cf. Jon. 4.3, 8), as one who lacks understanding of the divine or of the actual role of the prophet in the divine economy (and most likely both), as one attempts to fly away (cf. Jon. 1.3),[4] as one who is powerless before a mighty and merciful god, as a harbinger of salvation, as a sacrificial entity, and also as a beloved of a God who goes to substantial lengths to teach him a lesson, or at the very least, to enter into

3. Of course, many contemporaneous readers and rereaders may prefer to focus on Jonah and his tribulations, but they interact with the text from very different theological/ideological/discursive frameworks than that of the first, ancient rereadership of the book. See, for instance, and from various perspectives, M. Howell, 'A Prophet Who Pouts', *Bible Today* 33 (1995), pp. 75-78; Ch. Lewis, 'Jonah—A Parable for our Time', *Judaism* 21 (1972), pp. 159-63; L. Michaels, 'Jonah', in D. Rosenberg (ed.), *Congregation: Contemporary Writers Read the Jewish Bible* (New York: Harcourt Brace Jovanovich, 1987), pp. 232-37; Rosen, 'Jonah'; and cf. Eagleton, 'J.L. Austin' and Sasson, *Jonah*, pp. 342-50. On different readings of Jonah by diverse communities of readers see the Introduction to this volume.

4. For some of these associations see, for instance, Almbladh, *Studies*, pp. 16-17; A.J. Hauser, 'Jonah: In Pursuit of the Dove', *JBL* 104 (1985), pp. 21-37.

Fretheim (*Message of Jonah*, p. 43) adds also 'Israel' to the list of metaphors associated with the image of the 'dove'. But it bears noting that whereas Israel may be characterized as a dove (cf. Hos. 7.11; 11.11), it is less likely that the image of dove per se evoked the theological concept of Israel. Further, although Jonah is an Israelite, it is debatable whether he stands as a symbol of Israel in readings and rereadings of the story within a Persian period background (cf. Almbladh, *Studies*, pp. 16-17), and if so, in which sense? See Chapters 7 and 8 in this volume. For later readings, see Chapter 9.

dialogue with him (cf. Abraham in Gen. 18.23b-33).[5] Given the strong tendency in the book of Jonah to suggest and support a complex net of
multiple rereadings informing each other and in tension with one another,[6]
there is no reason to assume that the multiplicity of images evoked by the
'dove' must have been, or was missed by the readership.[7] Further, although
the name Jonah clearly activates the image of a 'dove', it has at least the
potential to evoke a secondary set of meanings, namely, mental associations with the root ינה whose basic range of meaning in the qal is to
oppress, to destroy. Thus, one finds חרון היונה (oppressing/devastating
fury) in Jer. 25.38, חרב היונה (devastating/destroying sword) in Jer. 46.16;
50.16, and עיר היונה ('the city of oppression', or better, 'oppressive city')
in Zeph. 3.1. Significantly, these associations are also coherent with some
possible understandings of the character of Jonah in the book.[8] Finally,
one may also mention that the choice of the name Jonah may have carried
some graphemic pun on the word Nineveh and that the two shaped a
leading sound 'n', that is, the one associated with the Hebrew letter nun.[9]

<hr />

5.   It is most likely that the story of the judgment of Sodom and Gomorrah and of
the related conversation of YHWH and Abraham (Gen. 18–19) informed the
composition and rereadings of the book of Jonah within the circle of literati for whom
the book was written. See Chapter 2.

6.   As demonstrated time and again in this work, and see Chapters 2, 3 and 5 in
this volume, for example. This tendency occurs elsewhere in prophetic literature and it
is related to both historical and literary constrains/concerns. See Ben Zvi, *Obadiah*, pp.
260-65; *idem*, 'Urban Center'.

7.   Some of these images easily led to christological understandings of the figure
of Jonah already in antiquity (e.g. Jerome). See Y.M. Duval, *Le livre de Jonas dans la
littérature chrétienne grecque et látine* (2 vols.; Paris: Etudes Augustiniennes, 1973),
passim; Steffen, *Die Jona-Geschichte*, passim, and for a short survey of the material,
with some bibliography, Magonet, 'Book of Jonah', esp. p. 620. On these matters see
also the Chapter 9 in this volume.

8.   Of course, יוֹנָה in these texts is grammatically a feminine participle, but still it
may have evoked at least the possibility of that connotation among the intended
rereaders of the book of Jonah. One may notice also that it is not impossible for
morphologically feminine participles to appear as the name of a male character (see
Qohelet). (It is likely that in those cases, they may point to a profession).

9.   נון means also 'fish' in Aramaic. Moreover, the word Nineveh itself probably
conveyed a pun on the word 'fish', that 'fish story' about a 'fish city'. See H.C.
Brichto, *Toward a Grammar of Biblical Poetics* (Oxford: Oxford University Press,
1992), p. 83; Marcus, *From Balaam to Jonah*, pp. 140-41; cf. Sasson, *Jonah*, p. 71. On
first impression, a necessary condition for the actual communicative value of these
proposed puns is that the intended audience is aware of the relevant forms in the other

Even the patronym, Amittay, fits well in the story, because it directly points to YHWH's reliability, faithfulness or trustworthiness,[10] namely, traits that figure prominently in the book. Its presence at the beginning of the story already hints at a satirical or ironical tone to be developed in the book.[11]

In sum, the name Jonah the son of Amittay not only identifies one of the main protagonists, but also hints at several of the main issues raised in the book, and at several of its possible interpretations. As such, it serves as a signpost to rereaders, similar to other signposts present particularly in the openings of other prophetic books.[12] There is no reason to assume, particularly in a book like Jonah in which well-crafted plays on words are abundant, that the literary and theological appropriateness of the name 'Jonah the son of Amittay' had nothing to do with its mention in Jon. 1.1b.[13]

Yet this is surely not the entire story. As it is well known, there is another prophet also called Jonah, the son of Amittay. He appears in the account of Jeroboam II in the book of Kings (see 2 Kgs 14.23-29, esp. v. 25). Neither of the names, separately let alone in conjunction—as pointing to father and son—is attested to elsewhere in the Hebrew Bible. Moreover, there is no case of two separate characters in the Hebrew Bible that carried the same name, the same father's name, and who both fulfilled the same social role, namely, to be prophets at seemingly more or less the same time, that is, the monarchic period and within it the time before the destruction of Nineveh.[14] It seems unlikely that the world of knowledge of

language (and script in the Assyrian case). In this regard, the pun based on the knowledge of Aramaic is much easier to account from the perspective of a community living in the Achaemenid period than the one that requires knowledge of Akkadian. Yet the latter may still be communicated if only a tradition about the association of Nineveh with fish was part of the world of knowledge of the community.

10. The final ' is most likely a hypochoristicon. See, for instance, Sasson, *Jonah*, p. 69. So the name may be rendered YHWH is reliable/faithful/trustworthy.

11. Cf. Wolff, *Jonah*, pp. 98-99; Marcus, *From Balaam to Jonah*, pp. 104-119; Fretheim, *Message*, pp. 43, 53-55, and Chapter 2 in this volume.

12. See Ben Zvi, *Obadiah*, pp. 37-43.

13. Cf. Holbert, 'Deliverance', pp. 63-64; Hauser, 'Jon⸱.h', pp. 22-23; Marcus, *From Balaam to Jonah*, pp. 104-105.

14. Even the most cursory reading of the narrative shows that the world of the book of Jonah is set at a time in which Nineveh was standing and was in fact a mighty, great city.

The reference to the king of Nineveh (rather than Assyria) directly correlates to the

the community within which and for which the book of Jonah was composed included two absolutely independent figures from the past who shared so much. Despite the many fantastic elements in the narrative in Jonah,[15] the text here is quite prosaic. Nothing within the world of the book could have led an ancient community of rereaders to doubt that the two Jonahs were actually one.[16]

Given that it is much more likely that the community of writers (and rereaders) within which Jonah was composed knew of the Jonah of Kings rather than vice versa,[17] it follows from the previous discussion that this is

scope of the divine judgment threatened in the book and to that of the described penance and repentance. It is Nineveh (not Assyria) that is about to be overturned and the Ninevites (not all Assyrians) are those who repent. This being so, and given the literary character of the narrative, it is erroneous to use the reference to Nineveh to narrowly associate the world of the book with historical periods in the neo-Assyrian empire, in which Nineveh served as the capital of the empire, and to exclude all others. In fact, it is erroneous to directly associate the world of the book with the historical neo-Assyrian empire in general. The most that can be said is that the book is set in a past in which Nineveh was an extremely large and accordingly, powerful royal city. This generalized past existed in the world of knowledge of the authorship and primary readership.

15.   E.g. the role of the fish, the rapid and complete repentance of the Ninevites in response to a short 'antirhetorical' (cf. Gitay, 'Jonah', esp. pp. 201-203) announcement. Cf. Marcus, *From Balaam to Jonah*, pp. 97-100.

16.   There is very long tradition of interpretation that identifies the two. See already Josephus, *Ant.* 10.205-14. See also, among many others, Ibn Ezra, Radak and Calvin. For contemporary treatments of this issue, see, among others, Ackerman, 'Jonah', p. 234; Bolin, *Freedom beyond Forgiveness*, pp. 72-75; Gitay, 'Jonah'; Sasson, *Jonah*, p. 342; Wolff, *Jonah*, pp. 98-99; H. Gese, 'Jona ben Amittai und das Jonabuch', *Tbei* 16 (1985), pp. 256-72.

Of course, from these observations it does not follow that there was one historical Jonah, the son of Amittay, whose deeds are recounted ('faithfully or unfaithfully') in two different places, nor that the two stories ever belonged to one single text, nor that any of them must be dated or go back in some related form to the monarchic times. For other positions, see, for instance, D. Schneider, 'The Unity of the Book of the Twelve' (PhD diss., Yale University, 1979, UMI order no. 7926847), p. 110.

17.   The book of Jonah seems to imply a readership aware of the Elijah and Elisha narratives embedded in the book of Kings. The latter are often considered are among the latest redactional elements in the book (see S.L. McKenzie, *The Trouble with Kings: The Composition of the Book of Kings in the Deuteronomistic History* [SVT, 42; Leiden: E.J. Brill, 1991], pp. 81-100). The book of Jonah is usually dated in the Achaemenid period, and later than Kings and much of biblical literature; see, for instance, Simon, *Jonah*, pp. xli-xlii, and see the introduction to this volume. Jonah

an instance of intentional association of a main character in a book with a positive figure of old that exists in the world of knowledge of the community of learned writers and rereaders (and its theological/literary repertoire).[18] This type of association is aimed at legitimizing the central character in the book within the discourse of the community, and indirectly the book itself as well as the teachings conveyed by it (e.g. the books of Baruch, of Enoch, or the ascription of a letter to Elijah in 2 Chron. 21). Thus, the mention of Jonah the son of Amittay may have contributed to the acceptance of the book in the community of rereaders and the impact of the rereading of the book in that social group, at the very least, by characterizing Jonah as a true prophet of YHWH.

Of course, one may argue that if Elijah or Elisha, for instance, had been chosen, then the potential for endorsement would have been maximized.

contains references and allusions to many Pentateuchal narratives (cf. the implicit comparison between Moses and Jonah; the connoted references to Sodom's fate), to other prophetic books and psalms. On Psalms see below. For a general discussion of the references and allusions to other texts, see A. Feuillet, 'Les sources du livre de Jonas', *RB* 54 (1947), pp. 161-86; Magonet, *Form and Meaning*, pp. 65-84, and K.J. Dell, 'Reinventing the Wheel: The Shaping of the Book of Jonah', in J. Barton and D.J. Reimer (eds.), *After the Exile: Essays in Honour of Rex Mason* (Macon, GA: Mercer University Press, 1996), pp. 85-101. In relation to the prophetic books in particular, see, for instance, Bickerman, 'Les deux erreurs', pp. 67-71; *Four Strange Books*, pp. 43-45. There is general agreement that the book of Jeremiah has influenced the composition of Jonah (see, for instance, Simon, *Jonah*, pp. xxxvii-xxxviii; Magonet, *Form and Meaning*, pp. 71, 76-77). There is, however, some debate about the direction of the influence between Joel 2.13-14a and Jon. 3.9a, 4.2b. Among those who maintain that Jonah follows and comments on the text on Joel see, among others, M. Fishbane, *Biblical Interpretation in Ancient Israel* (Oxford: Clarendon Press, 1985), pp. 345-47 and bibliography cited there, and Simon, *Jonah*, p. xxxix, but contrast with Magonet, *Form and Meaning*, pp. 77-79; and cf. T.B. Dozeman, 'Inner-biblical Interpretation of Yahweh's Gracious and Compassionate Character', *JBL* 108 (1989), pp. 207-23, and Landes, 'Case for the Sixth Century', esp. p. 107.

18. Prophets and other personages of old are assigned new texts in Chronicles (e.g. the letter of Elisha in 2 Chron. 21.12, which is the only reference to this prophet in Chronicles). One may also notice the association of Job and Daniel with the books of Job and Daniel respectively (see Ezek. 14.14, 20), of well-known characters (e.g. David, Solomon) with literary units in the books of Psalms and Proverbs. Further, some association with Solomon may have been alluded to in Qohelet. Of course, biblical characters are associated with the main personage of many postbiblical works (e.g. Baruch, the books of Enoch, and others). In addition a very similar process likely led to the characterization of Obadiah in the book of Obadiah, though the situation is more ambiguous there. See Ben Zvi, *Obadiah*, pp. 14-19.

However, one has to remember that, for instance, Enoch (see Gen. 5) and Obadiah, the one who was in charge of the palace of Ahab (see 1 Kgs 18)[19] were minor characters in their respective narratives. Thus, one may assume that other considerations were also at work (see below).

Further, the identification of one of the main characters in the book with a character in the world of knowledge of the community does more than convey legitimacy and authority. The act of reading a text implies that the readers are involved in developing some mental image of what the text is about. When the rereaders of the book of Jonah encountered the name 'Jonah, the son of Amittay', they turned to their prior knowledge about this persona. If the world of knowledge of the rereaders of the book of Jonah included the figure of the prophet Jonah the son of Amittay who lived in Northern Israel during the reign of Jeroboam II, as it is to be assumed, then they activated that image and brought it to bear into their rereading of the book.

Moreover, there even seems to be a textually inscribed marker encouraging this process. The book of Jonah opens *in medias res*.[20] Given the genre expectations associated with a narrative, it seems that Jon. 1.1a was written so as to develop in the community of rereaders a sense of an unfulfilled expectation. They are left pondering about what is 'missing' at beginning of the book. Perhaps some reference about temporal background? Or perhaps some other story?

In any case, ויהי דבר יהוה (translated as 'now the word of the LORD came' in the NRSV) in v. 1a serves as an attention getter that alerts the reader to these issues. It also serves as a signpost for successive rereadings. The reference to Jonah the son of Amittay in the following part of the verse does not solve these issues completely, but it provides the rereaders with a clear lead, namely, that it is likely that there is close link between this story and the character described in Kings, and thus it draws the attention of the rereaders to the particular account in 2 Kgs 14.23-29.

It should be emphasized, however, that the narrative in Jonah does not explicitly stress the identity of the two characters, nor is it interested in a kind of 'complete biography of Jonah'. For instance, there is no recounting or clear, direct allusion to the deeds of the Jonah of Kings in the book of Jonah (one may contrast this with the narrative in Josephus, *Ant.* 10.205-14). There is no temporal or regnal reference in Jonah that may strengthen

19. See Ben Zvi, *Obadiah*, pp. 14-19, 38-39.
20. See, for instance, Trible, *Jonah*, p. 129; Sasson, *Jonah*, pp. 66-68; cf. Bolin, *Freedom beyond Forgiveness*, pp. 74-75.

the bond between the two. Moreover, except for the name of the protagonist, the book of Jonah is not written to be textually reminiscent of the account of Jonah or Jeroboam II in Kings. Thus, one cannot find shared idioms, or quotations from the account in 2 Kings in Jonah. In other words, on the one hand, the text of Jonah is written so as to strongly suggest to its rereaders that they should approach it from a perspective informed by their knowledge of the Jonah of Kings, while, on the other, there is no attempt in Jonah strongly to interweave the two accounts of Jonah, but rather to maintain a certain discursive distance between them. The latter issue will be discussed in section 3.[21]

2. *Two Jonahs: Between Jonah the Son of Amittay in Jonah and on Jonah the Son of Amittay in Kings. Implications for Ancient Rereadings of the Book of Jonah*

a. *First Set of Considerations*
If the community of literati for whom the book of Jonah was written[22] identified the character in the book with the Jonah in Kings, then they constructed Jonah as a northern Israelite who lived during the reign of Jeroboam II. This Jonah, according to the story, delivered a psalm of thanksgiving while in the belly of the fish (Jon. 2.3-10). This psalm contains a remarkable number of textual allusions even to the point of direct quotations from a significant number of psalms,[23] and as such it calls

21. And see also Chapter 6 in this volume, esp. section 4.
22. See Chapter 1 and Ben Zvi, 'Urban Center', and, more recently, 'Introduction: Writings, Speeches'.
23. Thus, for instance, the following parallels have been noticed:

Jon. 2.3	Pss. 18.7; 30.3; 118.5; 120.1; 130.1, 2
2.4	42.8
2.5	31.23
2.6	18.5-6; 69.2
2.7	30.4; 71.20
2.8a	142.4; 143.4
2.8b	5.8; 18.7; 88.3
2.9a	31.7
2.10a	42.5; 50.14, 23; 66.13
2.10b	3.9

This table is based on the one in Dell, 'Reinventing the Wheel', p. 94; and cf. A. Brenner, 'Jonah's Poem out of and within its Context', in P.R. Davies and D.J.A. Clines (eds.), *Among the Prophets* (JSOTSup, 144; Sheffield: Sheffield Academic Press, 1993), pp. 183-92 (184-85). J. Mather ('The Comic Art of the book of Jonah',

attention to both an accepted repertoire of psalms in general[24] and to
certain psalms in particular.

Further, the thanksgiving psalm in Jonah 2 is placed in the mouth of a
character that was construed as a northern Israelite. Thus the text advances
a characterization of a northern prophet who was not only familiar with
many psalms[25] and the genre considerations governing their structure, but
also as one who considers them as a normative standard of piety, theological thought and literary expression. The text implies even more. Since
the prophet Jonah is set in the time of Jeroboam II, the text indicates to its
primary and intended readership that at the very least the psalms to which
explicit allusions are made, and perhaps much of the corpus of Yehud's
psalmic literature, were in existence during the monarchic past,[26] and,
even more important, that they already commanded a sense of normativeness (and accordingly, authority) at that time, not only among Judahites,
but also northern Israelites.[27]

To be sure, in principle, the presence of the same or similar expression
in Jonah's poem and in a particular psalm does not necessarily mean that
the intended audience construed Jonah as knowing the psalm rather than
the particular expression. Yet a number of considerations point in the other
direction:

(1)   The sheer weight of shared or alluded expressions appearing in
       almost every verset in the poem.
(2)   The fact that this 'exaggeration' of repetition is consistent with
       (a) the use of hyperbole elsewhere in the book of Jonah (which
       serves parody, satirical or humoristic purposes, or likely a
       combination of them)[28] and (b) the context because it conveys a

---

Soundings 65 [1982], pp. 280-91 [285]) calls the psalm of Jonah 'a pastiche of these
and other phrases from the psalms'; Brenner claims that 'disregarding v. 9…each verse
of the Jonah poem has an identical or closely parallel counterpart in the Psalms'
('Jonah's Poem', pp. 184-85).

24. The question of whether this repertoire was already present in the form of a
'book of Psalms' (either identical or a forerunner to the eventually canonical book of
Psalms) is beyond the scope of this work.

25. It is possible to argue that Jonah is not quoting from psalms but uses 'coined
phrases' and 'typical languages' present in psalmic literature, but see below.

26. Cf. with the relationship between 1 Chron. 16.8-36 and Pss. 105.1-15; 96.1-13;
107.1; 106.47-48 and 2 Chron. 6.41-42 and Ps. 132.8-10.

27. On this matter and its implications see Chapter 8, esp. section 5.

28. See, for instance, Miles, 'Laughing'; Mather, 'Comic'; Marcus, *From Balaam
to Jonah*, pp. 97-141; Orth, 'Genre'.

(burlesque?) sense of a most 'psalmic' psalm, which may connote a sense of the 'most perfect and therefore, normative (at least, from a genre perspective) psalm'.

(3)   The use (and 'abuse'?) of genre characteristics implies a community in which psalms do exist and this being so, then either Jonah's poem quotes or alludes to psalms that eventually were gathered in the Psalter (or to similar psalms for which there is no evidence, but if so Ockham's razor favors the first alternative).

(4)   The quoted or alluded expression appears in a set of individual psalms that at least at some time during the Achaemenid period—within which one is to situate the authorship and original rereadership of the book of Jonah—were associated with some degree of authority or normativeness.

In the light of these considerations, it is clear that Jonah is described as aware of psalms (not only of 'floating, common expressions'), and of a certain repertoire of psalms to which a sense of normativeness was attached.

The list of psalms to which some form of reference or allusion is made in the poem of Jonah includes, among others, Pss. 3, 5, 18, 30, 31, 42, 50, 66, 69, 71, 88, 118, 120, 130, 142 and 143.[29] Given the considerations advanced above, it is reasonable to assume that, from the viewpoint of a rereadership who is aware of at least some of these psalms, the world of knowledge of Jonah and by extension of a northern, true prophet in (what we call) the ninth century BCE included normative literature and theology of the postmonarchic Jerusalemite.[30] This included the latter's stress on Zion, the Jerusalemite temple, David,[31] and their construction of the concept of Israel.[32]

---

29. It is worth noting that these psalms appear in most of the collections that form the present psalter. For instance they occur among the psalms of 'elohistic psalter' (Pss. 42–83), and among the collection of 'the songs of the ascents' (Pss. 120–34). The question of whether the psalmic repertoire of the period was already organized in a way similar to the known book of Psalms cannot be answered on the basis of the evidence from the book of Jonah.

30. For a similar process of characterization of a 'northern' prophet, see Ben Zvi, *Obadiah*, pp. 38-39.

31. To illustrate, these psalms include such verses as:

(a) מציון מכלל-יפי אלהים הופיע ('Out of Zion, the perfection of beauty, God shines forth'; Ps. 50.2, NRSV);

This state of affairs is not surprising since the book of Jonah was most likely composed within and for that Jerusalemite center. This being so, it is only to be expected that a reconstruction of the past in which an image of the world of knowledge, horizon of thought and education of someone described as a good (northern) Israelite prophet of old be shaped so as to reflect that of the members of the community in which the book is written.[33] Such a reconstruction conveys authority and antiquity to the traditions, viewpoints and literature of the center. Of course, the closer the prophet of old and his theological world comes to that of the later community of writers and rereaders of the book, the less pronounced is the otherness of the image of the northern Israelites of old. In fact, to some extent, one could argue that this otherness is brought to the book for the sake of its disappearance. Scholars who work within the framework of postcolonial studies may claim that the images of the good prophets of the northern kingdom were colonized by the Jerusalemite elite of the Achaemenid period. I would prefer to regard this process in terms of acculturalization and integration. The same process is at work in numerous places in the Hebrew Bible as well as in Jonah. Thus, for instance, the

(b) כי אלהים יושיע ציון ויבנה ערי יהודה זרע עבדיו ינחלוה ואהבי שמו ישכנו־בה ('For God will save Zion and rebuild the cities of Judah; and his servants shall live there and possess it; the children of his servants shall inherit, and those who love his name shall live in it,' Ps. 69.36-37, NRSV);

(c) מגדל ישועות מלכו ועשה חסד למשיחו לדוד ולזרעו עד עולם ('great triumphs he gives to his king, and shows steadfast love to his anointed, to David and his descendants forever', Ps. 18.51, NRSV), and

(d) יאמר־נא ישראל כי לעולם חסדו יאמרו־נא בית־אהרן כי לעולם חסדו ('let Israel say, His *hesed* endures forever;' let the house of Aaron say, His *hesed* endures forever', Ps. 118.2-3) in which the concept of Israel is certainly not that of the northern kingdom.

Significantly, the elements of contrast and irony that are so abundant and crucial within the book are strongly reinforced by any perspective that informed by the texts of the psalms alluded to in the text. See, for instance, on the one hand Ps. 118.6-9, and, on the other, Ps. 3.8. See also Chapter 8.

32. The concept of 'Israel' in postmonarchic communities is discussed in detail in my previous work, Ben Zvi, 'Inclusion in and Exclusion from'. See also my 'What is New in Yehud?'

33. Allusions to other biblical texts—see above—characterize the prophet as one who is well aware of them. Thus, for instance, the readers of Jon. 4.2 learn that the list of (traditional) attributes of YHWH mentioned there was known in ninth-century northern Israel, and not only in a generic way, but in one very similar to the one that appears in Joel 2.13.

construction of 'pious' foreign kings in Chronicles,[34] of the nations in the ideal future in Mic. 4.2 (// Isa. 2.3),[35] and of the Ninevites and the sailors in Jonah all include an image of them as people who behave, at least in part, as (pious) Israelites are supposed to.

b. *Second Set of Considerations*
When the primary community/ies of rereaders approached the book of Jonah in the light of their identification of the character Jonah in the book with the one in Kings—as the implied and likely historical author intended to, they let their knowledge of the text of Kings inform their understanding of the book of Jonah. It is only reasonable to assume that such readers would tend to build their image of Israel's past on the basis of the information given in Kings.[36] It bears noting that if the intended readers were asked to approach the book with Kings in mind, and if the primary rereaders did so, then they had to set the prophet Jonah in a time period not only well before the destruction of Nineveh, but also prior to any contact between Israel and Assyria. The first reference to Assyria in the book of Kings is in 2 Kgs 15.19, that is, in the account of Menahem's reign.[37] In fact, within the world of Kings, the main foe of Israel during the reign of Jeroboam (and the entire dynasty of Jehu, and even from the time

34. Cf. Ben Zvi, 'When a Foreign Monarch Speaks', in M.P. Graham and S.L. McKenzie (eds.), *The Chronicler as Author: Studies in Text and Texture* (JSOTSup, 263; Sheffield: Sheffield Academic Press, 1999), pp. 209-28.

35. See Ben Zvi, *Micah*, esp. pp. 97-98, 105-106.

36. Although the book of Chronicles might have supplied another source of information for constructions of Israel's past to these readers, since Chronicles does not cover the reign of Jeroboam II, it would not have been relevant to the points advanced here.

37. According to G. Galil, the reference in Kings to the submission of Menahem is likely associated with the year 740/39 and the conquests of Jeroboam II mentioned in 2 Kgs 14.24-25 'most probably took place after the campaign of Shalmaneser IV against Damascus in 773'. Jeroboam II reigned from about 790 to 750/49 and Menahem from 749 to 738 BCE. See G. Galil, *The Chronology of the Kings of Israel and Judah* (Leiden: E.J. Brill, 1996), pp. 59, 64. It is worth stressing, however, that historical reconstructions of biblical chronologies are based on sources that were not available to the literati in Yehud (e.g. neo-Assyrian material), and accordingly, irrelevant for their understanding of the text. The book of Kings was most likely the only historiographical source for literati's image of the reign of Jeroboam II. (To state the obvious, the conceptual set up of chronological data in terms of a continuous era beginning with the supposed date of the birth of Jesus, or any kingly figure, was surely not part of their discourse.)

of Ahab) was Aram.[38] Assyria is simply not mentioned.

Thus, if the rereaders of the book of Jonah thought of Jonah as a prophet being sent to Nineveh during the reign of Jeroboam II, then this prophet was sent to a nation that had no contact with Israel. Such a feature would have strongly affected their understanding of Jonah, and the book. For one, there would be a level of readings in which Nineveh would be imagined as a distant, exotic land rather than as a foe of Israel,[39] to which a prophet is sent. Jonah's reluctance, in this reading, would not have anything to do with the future (from the prophet's perspective) actions of Nineveh, for the latter would not be aware of them. Thus, it is certainly significant that, in sharp contrast with other prophetic books (e.g. Nahum), nowhere in the book of Jonah does the character Jonah explicitly refer to, or show, an unequivocal awareness of Nineveh's future actions against Israel or Judah, or of its violent record against other nations.[40] To be sure, this type of readings would have been interwoven with those strongly informed by their image of Nineveh's (/Assyria's) behaviour later on, during the reigns of kings of Israel and Judah later than Jeroboam II.

38. In this regard, there is agreement between the narrative of Kings and the historical events, because the main threat to the northern kingdom during Jehu's dynasty was Aram, not Assyria. If Assyria was a 'shadow' over Israel, at that time it was a protective shadow. The repeated Assyrian campaigns against Aram (841, 838, 805, 804–802, 796, 773 BCE) allowed Israel to stand against Aram, and at times to fight back. In fact, the enigmatic reference to a מושיע, 'saviour', that YHWH gave to Israel in 2 Kgs 13.5 is likely to be a veiled reference to Adad-nirari III and a faint echo of the actual circumstances of the period. For bibliography and a different position regarding 2 Kgs 13.5 see N. Na'aman, 'The Contribution of Royal Inscriptions for a Re-evaluation of the Book of Kings as a Historical Source', *JSOT* 82 (1999), pp. 3-17 (11-12).

Incidentally, this reference in Kings is particularly interesting given that those responsible for the writing of the book seem aware of earlier events in the history of the northern kingdom such as Adad-nirari's campaigns, but unaware of later events, such as Sargon's activities against Samaria. On similar matters, and particularly regarding knowledge of Shishak's campaign cf. Na'aman, 'Contribution of Royal Inscriptions'.

39. Cf. the other 'exotic' or distant spaces referred to by the narrative (e.g. Tarshish, the bottom of the sea, the big fish).

40. As it is well known, there is a very long history of interpretation according to which Jonah does not want the salvation of Nineveh because he knows what Assyria will do to Israel. For a survey see Bickerman, *Four Strange Books*, pp. 14-19. Still, there is no explicit remark anywhere in the Jonah narrative that supports such a position. Such a reading may come only from the meta-narratives from which readers approach the text. See below and Chapter 9.

Prophetic literature would have also contributed to such a characterization of postsalvation Nineveh.[41]

It is possible, and even likely, that the negative characterizations of Nineveh and Assyria that existed in the world of knowledge of these communities had a bearing in their rereadings of the text in general, and in their understanding of Jonah's reluctance. If this was the case, and Jonah was assigned to the time of Jeroboam II, then they had to imagine him as one who could foresee events, such as the destruction of Israel, which stand beyond the horizon of his time (as shaped in Kings), or at least unknowingly acted as if he had sensed them. In other words, he was imagined as prophet who could see far beyond his own time (i.e. like Moses), even if it is nowhere stated that YHWH informed him of Assyria's future actions against Israel.

Alternatively, the rereaders may have construed Jonah as being sent to Nineveh many years after he prophesied Jeroboam's victories, and already into the period of confrontation between Israel and Assyria. In other words, they could have split the prophetic character and his own knowledge of Nineveh according to a diachronic axis, so the Jonah of the book of Jonah knew much more about Assyria than the Jonah of Kings. However, the text in Jonah nowhere claims that this is the case. [42] In fact, although the book of Jonah condemns—as it has to[43]—the behavior of Nineveh before Jonah's commission, the condemnation is phrased in such a way that it contains no reference to any action of Assyria against Israel, Judah, or any nation for that matter. The sin attributed to Nineveh in the narrative is חמס (Jon. 3.8), a term that is often translated as 'violence'. חמס most likely points at violence in the realm of social, interpersonal interaction rather than mainly or particularly in that of international affairs.[44]

---

41. Cf. *Targ. Nah.* 1.1.

42. On the relations between the account of Jonah in Kings and in the book of Jonah, see below.

43. If the city was to be threatened with evil from YHWH, it must have done something to merit it.

44. Cf. Gen. 6.11, 13; also Ezek. 8.17. On חמס see H.J. Stoebe, 'חמס', *TLOT*, I, pp. 437-39. The REB translated the relevant portion of the verse, 'the injustice they practise'; NJPS, 'the injustice of which he is guilty'. Cf. already *b. Ta'an.* 16a, 'Let them turn everyone from his evil way and from the violence that is in their hands. What is the meaning of, "From the violence that is in their hands"?'—Samuel said: Even if one had stolen a beam and built it into his castle he should raze the entire castle to the ground and return the beam to its owner' (ET Soncino Talmud). See also *b. Ta'an.* 7b, and see Chapter 9.

In sum, even when the text of Jonah asks its intended and first rereaders to approach the character in the book within the frame of their knowledge of the Jonah in Kings, such a request does not lead to a minimization of the number of potential readings. The text of Jonah is written in such a way that it is remarkably open. This textual openness is conducive to different understandings, which are all consistent with the text itself and the social, cultural and theological context from within which it was written and first reread. These different rereadings inform and comment on each other and create a richer theological/ideological texture. In addition they contribute to the necessary rereadability of the book and to its likelihood of being be passed from generation to generation.[45]

3. *Between the Two Accounts of Jonah*

As mentioned above, the readership for which the book of Jonah was composed was asked to approach this book from a perspective that was informed by the identification of the main human character in the narrative with the Jonah of Kings. Conversely, such an identification and the consequent sets of readings that it leads to influenced the way in which the Yehudite (and later; see Josephus, *Ant.* 10.205-14) literati read and reread the account of Jonah in Kings, for once both Jonah and Kings are integral to their repertoire, these texts begin to influence each other.

Yet is remarkable that the two written accounts (i.e. Jonah and 2 Kgs 14.23-29) were presented to their readerships from the very outset as quite separate and remained so, at least at the level of textually inscribed markers. For instance, the language of Jonah contains allusions to many other texts within the repertoire of the Yehudite literati,[46] but none to 2 Kgs 14.23-29, beyond the obviously important reference to Jonah the son of Amittay. But does not this shared reference create an expectation of more shared material? And if so, what kind of rhetorical (and theological) message is reflected and conveyed by the lack of fulfilment of this expectation?

The voice in Jonah uses a different language than the one in Kings,[47] and deals with separate issues—see below.[48] These textually inscribed

---

45. Such is the case in other prophetic books. See my previous work on Obadiah and Micah. See Introduction to this volume.

46. See Chapter 2.

47. Notice, for instance, the absence of dtr. language in the book of Jonah, and the relative high proportion of 'Aramaisms'.

48. To be sure, 'separate' within the limitations of a basically shared discourse.

differences—there is no real ambiguity on this point—indicates to the intended rereaders of Jonah that they are to approach this book as a separate literary/theological unit.[49] These tendencies are consistent with the organization of the theological and literary repertoire of the Jerusalemite center into 'sets' (e.g. the so-called dtr. history, prophetic books) that, although they inform each other, remain separate, each with its own voice and its own story about the past of the community of rereaders.[50]

Furthermore, granted that the account of Jonah in Kings and the book of Jonah were intended to be read as separate works, and the genre difference between a prophetic and a historical book were clearly conveyed to the targeted readership, still the fact remains that, because of the shared reference to a prophet named Jonah the son of Amittay, they *did* inform each other in some ways. Since Jonah was composed later than Kings, the prophetic book was written from the outset to activate in the memory of its intended readers the account in 2 Kgs 14.23-29.[51] This being so, one may ponder whether some kind of 'seed' of the narrative in Jonah is to be found in the account in Kings? Was there a potential 'trigger' for the narrative in Jonah within the account in Kings? Did the narrative in Jonah reflect in some way the account or the issues raised in the account in Kings?[52] And if this is the case, what would be the effect of this compositional feature on the intended readership?

49. This situation is similar to the one encountered in Obadiah (see above) and it is consistent with the eventual placement of the book of Jonah within the general corpus of the prophetic books rather than within that of the deuteronomistic history.

50. One may notice that even Jeremianic dtr. language shows a particular flavor. On these matters see Ben Zvi, 'Looking at the Primary (Hi)Story and the Prophetic Books as Literary/Theological Units within the Frame of the Early Second Temple: Some Considerations', *SJOT* 12 (1998), pp. 26-43. The relevance of this feature for the study of the organization of the knowledge of the past, and the world of knowledge of these literati is an issue that certainly deserves further study, but stands beyond the scope of this study of Jonah. See P.R. Davies, *In Search of 'Ancient Israel'* (JSOTSup, 148; Sheffield: Sheffield Academic Press, 1992), esp. pp. 106-15; and cf. Ben Zvi, 'Introduction: Writings, Speeches'.

51. To be sure many prophetic superscriptions asked their readers to associate the world of the book with the knowledge of Israel's past (e.g. Hos. 1.1). But the case of Jonah is different because it does not focus on a particular regnal period but on the figure of a prophetic character in Kings.

52. Cf. the narratives about Elijah in Kings and the appearance of the letter of Elijah in Chronicles, the reference to Enoch as a friend of YHWH who just disappeared and development of the Enochic tradition, or the references to Baruch in Jeremiah, and the development of the books of Baruch.

Neither the basic narrative of the two accounts, nor their details, nor their respective languages, point to any such 'trigger' or 'seed'. On the surface, however, both accounts seem to share what may be perceived as a case of lack of coherence between human behaviour and divine response. One of the most interesting proposals in this regard is the one advanced by Gitay.[53] He develops the following argument:

> The deliberate attempt of the author of Jonah to relate his prophet to the Jonah of Kings sheds fresh light on the meaning of the escape [of Jonah in the book of Jonah]… It [Jonah's mission to King Jeroboam II] was not the divine act of trial but an act of mercy. Consequently… Jonah might wonder whether he is being ordered to follow the steps of Jonah of Kings and to deliver the message of the absurd [Gitay here refers to something that contradicts what he calls 'the Deuteronomistic concept of the doctrine of retribution'.] to the wicked Nineveh (1.2). Therefore Jonah escapes. This escape is not a total surprise for the learned audience who is already familiar with the nature of the mission of Jonah of Kings… Because Jonah might suspect that his mission to Nineveh should be a duplicate of his predecessor's mission to Jeroboam of Israel, he escapes.[54]

If this were so, to some extent the lack of the coherence just indicated in Kings may be seen as the 'trigger' for the story in Jonah. But several issues undermine Gitay's proposal. To begin with, there is no reason to differentiate so tightly between two Jonahs, between the 'predecessor' (i.e. the Jonah of Kings) and a 'second Jonah'. More importantly, there is no reason to assume that the learned rereadership of the book of Jonah *had* to imagine, or only imagined their Jonah as later than the one of Kings. In fact, one temporal sequence (e.g. first Nineveh, then the prophecy in Kings) is as good as its opposite, because neither of the two is actually marked in the text. In both cases we are dealing with an act of 'filling gaps' according to a preconceived narratives about the prophet.[55]

On the history of interpretation of Jonah as a 'midrash' either on 2 Kgs 14.25, Jer. 18.8 or Exod. 34.6 and the problems of such a characterization see Sasson, *Jonah*, p. 345 n. 32; Trible, 'Book of Jonah', pp. 472-74; Salters, *Jonah*, p. 47. Cf. Trible, *Studies*, pp. 161-68, 273-79; J. Wellhausen, *Skizzen und Vorarbeiten*. V. *Die Kleinen Propheten* (Berlin: Reimer, 1892), p. 211.

53. Gitay, 'Jonah', esp. pp. 197-201.

54. Gitay, 'Jonah', esp. pp. 199-201.

55. So, for instance, 'for those who view Jonah as a prophet zealous for strict divine justice, his eponymous book is a sort of consecration story, in which his mission to Nineveh prepares him for his second mission—bringing good tidings to those who

Even if, for the sake of argument, one would agree that the learned readership followed the only path of interpretation that Gitay allows them and are unequivocally convinced that the Jonah of Kings precedes the one of the book of Jonah, they could still have developed more than one set of expectations on the basis of the record of the prophet from Kings.

Significantly, Gitay presupposes that Jonah was particularly ill-disposed to Nineveh,[56] but, to begin with, if he is the prophet of the days of Jeroboam, then he has no major reason for that hostility unless he is aware of what the future holds, but nothing of the kind is explicitly mentioned in the book. Moreover, as some scholars have pointed out, Jonah is not described as expressing hostility against the Assyrians in particular, or against any nation for that matter.[57] Such hostility is not textually inscribed in the book but brought about by the interaction between the worldview of the readers and the text of Jonah.[58] Ancient rereaders strongly informed by the image of Nineveh as a terrifying oppressing city were likely to view Jonah as strongly hostile to Nineveh from the outset; whereas ancient rereaders strongly informed by the world of the text and its setting within the history of Israel agreed among them were far less likely to view Jonah in this perspective. Again, these rereaders may have approached the book and the figure of Jonah in one occasion and under certain circumstances in one way, but in a different manner in another.[59]

In any event, the starting point of the narrative in the book of Jonah is a case of unexpected prophetic behaviour. No other prophet in the Yehudite theological and literary repertoire attempts to escape as Jonah does. Of course, the implied author uses this astonishing behavior for literary and rhetorical reasons. In fact, it serves to reinforce the image of what a normative prophet should do. But the same may be said of the conclusion of the book. The entire plot in ch. 4 begins with another instance of unexpected behaviour; after all, no other prophet strenuously objects to

have not and will not repent' (Simon, *Jonah*, p. xxxvi). Simon discusses also other possibilities, including the opposite temporal sequence.

56. Gitay, 'Jonah', p. 200.

57. Cf. H.C. Brichto, *Toward a Grammar of Biblical Poetics* (Oxford: Oxford University Press, 1992), p. 80. The construction of Jonah as a 'chauvinist'.

58. In other words, the construction of the prophet Jonah as a 'chauvinist' (or the like) is neither inscribed in the text nor necessarily the only possible one; it results from a reading of the text that is informed by certain worldviews and a number of premises. See Chapter 9.

59. See Ben Zvi, 'Introduction: Writings, Speeches'.

YHWH's mercy as Jonah does. Similarly, the astonishing behaviour of the prophet serves to reinforce the image of what a normative prophet should do and think. To be sure, if this understanding of the text is *one of* those the book intends its rereadership to grasp, then such a situation does imply that the implied author's expectation of the ancient rereaders was not that the Jonah of Kings would oppose YHWH's decision to spare Nineveh.[60] The same probably holds true for the historical author.[61] Significantly, even after Jonah 4 is taken into account, the text still leaves open the real reason for Jonah's opposition to YHWH's 'repentance' and accordingly, it also leaves open the ultimate reason for the 'unexpected escape' of Jonah.

To put this another way, although it is possible that some ancient rereaders followed at times the path suggested by Gitay, it is also likely that some of them would have noticed that the argument of Jonah in Jon. 4.2b—which is the crucial text—is phrased in such a way that it does not refer to Nineveh at all. It deals, however, with attributes of YHWH that within this discourse appear to be eternal and noncontingent. It is worth stressing that the final note in Jon. 4.11 does not condition YHWH's relent from punishing Nineveh on the latter's repentance.[62] Jonah's words in 4.2b also do not presuppose the necessity of Nineveh's repentance for YHWH's relenting. Within these types of readings, that is, readings in which the fate of Nineveh is salvation not destruction, YHWH and Jonah are characterized as essentially agreeing on the attributes of the latter; they differ, however, on how they evaluate them. Was Jonah very zealous of these divine precise attributes—and implicitly zealous for others within the tradition?[63]

---

60. M. Sternberg reconstructs the reaction of the readers of Jon. 1 as follows: 'Why does Jonah flee when God orders him "go to Nineveh, that great city, and cry against it, for their wickedness has come up before me" (1:2)? The narrator does not say, but apparently only because the reason is self-evident: Jonah is too tender-hearted to carry a message of doom to a great city. He obviously protests against a wrathful God not with words, like Abraham or Moses or Samuel, but with his feet' (*The Poetics of Biblical Narrative* [Bloomington: Indiana University Press, 1987], p. 318). According to Sternberg, it is only in ch. 4 that the readers understand that they have been misled, that Jonah is not merciful but ruthless. For Sternberg, the image of an Israelite prophet who refuses to carry a message of doom to Nineveh is not a logical impossibility, but a basic assumption essential to the narrative art of the text. It is a narrative surprise that Jonah objects to YHWH's mercy. See Sternberg, *Poetics*, pp. 318-20.

61. See Chapter 1.

62. Contrast with the theology advanced in, for instance, Jer. 18.1-12, though notice the motif of divine foreknowledge in Jer. 18.12.

63. E.g. Num. 23.19; 1 Sam. 15.29. It is a marker of majesty that the king's decree

And if so, and within the horizon of thought of that discourse, what did they think that the character Jonah would have thought of YHWH's decision to relent, or not to relent, from punishing another great city, Jerusalem, in which חמס was in abundance (cf. Jer. 6.7; Ezek. 7.23-24; and see Amos 9.7)?[64] Or was Jonah concerned only about the lack of correspondence between his prophetic proclamation, as he understood it, and the divine actions? Or did he think that a prophet should have something more than a secondary, at best, role in the administration and manifestation of the divine economy?[65]

Scholars have recognized the rhetorical importance of the suspense created by the unanswered question of why Jonah escaped in Jonah 1. They have also recognized its role in channelling attention in the narrative.[66] But Jon. 4.2 does not really resolve the question. The reason for his flight is not textually inscribed in the book. This fact substantially contributes to the phenomenon of multiplicity of partial meanings informing each other.[67] The text therefore channels the attention of the rereaders to a question, or better to a set of possible answers that suit well the theological discourse/s of the literati. None of these answers can rule out of existence the other, and all of them together shape and reflect the horizon of thought of the literati of the period.[68]

Gitay's approach *presumes* rather than proves that a perceived lack of

---

cannot be changed. For ironical representations of this motif see Est. 1.19, 8.8 and Dan 6.9, 13.

64. On these matters, see Chapter 8 in this volume.

65. On these matters see Chapter 2 in this volume.

66. See, for instance, Simon, *Jonah*, pp. xxiii-xxiv.

67. See above, and Chapters 2, 3 and 5.

68. I wish to stress that the point I am making is *not* that anything could go in ancient Israel, or that readings are so indeterminate that there is no practical purpose in trying to reconstruct likely readings in ancient Israel. The point is that there is a set of potential readings that suits well the discourse of the period. Given that these texts were read, reread and studied, it is likely that all these readings would occur at some point and then enter into the discourse of the community. Moreover, since the possibility of particular multiple readings is directly dependent on textually inscribed features of the text, and since one may assume that the authors of prophetic books knew that their work was supposed to be read and reread, it is likely that some of these multilayered meanings were intended by the actual authors. In any case, the rereaders attributed them to the communicator or implied author of the book (see Introduction). It is worth stressing that just as the text was textually inscribed to allow multiple meanings in some regards, it was quite unequivocal in others, for instance, regarding the secondary role of the prophet in the divine economy. See below and Chapters 2 and 7.

coherence between human behaviour and divine response is (a) *the* reason that led the author of the book of Jonah to link the protagonist of that book to Jonah of Kings, (b) the actual bond keeping the two texts together in the mind of the audience, in addition to (c) *the* reason for Jonah's escape in the narrative as presented by the text and as understood by the ancient readership (/audience) of the book. But does this lack of coherence serve as a particularly close link between the two texts?

The account in Kings reports of an explicitly sinful king of Israel who not only avoided divine judgment, but was given victory against his enemies, and even expanded Israel's territory—both seeming markers of divine blessing. All this is not because of the king's or Israel's repentance—which are notoriously absent in the account—but because YHWH was mindful of Israel's distress.

In the narrative of the book of Jonah, Nineveh is a sinful city saved from the divine judgment, but here its king and its people do repent. This lack of punishment is probably expected within the discourse of the rereaders (cf. Jer. 18.18; 26.3, 13) and broadly hinted at by the narrative's hyperbolic account of Nineveh's repentance.[69]

The unexpected element in Jonah—in fact, unparalleled in the entire Hebrew Bible—is that the (true) prophet expressed such a distress over a divine lack of judgment in the face of massive repentance (see Jon. 4.1).[70] Thus, the tension in the book of Jonah does not reside in a perceived lack of coherence between human actions (i.e. those of the Ninevites both before Jonah came to town and following his announcement) and divine response, but rather between YHWH's actions and a prophet's response to them. In sum, if the assumption is that the main theological relation between the two texts is centered on the opposite pairs 'YHWH–Israel' and 'YHWH–Nineveh', then this position is strongly undermined by a close comparison of the two texts because they advance a different set of pairs, namely, 'YHWH–Israel' or 'YHWH–Jeroboam' in Kings and 'YHWH–Jonah' in the book of Jonah.[71]

---

69. Despite a text such as Num. 23.19, but contrast with Exod. 32.14, in which repentance is not mentioned.

70. Significantly, there is no textual support in the book of Jonah for the idea that Jonah doubted the Ninevites' repentance. Such a position represents an attempt to fill a gap in the narrative in a manner that, on the one hand, justifies Jonah's position and, on the other, maintains the position that people who repent are to be spared from the divine judgment.

71. In other words, in the book of Jonah, the Nineveh episode becomes a foil, like

This being so, one may wonder whether, alternatively, there is some form of a substantial link between the texts around the polarities of Jonah–('theologically ideal') Israel. Although the character of Jonah is far from being construed as the typical and ideal Israelite (or Israelite prophet) within the theological world communicated by the book of Jonah to its original rereadership,[72] it is doubtful whether this polarity is central to the book of Jonah,[73] beyond the obvious, namely, that any attempt to characterize a person separates him/her from the larger group and advances a set of 'differences'.

A different set of polarities may be brought into the discussion. If the focus of attention is on Jonah's attitude, it may be proposed that the main pairs are 'Jonah–Jeroboam/Israel' in Kings, and 'Jonah–Nineveh' in Jonah.[74] But the account in Kings is of no help in this regard, because there is no reference to the prophet's thoughts about the divine action that he had to proclaim.[75]

It is possible, given the tendency to identify with one's group in the social systems of ancient Near Eastern/eastern Mediterranean cultures, that the Jonah of Kings was construed by the community of rereaders of Jonah as thoroughly supportive of his prophecy.[76] However, this understanding is not necessarily the only one allowed by the text, which is silent in this regard, nor does it seem to be the most likely once the general theological discourse of Kings is taken into account.

---

the episode of the plant, for the private education of an individual prophet by YHWH. On YHWH and Jonah as the two main protagonists of the book of Jonah, see above. It goes without saying that YHWH's education of the prophet in the world of the book serves as a foil for the theological education of the readers of the book and of those to whom the book was read.

72. One may notice, for instance, how the authorial voice sets YHWH as the main opponent of Jonah's viewpoint, and the burlesque characterization of Jonah.

73. Israel as a social group is not mentioned in Jonah, and no Hebrews are mentioned in the book, except Jonah.

74. If this were so, then a main underlying issue would have been the relation between 'Israel' and Nineveh and perhaps by extension that between Israel and 'the nations', but see below.

75. That prophets were construed as having no choice but to proclaim the word of YHWH as they were commanded is exemplified in Jonah, who, after all, proclaims. Cf. Amos 3.8.

76. The characterization of Jonah the son of Amittay as a 'nationalistic', narrow-minded prophet cannot be supported on the basis of the account of Kings, nor on the basis of the narrative of Jonah (see below).

The odd character of the pair 'a sinner king and divine blessing' is certainly recognized by the narrator in 2 Kgs 14.23-29 and communicated to the intended readers of Kings. It is most reasonable to assume that the Yehudite literati within whom and for whom the book of Jonah was composed recognized the oddity of the case. Since these literati construed the prophets of old as figures who shared their own theological conundrums, it is likely that they imagined Jonah (i.e. the one in Kings) as baffled by a seeming divine inconsistency, and particularly so given that Jonah was characterized there as a true, good prophet.[77] Such a good prophet was most likely construed as one who stood up against what is wrong in the sight of YHWH and, accordingly, as a strong opponent of Jeroboam II and his elite, just those whose success he was commanded to proclaim. It almost goes without saying that prophetic voices that understood and accepted YHWH's right to punish Israel if it was considered sinful populate the books of Kings, the Latter Prophets and Chronicles. These voices endorsed a principle of consistency between human behaviour and divine retribution.

Significantly, in 2 Kings 14 the 'answer' provided to the inconsistency between human activity and divine response is *not* placed in the mouth of the prophet Jonah, nor is it associated with him at all. It is the narrator's voice. In any case, the simple fact is that the text is silent and therefore open about Jonah's state of mind in Kings.

The situation is to some extent similar in the book of Jonah, because it is still unclear why Jonah felt dismayed, or even perhaps betrayed by YHWH's actions. It is worth stressing in this regard that Jonah himself is nowhere presented in the book as one claiming that he opposes the non-punishment of Nineveh because they were non-Israelites. Quite the opposite, the interaction between Jonah and the sailors in Jonah 1 makes such a claim quite improbable. Further, the main 'pair' of the book as a whole is certainly not 'Jonah–Nineveh',[78] as required by this proposal, but

77. His prophecy is presented as an integral part of a pattern of 'proclamation and fulfillment' (cf. G. von Rad, 'The Deuteronomistic Theology of History in the Book of Kings', in *Studies in Deuteronomy* [SBT, 9; London: ACM Press, 1953], pp. 74-91) in which the prophet character is surely seen in positive terms (cf. Deut. 18.21-22).

78. Nor 'Jonah–the nations'. It is worth stressing in this regard that there are no explicit references to any tension between Israelites and non-Israelites in the book of Jonah. Further, as Radak (commentary on Jon. 1.1) has noticed, the book of Jonah is the *only* prophetic book in the Hebrew Bible that contains no reference to Israel at all. On these matters, cf. among others Bickerman, *Four Strange Books*, pp. 27-28; Rofé,

'Jonah–YHWH'. In sum, neither the account in Kings nor the book of Jonah supports this proposal.[79]

There is, however, one clearly shared common theological supposition that is reflected and communicated by these two texts. In both accounts, the prophet's proclamation of YHWH's word is presented at first as having great impact on the events, but in both cases it is shown to carry no real importance. In Kings, following the negative note of evaluation (i.e. 'the king did evil in the eyes of YHWH', 2 Kgs 14.24), the text reports Jeroboam's military and political success, which is described as the fulfillment of the prophecy of Jonah the son of Amittay (v. 25b). But what was the putative weight of this prophecy in the political and military events? According to the next two verses (i.e. vv. 26-27), almost none, 'for YHWH saw that the affliction of Israel was very bitter…so YHWH saved them by the hand of Jeroboam son of Joash'. Significantly, this is only one example of the tendency to place prophecy in its 'proper proportion' in the book of Kings, and in the Deuteronomistic History as a whole.[80] In the book of Jonah, the narrative tells about the immediate, great success (Jon. 3.5-9) of what is arguably the prophetic proclamation with the least persuasive appeal (Jon. 3.4b) in the Hebrew Bible.[81] This consideration, along with the explicit reference to Jonah's conviction that no matter what the prophet will do or attempt to do, YHWH will save the city (Jon. 4.2), raises the issue of the putative weight of the prophet and his actions (or lack therof) in the divine economy.[82] Yet this observation about the tendency to

Prophetical Stories, pp. 160-63; Clements, 'Purpose', esp. pp. 17-19.

79. So why was Jonah so disappointed with YHWH's decision not to execute judgment against Nineveh? To mention a few options, was it because he begrudged Nineveh's fate, despite its repentance? Or was it because of the role he had to play in the divine economy? Or was it because he held a particular (and quasi-burlesque within the world of the book) understanding of what prophecy is about? Or a combination of the above? Or do these options present a net of complementary answers each informing one another and shaping together a kind of multivocal message to the community of rereaders?

80. See Ben Zvi, 'Prophets and Prophecy'.

81. One cannot but notice that this is one of the shortest prophetic proclamations and that it provides no ground whatsoever for what it announces; yet it is precisely this proclamation that achieves a success that is unparalleled in other prophetic texts. On these issues see Gitay, 'Jonah'.

82. If the text of Jonah suggests to its intended rereaders that the contribution of Jonah (and by implication, likely that of any prophet) to the implementation of YHWH's will on earth is secondary at best—and perhaps bordering on nil—then they

convey the 'proper place of prophecy' in the divine economy is more likely to be a reflection of a shared worldview than of a one to one particular link between these two accounts, and the more so since this tendency is present not only in these two accounts but also in the Deuteronomistic history at large.[83]

may approach the central confrontation in the book, that is, that between Jonah and YHWH from a different perspective, something like Jonah saying to YHWH, 'Why do you want me to go through all this ordeal when my role is actually not necessary, since no matter what I will do, you will still able to carry out your will?'

For a very different perspective, but still touching on these issues, see Eagleton, 'J.L. Austin'.

83. See Ben Zvi, 'Prophets and Prophecy'.

Chapter 5

JONAH, THE RUNAWAY SERVANT/SLAVE

1. *The Motif of the Runaway Servant/Slave: General Considerations*

The purpose of this chapter is to explore the network of possible meanings and connotations raised by a characterization of Jonah as a 'runaway servant or slave' among the literati of Yehud, that is, the ancient communities of readers and rereaders of the book of Jonah among whom and for whom primarily the book as such was written.[1] Jonah embodied multiple social and ideological (or theological) constructions. To mention two: (a) an ancient prophet from the northern kingdom in the monarchic

---

1.   I wish to express my debt to R.J. Ratner, whose article 'Jonah, the Runaway Servant', *Maarav* 5–6 (1990), pp. 281-305, drew me to the study of this matter. This chapter builds on his observations and leads the discussion into new directions.

The narrow focus here on a particular time and type of readers is fully intentional and absolutely necessary. The connotations and meanings raised by the imagery of a runaway slave depend on the social location, world of knowledge, ideology and general discourse of those who develop the mentioned meanings and connotations. The images and concepts evoked by references to slavery and to runaway slaves among the literati in Yehud were surely different from what these references evoke among, for instance, present-day Americans, Canadians and Danes. They are also different from those of actual slaves in Yehud. It would be a mistake to assume that all members in society, slaves and bearers of high literacy—some of whom may have owned slaves—shared the same viewpoint regarding slavery. Cf. J. Glancy, 'The Mistress–Slave Dialectic: Paradoxes of Slavery in Three LXX Narratives', *JSOT* 72 (1996), pp. 71-87.

The book of Jonah was written primarily among and for a particular group in society, namely, bearers of high literacy and as such it bears testimony to their views.

As pertinent to the genre of this volume, this chapter deals only with matters of ancient history, and therefore does not address theological issues that may and do arise today from the fact that neither the Hebrew Bible—nor for that matter the New Testament or rabbinic literature—call for the abolition of slavery. I would leave that matter to theologians. From a historical point of view, it suffices to state the obvious, the institution of slavery existed among all peoples in the ancient Near Eastern world including, of course, Israel.

period; (b) a person who is knowledgeable of authoritative texts, knows how to quote them, claims to know about God's attributes on the basis of his knowledge of these texts, and to a degree fails because of the limitations of such a knowledge.[2] These partial constructions of Jonah inform each other, and through this process lead to a multidimensional and multivocal characterization of Jonah in the book, within the frame of the worldview and world of knowledge of these readers and rereaders. The focus in this chapter is on another feature of the constructions of Jonah in this milieu: as a runaway servant or slave, and its potential implications for readings of the book within its intended and primary rereadership.

Before studying the possible implications of the motif of the runaway servant or slave within the Yehudite literati, one first has to demonstrate the relevance of the motif to the matter at hand. One has to show that (a) Jonah was likely understood as a 'servant or slave of YHWH', (b) Jonah was characterized in the book as runaway from YHWH, and (c) the likely presence of the ideological motif and social realia of running away slaves among these ancient Near Eastern communities of literati. Point (b) does not require much elaboration. Jonah is explicitly characterized as a runaway (Jon. 1.1-3, 10; 4.2). Similarly, references to runaway slaves occur in many documents and literary texts of different sorts and across time in the ancient Near East, including the Persian period.[3] Point (a), however, demands some attention.

To be sure, different people and groups are referred to in the Hebrew Bible as 'servants of YHWH' (עבד יהוה, either in singular or plural depending on the case). The list includes Moses (see Exod. 14.31 and passim), Joshua (e.g. Josh. 24.29), Caleb (Num. 14.24), David (see 2 Sam. 3.18 and passim), Hezekiah (2 Chron. 32.16); Zerubbabel (Hag. 2.23), Abraham (Gen. 26.24; Ps. 105.6, 42), Isaac (Gen. 24.14), Jacob (e.g. Ezek. 37.25), Job (see Job 1.8; 2.3; 42.7-8), cultic officials who praise YHWH, likely Levites (e.g. Pss. 134.1; 135.1), pious people in general (e.g. Pss. 34.23), worshippers of YHWH (2 Kgs 10.23); Israel as a people (e.g. Lev. 25.42, 55; Isa. 41.8-9; 54.17; Ezek. 28.25; Ps. 69.37), and perhaps some

    2.   See Chapters 4 and 7.
    3.   R.J. Ratner summarized the Near Eastern evidence from law codes, legal documents, treaties, letters and wisdom literature on the matter of the runaway slave, as well of the relevant biblical texts (see 'Jonah, the Runaway Servant'). For runaway slaves in Babylonia, see M.A. Dandamaev, *Slavery in Babylonia: From Nabopolassar to Alexander the Great (626–331 BC)* (ed. M.A. Powell and D.B. Weisberg; trans V.A. Powell; Dekalb, IN: Northern Illinois University Press, rev. edn, 1984), esp. pp. 490-99, 590-91.

'angelic' beings in Job 4.18. This lengthy list is not surprising given that YHWH was construed as the divine lord, whom every pious person was supposed to serve, and accordingly be a servant of.[4]

For the purpose of the present study it suffices that prophets were explicitly characterized as 'servants of YHWH' numerous times (e.g. 1 Kgs 14.18; 2 Kgs 9.7, 36; 21.10; Isa. 20.3; Jer. 7.25; Ezek. 38.17; Zech. 1.6; passim). In fact, there are passages that effectively equate the terms 'servants of YHWH' and 'the prophets' (e.g. 2 Kgs 17.23; 21.10; Amos 3.7; Jer. 7.25; Ezek. 38.17). It bears noting also that the readers of the book of Jonah were asked to associate the Jonah of their book with Jonah the son of Amittay,[5] and that the latter is explicitly characterized as 'a servant of YHWH' in 2 Kgs 14.25. In sum, it is most likely that the mentioned readership and rereadership of the book conceived the prophet Jonah as עבד יהוה (i.e. 'a servant of YHWH'). It is worth mentioning that according to the LXX, Jonah explicitly claims, 'I am a servant of YHWH' (LXX, Jon. 1.9). Although it is most likely that the LXX text does not represent the original Hebrew,[6] still it implied and reflected a well-rooted understanding of the prophet as a servant of the divine.

This being so, the question is whether the image of Jonah as 'runaway *servant* of YHWH' evoked among these readers the common images and ideological views associated with the motif of the 'runaway *slave*'? To be sure, the ancient readers knew well the distinction between a servant of a king and an actual slave. But was this distinction so categorical as to preempt the relevance of a metaphor based on the one (literary) image from being substantially relevant in case of the other?

Leaving aside present meanings and connotations of these two terms, and the actual, social and ideological differences between servant (e.g. the son of a king) and slave in the ancient Near East,[7] the evidence strongly suggests that two terms were closely associated particularly in figurative language, which is the language that concerns us in the book of Jonah. It is not by chance that in *Sefire* 3, the language for the extradition of fugitive servants is that used for runaway slaves.[8] Greek and Hellenistic his-

---

4. In fact, all creation may be conceived as 'servants/slaves' of YHWH. For the explicit use of this metaphor in relation to the Leviathan, see Job 40.28.

5. See Chapter 4.

6. See, among others, E. Tov, *Textual Criticism of the Hebrew Bible* (Philadelphia: Fortress Press, 2nd edn, 2001), p. 257; Simon, *Jonah*, pp. 11-12.

7. On this matter, see, for instance, Dandamaev, *Slavery*, pp. 67-102.

8. See *Sefire* 3.4-7: 'If any of my officers flees from me as a fugitive or any of my kinsmen or any of my eunuchs or any of the people who are under my control, and

toriography provides also clear examples in which servants of an ancient Near Eastern king are construed as his slaves (e.g. Herodotus 7.135.2; Xenophon, *Anabasis* 2.5.38; *Hellenika* 6.1.12). Moreover, the fact that in biblical Hebrew—and other Semitic languages—the same word denotes both servant and slave not only facilitates metaphorical associations, but also hints at some conceptual links between the two. Thus, for instance, prophetic servanthood implied not merely a general acknowledgment of a relation lord/patron–servant/client but unfree work imposed by YHWH on the servant. The prophet was never really free to accept or reject YHWH's command to prophesy (cf. Amos 3.8, and of course Jonah). Further, as YHWH's workers, prophets received no daily wages as any other hired worker (cf. Deut. 24.15). In addition, within this discourse, prophets, and any human being for that matter, belong to YHWH, since heavens and the heavens of heaven and the earth and all that is in it and all those who dwell in it belong to YHWH (cf. Deut. 10.14; Ps. 24.1). Thus, it is not surprising that YHWH may *sell* (מכר) YHWH's servant Israel (see Deut. 32.30; Judg. 2.14; 3.8; 4.2; 10.7; 1 Sam. 12.9; Ps. 44.13; Isa. 50.1; 52.3; the element of property that is involved in this metaphorical language is even emphasized in Isa. 50.1; 52.3) nor that YHWH has the power of life and death over all human beings. It goes without saying that these or less stringent features do apply to slaves.[9]

they go to Aleppo, you shall not provide them with food, nor shall you say to them, Enjoy yourselves in your place, nor shall you alienate them from me; you must conciliate them, and send them back to me. If they will not [remain] in your land, be conciliatory (and keep them) there, until I come in person and make reconciliation with them. But if you alienate them from me and provide them with food and say to them, Remain where you are and do not return to his allegiance, you have been false to this treaty' (J.C. Gibson, *Textbook of Syrian Semitic Inscriptions*. II. *Aramaic Inscriptions Including Inscriptions in the dialect of Zenjirli* [Oxford: Clarendon Press, 1975], p. 47).

9.   In fact, some aspects of the treatment of a Hebrew slave seem more relaxed. For instance, according to Exod. 21.20 a master does not have the power of life and death over a Hebrew slave, male or female. See also Exod. 21.2-11; Deut. 15.12-18; Lev. 25.35-43. There are some limitations also regarding non-Israelite slaves; see Deut 21.10-14. See L.G. Perdue, 'The Israelite and Early Jewish Family: Summary and Conclusions', in L.G. Perdue, J. Blenkinsopp, J.J. Collins and C. Meyers (eds.), *Families in Ancient Israel* (Louisville, KY: Westminster John Knox Press, 1997), pp. 163-222, esp. 195-98.

To be sure, in some texts servanthood to YHWH carried also a positive connotation of divine favor (e.g. Isa. 41.8; 42.1-5; Ps. 69.36-37), but within the theological discourse of Yehud this connotation is not incompatible with all the attributes of servanthood mentioned above, but rather it complements them.

In sum, metaphorical and ideological constructions associated with the image of a slave running away from his or her master strongly informed those associated with that of a servant running away from his or her master. This being so, and given that Jonah is explicitly described as running away from YHWH, the master of masters, the heuristic question is which expectations about the behavior of these characters can be linked to the motif of the runaway slave (or slave) among the intended and primary readership of the book, and how did these expectations likely inform their reading of the book? What kind of implicit logical implications and issues arise because of the presence of the motif of a runaway slave in the world of knowledge of early community of readers?

To address these questions, first one has to identify the main attitudes regarding runaway slaves that were common in the Persian period, and among the social strata from which one would expect the relevant literati to come. Biblical and general ancient Near East material are very helpful in this regard.

First and foremost, across all periods in antiquity, there is a clear consensus that the slave must return to his or her master.[10] The 'rightful order' must be restored. To be sure, this may not reflect the opinion of the runaway slaves themselves, but certainly that of the written texts and literary documents.[11] Moreover, the owner of the runaway servant in this book is none but YHWH, the heavenly lord. If runaway slaves must return to their human lords, certainly they should return to the heavenly lord. The book of Jonah is a written text that was neither written by, nor for, slaves.[12]

It bears noting that in another written text, Genesis 16, even when YHWH is clearly sympathetic to the plea of an individual runaway slave and heard her cry (Gen. 16.11), still YHWH's messenger orders her to return to her master (Gen. 16.9). Running away is simply not an acceptable option. One may note that even Joseph, who at the relevant point in the story is already characterized as a paragon of virtue, does not attempt to run away from Potiphar's house (see Gen. 39). The 'classical' case of Exodus does not contradict, but rather supports the interpretation

---

10. See texts mentioned in J.H. Tigay, *Deuteronomy* (JPS Commentary; Philadelphia: Jewish Publication Society of America, 1996), p. 387 n. 57; Ratner, 'Jonah, the Runaway Servant'; and cf. the behavior of Achish in 1 Kgs 2.39-40; on Genesis 16 see below.

11. Cf. Glancy, 'The Mistress–Slave Dialectic'.

12. But very likely by and for people who owned slaves.

advanced here. To begin with, it refers to an entire people rather than individuals. But more importantly, one of the central issues there is that YHWH not Pharaoh is the master or patron of Israel. Within this meta-phorical discourse, it is good for the Israelites to leave their *false* master, but surely it is not good for them to leave their real master?

Second, runaway slaves were often considered to be no good. They were unreliable people. They transgressed the moral norms of their society. To acquire such slaves was a kind 'corrupt behavior'.[13]

Third, some texts reflect also an expectation that masters should not create circumstances that will incite the slave to run away. In these texts, masters who mistreat slaves to the point that the latter run away are negatively portrayed.[14]

Fourth, and from a societal perspective, the presence of runaway slaves was often considered as a chaotic element. They pointed at, and even embodied, an ideologically based sense of social breakdown. Their multi-plication was considered a sure marker of troubled times. Thus, for instance, Nabal says in 1 Sam. 25.10, 'Who is David and who is the son of Jesse? There are many slaves nowadays who are breaking away from their masters.' Of course, the readership of 1 Samuel knows that Nabal was wrong, not because the multiplication of breakaway slaves was an acceptable social development, but rather because of his inability to under-stand that David was not a fugitive slave, but the rightful master, the one whom YHWH has designated as king. This being so, Nabal becomes a refractory subject/servant, a point that his wife quickly understands in the narrative. In any case, the seemingly multiplication of 'outlaws' in the text points to a situation of social and political instability and of contending claims to lordship.

Fifth, the honor of masters of runaway slaves was tarnished by the fact that they were unable to control them well, to preempt their running away. This being so, masters were expected to do their best to retrieve not only their property but also to restore their honor.[15] So, they were expected either to take personal steps to catch their slaves, or to make sure that their

---

13. See 'He who acquires a runaway slave or a thievish maid [...and ruins] the reputation of his father and his progeny by his own corrupt behavior' (Ahiqar col. 6.6; see J.M. Lindenberger, 'Ahiqar', *OTP*, II, p. 498).

14. See Gen. 16 (and esp. vv. 5b and 11b); Sir. 33.30a, 31-33.

15. One may note with much regret that slavery and viewpoints similar to those presented in these texts led to incommensurable misery to myriads of human beings all throughout history. The issue is, of course, beyond the scope of this work.

slaves be caught and returned to them, even when such actions were potentially costly (see 2 Kgs 2.39-46). Further, masters were expected to ensure that runaway slaves did not escape again, and that refractory slaves in general accepted their authority. Different types of punishment, hard work and putting the person in shackles were among the common options.[16]

Sixth, there was a clear negative evaluation of those who hide runaway slaves and actively help them to avoid their 'lawful' return to their masters. Although it is true that a punishment was not always explicitly prescribed against those who so behaved, there is no doubt that the behaviour itself was almost universally condemned (on Deut. 23.16-17 [ET 15-16] see below).

2. *Readings of Jonah Informed by the Motif of the Runaway Servant/Slave*

One may begin by analyzing the sailors' actions in light of this motif and its associated expectations. If Jonah was construed as a runaway slave or servant, then the usual expectation would be for the sailors to do their best to return him to his master and surely not to assist him in his escape. Do they fulfill that expectation? Do they follow what seemed to them the desire of Jonah's master?

Here, as in other primary or even secondary key points in the book,[17] the text allows or encourages polyvalence. In fact, two substantially different sets of readings are possible within the discourses of Yehudite literati. According to the first, the sailors recognized the magnitude of Jonah's transgression, terribly feared its consequences for them (1.10), and therefore turned the ship around to return Jonah (1.13). Within this reading, their unwillingness to throw Jonah overboard—contrary to the advice of

16. See, for instance, 'Fodder and whip and load for an ass; food, correction and work for a slave. Make a slave work and he will look for his rest; let his hands be idle and he will seek to be free. Yoke and harness are a cure for stubbornness; and for a refractory slave, punishment in the stocks. Force him to work that he be not idle, for idleness is the teacher of much mischief. Give him work to do such as befits him; but if he fails to obey you, load him with chains' (Sir. 33.23-27; translation according to P.W. Skehan and A.A. Di Lella, *The Wisdom of Ben Sira* [AB, 39; New York: Doubleday, 1987], p. 402).

See also Dandamaev, *Slavery*, pp. 490-99, for the case of institutional lordship, that is, slaves who belong to the temple and their escape from their overseers.

17. E.g. the meaning of Jonah's proclamation in Jon. 3.4.

the transgressor—could have been motivated by their reluctance to murder in general and especially to kill rather than keep and return a slave who is the property of such a powerful god/master.[18] Moreover, Jonah's request was probably understood as another attempt to escape the service of his owner,[19] and accordingly, the sailors could not have agreed without risking the anger of Jonah's master. The sailors desired to return Jonah to dry land, or to the land from which he escaped, so his lord could take possession of him. To be sure, within this frame of readings, the sailors fulfilled the typical expectations raised by the motif of the runaway slave in the ancient Near East. True, they were unaware that they were helping Jonah to run away from his master when they allowed him to come aboard, but as soon as they learned that Jonah was a runaway servant or slave, they did their best to restore the slave to his owner, or at least to keep him safe until the master could take care of him. Within this reading, the implied logic of the sailors' actions is easy to understand. From the sailors' perspective, YHWH's storm was probably not only the means by which the owner derailed Jonah's attempt to escape, but also a rightful action against them, because they seemed to harbor and collaborate with a runaway slave. The sailors knew, however, that they were innocent. Their efforts to return Jonah and to keep him alive, so as to be returned, serve to demonstrate their innocence before the master of Jonah and, accordingly their actions were expected to cause the storm to calm.

In other words, the sailors behaved as good (non-Israelites) were expected to do. Yet they failed to understand YHWH. Their failure is directly associated with central issues in the discourse of the readership of the book. Because either (a) the sailors did not take seriously Jonah's claim that YHWH is the lord of both the dry land and the sea (1.9) and, accordingly, they failed to understand that there was no need to return

---

18. As a rule, those who found a runaway slave were not supposed to kill them, but to return to their owners. Attacks on servants or slaves of a master are likely to be considered an attack on the master himself or herself (cf. Lev. 25.42). The sailors have no legal reason to execute Jonah: killing him would most likely be considered a case of shedding innocent blood, as they themselves are well aware (see 1.14).

19. This is consistent with Jonah's desire to die in 4.3, 8 and his retreat to the hold of the vessel and his 'deep sleep' during the storm. On death as a way to remove oneself, or to be removed from a prophetic mission, see Num. 11.10-15; 1 Kgs 19; Jer. 11.21, among many others. (There is an element of demeaning irony in the comparison between Moses and Elijah, on the one hand, and Jonah on the other; see Jon. 4.3, 8 and cf. Num. 11.15; 1 Kgs 19 and see Simon, *Jonah*, p. 38). On death and the lack of ability to even praise YHWH see Ps. 30.10.

Jonah to the land from which he escaped, or to any land for that matter, since all the earth is YHWH's, or (b) they rejected the unequivocal advice of the prophet of YHWH (1.12) or (c) they thought that they knew better than YHWH—the creator of the storm—what to do with YHWH's runaway servant, or far more likely (d) a combination of all the above. One may notice that none of the options excludes the others. In fact, they seem to cohere into a multi-dimensional 'grammar' of understanding and action.

The first possibility resonates with theological misconceptions that were at times associated with non-Israelites in the discourse of the time. From this perspective, the episode is a particular case of the motif of non-Israelites who acknowledge the power of YHWH, but fail to recognize that YHWH is not a geographically based god. YHWH is not one among many local gods, but an absolutely universal god (cf. 1 Kgs 20.23; and contrast with the theological position embraced in Ps. 139.7-10).[20]

The second possibility brings the importance of accepting the words of the prophet of YHWH, no matter who is the prophet, to the forefront (and cf. 3.5).

The third option resonates with issues that are raised, for instance, in Job 38. It draws attention to the sailors' failed attempt to imagine the power of YHWH. After all, contrary to their expectations, precisely by throwing Jonah into the sea they facilitated his coming to an environment that kept him safe and eventually brought him back to the work of his master.[21] In other words, their thoughts and actions reflect rational

20. For instance, according to Ratner the sailors decided to 'turn the ship around and return Jonah directly home…they will right Jonah's wrong for him by returning his body (with or without his consent) to his god's homeland' ('Jonah', pp. 301-302). The question of whether there is some geographical limitation to YHWH or to YHWH's actions or interactions with human beings is already raised by Jonah's escape (Jon. 1.3; cf. Gen. 4.16). His escape to the sea makes sense only if, from his perspective, geography mattered. Some medieval Jewish interpreters faced this problem and, with the impossibility from their viewpoint that Jonah actually tried to escape God, claimed that he escaped to the sea to avoid a second call from YHWH, for prophetic revelations do not take place either at sea or outside the land of Israel (see Abrabanel). A variant of this proposal is that Jonah was looking for a place in which the shekhinah does not reveal itself (see already *Mechilta* דפסחא מסכתא, 1.71-81, pp. 6-7; Lauterbach edition) or 'to place where his [i.e. YHWH's] glory is not manifested' (למקום שלא נראה כבודו שם , *PRE* 9; Radak). Of course, the plain meaning of the text is that YHWH does communicate with a Hebrew prophet in Israel and outside Israel. The similarity in the wording of Jon. 1.1 and Jon. 3.1 clearly suggests that there was no difference between the two instances.

21. As explicitly expressed by the language of Jon. 3.1, the narrative and Jonah

endeavor but lack 'proper knowledge'. They should have obeyed YHWH, even if doing so did not make sense to them, and even if it seemed to them that doing so meant that their actions not only bordered on murder but also directly involved destroying YHWH's property, and even dishonoring YHWH.[22] Moreover, as suggested by option (b), they should have obeyed YHWH and followed the words of YHWH's prophet.

The second set of readings is substantially different from the first. Faced with impending doom, the sailors, as the Ninevites later, accepted the words of the prophet of YHWH, Jonah, as fully reliable. Significantly, this was the correct choice according to the narrator, the authorial voice and YHWH. According to these readings, the sailors learned not only the true reason for the tempest, but what they should do to stop it, namely, to cast Jonah overboard (1.9-12). Such an action would have been tantamount to bringing Jonah to his lord, who is also the lord of the sea and who was in any case carrying out impressive actions at sea aimed at stopping Jonah's escape. According to this set of readings, the sailors were convinced that throwing Jonah overboard was YHWH's will (cf. 1.14). Still, despite doom looming over them, the sailors decided to confront YHWH and to try to force their way out of the storm by rowing hard towards the dry land (v. 13), carrying Jonah and themselves out of the area in which YHWH was attacking them. Read in this way, the sailors' act was clearly an act of defiance.[23] If so, the sailors were behaving just opposite to the common

move as it were to square one, that is, Jon. 1.1, only that Jonah learned from his failure and is not about to run away now.

22.   The story here compares and contrasts the behavior of the sailors and of the fish as carriers of YHWH's purposes. The former, though described as pious, and as motivated on a reasonable fear of shedding innocent blood, are less willing to fulfill their role in the salvation of Jonah as designed by YHWH than the latter. Their problem is grounded in their humanity.

23.   To be sure, real sailors in the eastern Mediterranean would have avoided the coast at all costs if they faced a storm. Yet Jonah's sailors live in the world of the narrative. The narrative provides a contrast of dry land and sea. They were all but lost in the sea. What was their alternative in that world once capitulation to YHWH's will—that is, to throw Jonah overboard—is ruled out?

The verb חתר in the qal is used elsewhere with the meaning of 'dig', most often in the sense of digging through a wall (e.g. Ezek. 8.8; 12.5). Here it may connote an image of a severe obstacle that is to be overcome. The sailors' choice is certainly a difficult one. One may paraphrase this connoted meaning by 'the sailors tried to dig themselves out (or tunnel themselves out) of the storm.'

The gap between what real sailors would have done during an eastern Mediterranean storm and what the sailors in the narrative do may be indicative of a community of

expectations raised by the motif of the runaway servant/slave. Such behavior raises an obvious question in the intended readership: why did they
do so? To be sure, the text does not allow any explanation of their behavior
as due to their base character, or as aimed at personal profit, or both.

At this point it is worth mentioning that the book of Jonah construes a
Ninevite king who speaks in a way reminiscent of Moses and acts as an
intermediary and even as a good Israelite theologian.[24] The sailors fear
YHWH and when they talk about theological matters their language carries
expressions and connotations that were well associated with the inner
discourse of the postmonarchic community (e.g. דם נקיא, 'innocent
blood', in Jon. 1.14 and see, among others, Deut. 21.8; 2 Kgs 21.16; 24.4;
Ps. 106.38; Prov. 6.17; Isa. 59.7; Jer. 7.6; 22.3; 26.15; and see כאשר
חפצת עשית, 'you have done as it pleased you', in Jon. 1.14 and Ps. 115.3;
also cf. Ps. 135.6).[25] Given the partial Israelitization of the characters of
the pious sailors and of the king and people of Nineveh,[26] it is reasonable
to assume that the attitude of the sailors here be associated at least with the
sentiment of Deut. 23.16-17, and the more so since this text is exceptional

readers and writers in Jerusalem in which practical knowledge of sailing was not widespread. But narrative considerations may outweigh widespread technical knowledge in
the target readership of literary works. Cf. Sasson, *Jonah*, pp. 141-42.

24. See Jon. 3.8-9 and cf. Exod. 32.12b (and see Exod. 32.14); see, among others,
Simon, *Jonah*, p. xxxvii; Magonet, *Form and Meaning*, pp. 71-72. See 2 Chron. 7.14;
Amos 5.15; Zeph. 2.3; Joel 2.14; and cf. Jon. 3.9. On some of these issues, see Simon,
Jonah, p. xxxvii, and Chapter 6 in this volume.

25. See also Magonet, *Form and Meaning*, pp. 70-73, and the discussion below.
It is possible that the (relatively late) Hebrew expression כאשר חפצת עשית (you
have done as it pleased you) entered into Hebrew through Aramaic influence—and
earlier into Aramaic because of Akkadian influences, but the rereaders of these books
are not asked to read the expressions they found in them in the light of philological
explanations, but rather as Hebrew words which are part and parcel of their own
discourse. In sum, there is no reason to assume that the expression כאשר חפצת
עשית evoked non-Hebrew associations in its intended or primary readership (see Ps.
115.3; cf. Ps. 135.6). On a reconstruction of the history of כאשר חפצת עשית and its
role in the dating of the book of Jonah on the basis of its language, see B. Dan, 'לשון',
esp. pp. 356-58, and see also Hurvitz, 'History of a Legal Formula'.

26. On the Israelite-like characterization of pious foreigners see also Ben Zvi,
'When a Foreign Monarch Speaks'. To be sure, this process may be described as a
'universalist' trend or as a 'colonization' of the other. Both terms are highly evaluative.
The process itself was the result of a social and literary activity of imagining and
characterizing theologically or ideologically good foreigners and a social and culturally
based understanding of what theological or ideological goodness is. See Chapter 8.

in the Hebrew Bible and, to the best of my knowledge, in the ancient Near East. The text itself was surely known to the community of readers and writers responsible for the book of Jonah. Moreover it stood alone against the (ideological) consensus that slaves should be returned to their masters. Deut 23.16-17 (ET 15-16) reads:

לא־תסגיר עבד אל־אדניו אשר־ינצל אליך מעם אדניו
עמך ישב בקרבך במקום אשר־יבחר באחד שעריך בטוב לו לא תוננו

> Slaves who have escaped to you from their owners shall not be given back
> to them. They shall reside with you, in your midst, in any place they choose
> in any one of your towns, wherever they please; you shall not oppress them
> (NRSV).

It is true that this text most likely refers only to foreign slaves.[27] Further, it may reflect theological or ideological concerns[28] and a socio-ideological utopia rather than actual practice. But in any case, in this text people are commanded not only *not* to return the slave to his or her master, but also actively to provide refuge for the runaway slave.

The actions of the sailors, according to this set of readings, do resonate with this commandment. Within the limitations of their life aboard the ship, the sailors behaved as 'pious Israelites' whose actions were informed by Deut. 23.16-17.[29] The sailors, as the Ninevites later in the story, serve thus as examples of pious behavior.

Since there is no hint in the text that the sailors do know the text of Deut. 23.16-17—despite their partial Israelitization—the implicit question is: how do they know how to behave? Does the text suggest or reflect an underlying assumption that this particular teaching of Deuteronomy, devoid of its particular limitation to a non-Israelite who entered the land of the Israelites, resonates now as a general moral principle accessible to all? Within such a readings, this is probably the case. This position surely has implications for the general issue of the extent of divine knowledge that non-Israelites who are unaware of the authoritative writings of Israel may have.

---

27. See, for instance, Tigay, *Deuteronomy*, p. 215; for a different position see F. Crüsemann, *The Torah: Theology and Social History of Old Testament Law* (trans. A.W. Mahnke; Philadelphia: Fortress Press, 1996), pp. 159, 232-33.

28. Such as the general undesirability of transferring a person from the community of worshippers of YHWH to that of worshipers of other gods, or considerations associated with the concept of *ger*.

29. It bears note, however, that the sailors still retain their non-Israelite character. See Chapter 8.

Yet this is not the end of the matter. The sailors are eventually forced to return Jonah to YHWH, to cast him into the waters, to what they believe is his death. Thus, the readers have to imagine that these pious sailors had to settle with the idea of killing, destroying YHWH's creature and servant at the deity's request (a kind of inversion of Jonah's perspective of YHWH, at least in regard to the Ninevites). Obeying YHWH against their wishes and as a last resource implies—from their perspective—that their thoughts and morals are not YHWH's. The book seems to imply and evoke theological motifs similar to those expanded in Job (and particularly Job 38). More-over, from the perspective of the Yehudite readers of the book, it already hints at a central problem raised in Jonah, the relation between YHWH's behavior and YHWH's word as accepted in the accepted repertoire of the community, for the sailors' behavior is the only one consistent with Deut. 23.16-17.[30]

These two different sets of readings do not exclude each other, even within the same readership, and particularly so since the text was read, reread, meditated upon and read to diverse people. Both types of readings could have been part of the social and ideological interaction between the text and those for whom it was composed.

We can now address the question of the owner of a runaway slave. The honor of such a person was tarnished by the escape of the slave. Not surprisingly, masters were expected to take action to restore their honor and property to themselves and to prevent further escapes. A reading of Jonah that is informed by these perspectives and expectations will under-score that YHWH takes steps, even very dramatic steps, to catch Jonah. The messengers employed by YHWH to retake him include a vast array: the sea, the wind, the fish, and even the sailors and the (personified) ship. Thus the text reflects and shapes a theological construction of the entire world—including nature, people and the products of human hands[31]—used by YHWH to achieve this goal, and to convince the readers and Jonah of the futility of any attempt to escape. Rather than depicting a god whose honor is tarnished because he was powerless to preempt a slave from running away, the book explicitly points to a most powerful god who controls every aspect of the world, including the manufactured world. The 'chance

30. On this matter see also Chapter 8.
31. The ship is a product of human hands, but is also conceived as YHWH's creation, just as the fish. Both are YHWH's servants. The personification of the ship in 1.4 is not only a matter of style. It reflects and conveys an important theological message.

occurrences' that seem to bode well to Jonah's escape in 1.3[32] are nothing but a 'ploy' by YHWH, who never lost control of the whereabouts of the supposedly running away slave. Moreover, they show YHWH's control over time too.

Once the slave was caught, masters were supposed to ensure that he or she would not attempt to escape again. Different types of coercion were often used for that purpose. YHWH is characterized as one who possesses, and uses extremely intimidating powers. To be sure, Jonah is unequivocally and emphatically described as a person forced to fulfill his mission against his own will (see Jon. 3; 4.1-8). Yet divine force is not all that is present in the discourses reflected in the text. The book as a whole reaches its climax not at Jonah's forced proclamation, but with the final conversation between YHWH and Jonah in which the former takes the role of the divine teacher.[33] Thus the text communicates an image of YHWH whose final goal is not to continue to force Jonah and the readership for whom the book is intended against their will, but to persuade them.

As mentioned above, the multiplication of runaway slaves may be associated with a socially or politically chaotic situation. It bears note that the book of Jonah unequivocally proclaims the rule of YHWH over all creation, and all and every aspect of it. Chaos is then illusory. Jonah may attempt to escape YHWH, but fails completely and from the very beginning.

Just as important for the reconstruction of the theological thought of the period, the book clearly reflects and communicates a worldview according to which, precisely in this non-chaotic world, Israelite prophets, YHWH's servants, may confront YHWH and YHWH's actions, both past and future, on theological or ideological grounds (see Jon. 4). To be sure, the book of Jonah is certainly not unique in this regard; rather it reflects a theological discourse that is well attested in the Hebrew Bible[34] as well as some of the limitations of such a discourse.

---

32. See esp. באה תרשיש ('had just come from Tarshish'; note also the verb in the participle form), and for a discussion of this matter, see Sasson, *Jonah*, pp. 66 and esp. 82-83.

33. On YHWH as a teacher see, for instance, L.G. Perdue, 'The Household, Old Testament Theology, and Contemporary Hermeneutics', in L.G. Perdue, J. Blenkinsopp, J.J. Collins and C. Meyers (eds.), *Families in Ancient Israel* (Louisville, KY: Westminster/John Knox Press, 1997), pp. 223-57 (228).

34. Cf. with the words of Abraham (Gen. 18.20-33), Moses (Exod. 32.7-14), Elijah (1 Kgs 17.21), and the tone of Elisha's comment in 2 Kgs 4.27. On these matters, see Y. Muffs, *Love and Joy: Law, Language and Religion in Ancient Israel* (New York: Jewish Theological Seminary, 1992), esp. pp. 9-14. Still, as it is often the case in the

Did YHWH mistreat Jonah? Did Jonah have a reason to respond negatively to YHWH's request? Was Jonah no good? In sharp contrast to the cases of unequivocality just mentioned, the book of Jonah is clearly ambiguous, or better multivalent, when it comes to these matters. Although Jonah is ridiculed, he is still a prophet, and a very successful one for that matter. He is still a person knowledgeable of the religious literature of his period and who may have a theological or ideological reason for his refusal to prophesy against Nineveh. Jonah's theology may be criticized in the book, but the issues raised by Jonah and by Jonah's behavior do resonate and point to some of the central issues and self-assumed limitations of the theological discourse of the time.[35]

Moreover, if, at least from his viewpoint, Jonah has a reason for his behavior, then YHWH may be considered as the one who incited Jonah to flee. Since there is no book of Jonah unless Jonah opposes his mission, the implied author of the book necessitates Jonah's rejection of his master to bring forth the point of the book to the readership. The same holds true for the character YHWH within the book. This being so, the readership may well have construed YHWH as one who purposefully created a situation in which Jonah would be 'forced' as it were to escape, so as to teach him along with the readership of the book the required lesson. YHWH, the pedagogue, may well be a master who incites a slave to run away so that a lesson may be learned.[36]

In sum, rereadings of the text by the Jerusalemite literati, who were well informed by the motif of the runaway servant or slave, likely raised or evoked many of the central theological or ideological positions that were part and parcel of the interpersonal theological discourses of the period.

book of Jonah, there is a substantial twist in the presentation of this theological and literary motif. The examples mentioned above involve human beings confronting YHWH because they oppose YHWH's actions that lead, may lead or seemingly led to death and destruction. Jonah, however, is dismayed because YHWH is not about to destroy Nineveh.

35. See Chapter 7.

36. The case is comparable to YHWH's announcement to Abraham of the decision to destroy Sodom and Gomorrah. Such an action is necessary for the development of the theological point of the story in Gen. 18.20-33.

Chapter 6

ATYPICALITY AND THE META-PROPHETIC CHARACTER OF THE BOOK OF JONAH

1. *Introduction*

There is no dispute that the book of Jonah is unlike any other prophetic book. The differences between Jonah and the other books are many and in some cases obvious.[1] For instance, the book of Jonah is a narrative, whereas the others are not, though they may include some narrative sections. Prophetic books tend to allocate a large share of their text to reports of divine announcements and of prophetic addresses to a public other than the LORD or the prophet alone.[2]

Still, the fact remains that the book of Jonah was accepted, read and reread in antiquity as a prophetic book, as it is shown by its inclusion in the collection of prophetic books later called 'The Twelve', rather than for instance, in the Writings.[3] In fact, there is no evidence whatsoever for Jonah being considered anything but a prophetic book.[4]

The reasons that may have led the ancient rereaders of the book of

---

1.   For one of the best short summaries of these differences see Trible, *Studies*, pp. 126-27.

2.   On the significance of these matters, see below.

3.   I wish to stress that I am *not* claiming that Jonah was written so as to be included in the Twelve, but that its inclusion in the collection of prophetic books later named 'The Twelve' demonstrates that the book of Jonah was understood as a prophetic book. On the debate on the likely original placement of the book within the Twelve, see below.

4.   Jonah was most likely one of the twelve prophets mentioned in Sir. 49.12. Sections of the book of Jonah are included also in 4QXII^a, 4QXII^f and 4QXII^g, 8Hev XII gr, Mur XII. In addition, 4 Ezra (see 1.39-40), the *Martyrdom and Ascension of Isaiah* (4.22) and *The Lives of the Prophets* all include Jonah among the Twelve, as does, of course, the Septuagint. Further, the book of Tobit implies that a good Israelite is aware of the prophecy of Jonah regarding Nineveh (Tob. 14.4. 9, 15—according to Codex Vaticanus, Alexandrinus; on this matter see Chapter 2 in this volume).

Jonah to recognize the genre of the book as prophetic book[5] are various. For one, there is the fact that the two main characters in the book are YHWH and a prophet from the past.[6] This is probably a sufficient reason by itself, since no separate book in which the main human character is a prophet—as characterized and understood in books of the Hebrew Bible— was ever included in the Writings.[7] Further, the opening of the book with ויהי דבר־יהוה אל־יונה בן־אמתי לאמר ('Now the word of the LORD came to Jonah son of Amittai, saying…', NRSV) not only introduces the direct speech of YHWH in v. 2, but also at least connotes that the entire literary unit is YHWH's word (cf. Ezek. 12.1 and the usual characterization of entire prophetic books as YHWH's word[8]).

In addition, one may notice that some of the underlying issues in the book of Jonah (e.g. the status of the non-Israelite nations in the divine economy, the efficacy of repentance and of prophecy) as well as elements of its style (e.g. the tendency towards polyvalence and ambiguity) are common among prophetic books.[9]

In any event, the ancient rereadership's reception of Jonah as a book that belongs to a certain genre, that is, as a prophetic book brought expectations and suggested a particular orientation to the text.[10] Yet these

5. There is a plethora of proposals regarding the genre of the book of Jonah. See, for instance, Trible, *Studies*, pp. 126-84; *idem*, 'Jonah', pp. 466-74; Wolff, *Jonah*, pp. 80-85; Bolin, *Freedom beyond Forgiveness*, pp. 46-53; Salter, *Jonah*, pp. 41-50; E. Levine, 'Jonah as a Philosophical Book', *ZAW* 96 (1984), pp. 235-45; LaCoque and Lacoque, *Jonah*, pp. 26-48; Orth, 'Genre in Jonah'; Rofé, *Prophetical Stories*, pp. 159-60; and see also Sasson, *Jonah*, pp. 328-40, and Marcus, *From Balaam to Jonah*, pp. 93-141.

On 'prophetic book' as a biblical genre I have written elsewhere, see Ben Zvi, 'Prophetic', and *idem, Micah*.

6. See J.M. Sasson, *Jonah*, p. 86. The text relates this character to the Jonah of Kings. See Chapter 4 in this volume.

7. The term prophet was partially re-categorized towards the end of the Second Temple period. So, for instance, Joshua (*Ant.* 4.165, 311), and Daniel (e.g. *Ant.* 10.249, 267-69; 4Q174 = 4Qflor) were characterized as prophets. For a general survey and bibliography, see L.L. Grabbe, *Judaic Religion in the Second Temple Period: Belief and Practice from the Exile to Yavneh* (London: Routledge, 2000), pp. 236-41. The main mark that this recategorization of the concept of prophet left in later traditions is the inclusion of Daniel among the prophetic books in some of them (see already *Life of the Prophets*, the LXX and Vg.), though not in the masoretic tradition.

8. See, for instance, Hos. 1.1; Joel; Mic. 1.1.

9. I discussed these issues in my commentaries on Micah and Obadiah. One has to admit, however, that some of these features occur in other types of biblical literature.

10. I understand genre as 'historically specific conventions and ideals according to

expectations created some degree of dissonance within these rereader-ships, because they also noticed that several of the central features of the book set it apart from the others. The recognition of these features led them to sense that Jonah is not only a prophetic book and an integral part their literary repertoire of prophetic books, but also that it is very much 'atypical'. In other words, Jonah does not fulfill the usual expectations raised by the genre of prophetic book. Significantly, it is not only the book, but also the prophet Jonah who is characterized as atypical. He is unlike any of the other prophets populating the prophetic books accepted by the community.

In other words, literary genre and the image of past prophets are manip-ulated here for rhetorical purposes.[11] This chapter is concerned with the communicative messages served by the atypical characterization of book and prophet within the frame of the ancient—most likely Achaemenid period—communities of rereaders for whom the book was composed.[12]

which authors compose discourse and audiences receive it'. From this perspective, 'genres consist of orientating frameworks, interpretative procedures and sets of expec-tations'. See W.F. Hanks, 'Discourse Genres in a Theory of Practice', *American Ethnologist* 14 (1987), pp. 668-92 (670), and cf. G.M. Tucker, *Form Criticism of the Old Testament* (Guides to Biblical Scholarship; Philadelphia: Fortress Press, 1988), pp. 2-3.

Although the emphasis should be on the way in which the ancient communities understood the text rather than on the intention of an actual author of the text, it is clear that the implied author constructed by the ancient rereadership 'intended' Jonah to be read as a prophetic book, and the character Jonah to be understood as a prophet. Given that authors and rereaders shared a cultural horizon in Achaemenid Yehud, their very limited numbers and a tendency towards cultural continuity in traditional societies, the assumption that this 'implied author' was not too different from the 'actual author' is more likely than its opposite. I discussed elsewhere the implications of the low number of bearers of high literacy in Yehud. See Ben Zvi, 'Introduction' and 'Urban Center'.

11. Genre manipulation is a common rhetorical device in prophetic literature. The difference here is the level at which genre is manipulated. Here it is manipulated (or defamiliarized) at the highest possible level, that of the prophetic book itself. In the other prophetic books defamiliarization takes place at the level of the particular readings of which the book is composed. See my commentary on Micah (Ben Zvi, *Micah*, passim). For examples of genre manipulation in the ancient Near East outside Israel, see, for instance, D.B. Redford, 'Scribe and Speaker', in E. Ben Zvi and M.H. Floyd (eds.), *Writings and Speech in Israelite and Ancient Near Eastern Prophecy* (Symposium, 10; Atlanta: Society of Biblical Literature, 2000), pp. 145-218 (197-99).

12. A somewhat similar starting point is developed in a substantially different manner in E. Dyck, 'Jonah among the Prophets: A Study in Canonical Context', *JETS* 33 (1990), pp. 63-73. Neither Dyck's approach nor his conclusions are followed here.

This being so, this chapter will point at some of the most substantial differences between Jonah and the other prophetic books, or between Jonah and other prophets,[13] and then address the significance of each of these differences.

2. *Narrative Features, Thematic Focus and Meta-prophetic Character*

As it is well known, the book of Jonah is shaped as a narrative, unlike other prophetic books. The main narrative line is clearly marked by *wayyiqtol* structures, and as expected, secondary lines and direct speech are also present.[14] Of course, the larger prophetic books (i.e. Isaiah, Jeremiah, Ezekiel) also include narratives (e.g. Isa. 36–38; Jer. 41, 52) and the so-called 'Minor Prophets' may occasionally include a narrative (e.g. Amos 7.12-17), but no prophetic book in its entirety is shaped around a *wayyiqtol* series. Whereas the book of Jonah as a whole has a narrative plot, or combination of plots, the same cannot be said of Obadiah, Micah or any other prophetic book.

In addition, prophetic books tend to allocate a large share of their text to

13. The differences are many. A discussion of all of them is not required for the purpose of this study.

14. See A. Nicacci, 'Syntactic Analysis of Jonah', *LA* 46 (1996), pp. 9-32; cf. E.R. Wendland, 'Text Analysis and the Genre of Jonah', *JETS* 39 (1996), pp. 191-206.

The presence of a psalm (Jon. 2.3-10) well set within the narrative (notice the *wayyiqtol* introducing the poetic section) does not affect this observation. It is not uncommon for poetic texts in the Hebrew Bible to be included in a narrative frame (e.g. 1 Sam. 2.1-10), and on this matter see J.W. Watts, *Psalm and Story: Inset Hymns in Hebrew Poetry* (JSOTSup, 139; Sheffield: Sheffield Academic Press, 1992).

The issue of whether the 'Psalm' of Jonah was added at a later stage to a forerunner of the (present) book of Jonah is not relevant to the study of the latter as read and reread by ancient communities, unless one can prove that these readers were asked— and did agree—to read the book diachronically, in the light of its textual history. Significantly, there are no markers in the text asking its intended readers to approach the book in such a matter. To the contrary, the readership is asked to read and reread the psalm as part of the narrative and to assign it to Jonah, the main character of the narrative and to a particular time within the narrative. Numerous markers of a textual cohesion that encompasses both the narrative per se and the psalm are present; see, for instance, Jon. 2.1-2, and note, among others, the presence of the word-pair בטן-מעה in vv. 1-3 (NRSV translates the two words identically as 'belly') the reference to waters, and the play on ירד (qal; 'go down') in 2.7 and 1.3, 5. (On the basically interchangeable character of דג-דגה, 'fish', in 2.1 and 2.2 (cf. 2.11) see Sasson, *Jonah*, pp. 155-57, esp. 156-57). On the Psalm of Jonah, see, for instance, Brenner, 'Jonah's Poem'.

divine announcements and prophetic addresses to a public other than YHWH or the prophet alone. Moreover, when divine speech is addressed to the prophet, it often has purposes that go beyond the interaction between prophet and YHWH. Usually, even within the explicit world of the book, the speech is to be conveyed to other characters populating that world (Ezek. 13.2 and passim), or it explains circumstances associated with prophetic speech, or its reception by a public other than the prophet himself (e.g. Isa. 6.10; 49.3). All in all, much of the message communicated by the prophetic books is shaped around divine and prophetic announcements and speeches directly or indirectly addressed to a public other than YHWH and prophet (e.g. Israel, Judah, Jerusalem, a king, the social elite) but still present within the world of the book. In Jonah, these types of discourse are conspicuously absent, except for a five-word announcement to Nineveh (Jon. 3.4b).[15]

The main narrative line in the book of Jonah consists of verbal and non-verbal interactions between YHWH and the prophet. Within the world of the book, these interactions are focused, in the main, on the relation between these two characters rather than towards the world of nations and social groups that populate that textual world.[16] The main concern of YHWH in the narrative, and as expressed by YHWH's words and pattern of actions, is Jonah. YHWH attempts to persuade the prophet, shape his position and accept the role that YHWH has assigned to him as prophet. Conversely, the main concerns of Jonah as it becomes clear in Chapter 4 are centred on YHWH, in YHWH's character, behavior, demands from the prophet and the divine economy enforced by the deity. In other words, they and their relationship, the messages that they send one another stand at the center of the book of Jonah. In sharp contrast, the divine messages communicated—directly or indirectly—by either YHWH or the human prophetic voice to other addressees in the book stand at the center of all

15. On the announcement in Jonah, and their 'antirhetorical' character, see Gitay, 'Jonah'.

16. Nineveh is a secondary rather than a main character in the book as a whole, from the perspective of an ancient audience that accepts the viewpoint of the authorial voice. See Jon. 4. Although the two main characters in the book have been interacting with each other throughout the book, they reach the level of a verbal dialogue in which they explicitly advance their contrary positions—and let the readers know about them—in Chapter 4. The book does not conclude with the salvation of Nineveh, but with the education of Jonah, and the intended readers. See Chapter 9.

Yet the choice of Nineveh is not without significance. See below.

the other prophetic books, if they are viewed from the perspective of each book as a whole. To be sure, the larger prophetic books contain important verbal communications between YHWH and prophet. See, for instance, Isa. 6.8-13; Jer. 1.4-10; 12.1-6; 15.10-21. These texts deal, at least in part, with the relation between YHWH and prophet. No prophetic book, however, as a whole consists mainly or almost only of a series of verbal and non-verbal communications between prophet–YHWH whose main issue is the relationship between these two characters, along with their expectations of, and complaints about each other.

The atypical narrative character of this prophetic book draws the attention of the ancient rereaders to its plot, as opposed to the series of reported divine or prophetic oracles, sermons and prophetic addresses that characterize the other prophetic books. The narrative in turn brings to the forefront the crucial issue of the relation between YHWH and prophet.

A narrative book that focuses on the relation between YHWH and prophet and is included in a repertoire of prophetic books, in all of which YHWH and prophet are the main characters, was probably received by the ancient, primary readerships as what today we call a 'meta-prophetic' book, that is, a prophetic book that deals with or is even devoted to issues that are of *relevance for the understanding of the messages of other prophetic books*.[17] To be sure, there are comments and sections in other prophetic books that can also be considered meta-prophetic (e.g. Isa. 55.7-11; Amos 7.12-15), but clearly there is no prophetic book that can be considered meta-prophetic in its entirety. Jonah is unique in this regard.

It bears notice that the book of Jonah likely followed Malachi in the sequence preserved in a scroll of the Minor Prophets in Qumran, namely, 4QXII[a].[18] It may well be that this position does not reflect the primary order of the Twelve.[19] Yet the fact that Jonah is placed after Malachi in

17. Although he does not use this term, Sweeney may come close to a position that Jonah is a meta-prophetic book, but in a far more restricted sense and for reasons different than those advanced here. See Sweeney, *Twelve Prophets*, p. 332.

18. See R.E. Fuller, '4QXII[a]', *DJD* XV, pp. 221-32 and relevant plates, and esp. p. 222; *idem*, 'The Form and Formation of the Book of The Twelve: The Evidence from the Judean Desert', in J.W. Watts and P.R. House (eds.), *Forming Prophetic Literature: Essays on Isaiah and the Twelve in Honor of John D.W. Watts* (JSOTSup, 235; Sheffield: Sheffield Academic Press, 1996), pp. 86-101 (91-92).

19. See Sweeney, *Twelve Prophets*, pp. xxvii-xxxix. Cf. Fuller, '4QXII[a]', p. 222; B.A. Jones, 'The Book of the Twelve as a Witness to Ancient Biblical Interpretation', in J.D. Nogalski and M.A. Sweeney (eds.), *Reading and Hearing the Book of the Twelve* (Symposium, 15; Atlanta: Society of Biblical Literature, 2000), pp. 65-74 (68-69).

this manuscript indicates the early existence of some system of ordering the prophetic books that is different from the others, at least in the relative position assigned to Jonah. Such an order requires an explanation.[20] The concluding slot is often allocated to textually inscribed, interpretative keys for the understanding of the literary unit (e.g. Hos. 14.10; Ruth 4.18-22; Qoh. 12.13-14; Job 42.7-17) or corpus (see the place of Mal. 3.23-24 in the Christian Scriptures).[21] A probable explanation is that the writers of 4QXII[a] placed Jonah at the end because they considered it an interpretative key for the prophetic books. There is no reason to assume that the intended

In antiquity there were several sequences of the twelve prophetic books, see Ben Zvi, 'Twelve Prophetic Books', p. 134 n. 24.

20. And the more so if it does not represent the original order, but rather a recasting of a previous order. The ultimate position in the original order of a series of books may be somewhat arbitrary. After all, some book must be the last. To be sure, the same does not hold true for any variation from that original order, or in a case in which multiple orders are present, and by necessity 'competing' against each other in the social market.

21. An alternative suggestion is that the ultimate position of Jonah in 4QXII[a] was due to, or indicates that the book was added at a very late stage to the collection of the twelve prophetic books. But there is little merit to this proposal. After all, Deuteronomy is not necessarily the last book included in the Pentateuch, nor Chronicles in the Writings (and incidentally, see its position in L), nor Kings in the 'Latter Prophets', nor for that matter is Prov. 31 the last unit included in the book of Proverbs. The literati could have added books and units in positions other than the ultimate, as the very multiplicity of sequences of the Twelve in antiquity demonstrates. Further, why would this supposed principle of 'last to be included-last spot' be in effect only in 4QXII[a]? And if the order in 4QXII[a] was not the original, how likely is that some literati would decide to reshape a received sequence so as to reflect a diachronic reconstruction of the process that led to the assembly of this collection of twelve, authoritative prophetic books? Similarly, the fact that Jonah appears in different places in some sequences is probably due to such factors as the place of Micah and an interpretative tendency to associate Jonah and Nahum (see sequences in the LXX, 4 Ezra 1.39-40, and *Lives of the Prophets*; for a different kind of linkage between the two books see Tg.) and it has nothing to do with the question of whether Jonah was the last book to be included among the twelve prophetic (cf. the diverse places that Ruth, Chronicles and Lamentations found themselves). For other positions on these matters see Sweeney, *Twelve Prophets*, I, pp. xxxviii, and cf. p. xxvii; A. Schart, 'Reconstructing the Redaction History of the Twelve Prophets: Problems and Models', in J.D. Nogalski and M.A. Sweeney (eds.), *Reading and Hearing the Book of the Twelve* (Symposium, 15; Atlanta: Society of Biblical Literature, 2000), pp. 34-48 (37-38); B.A. Jones, *The Formation of the Book of the Twelve: A Study in Text and Canon* (SBLDS, 149; Atlanta: Scholars Press, 1995), pp. 129-69.

readers of 4QXII[a] were substantially different from the writer/s respon-sible for the sequence there. They too could have interpreted such a place-ment of Jonah as reflecting its meta-prophetic character of Jonah. In sum, even if 4QXII[a] reflects a marginal textual tradition that eventually faded, the very existence of such a tradition seems to reflect both acknowledg-ment of Jonah as a prophetic book with an awareness of its particular character.[22]

3. *The Atypical Characterization of the Prophet and the Character of the Book*

The figure of Jonah is central to the book. Unlike other prophetic books, most of the text serves to characterize the figure of the prophet. As such the large allocation of textual space for that purpose draws much of the attention of the rereadership to Jonah, the personage. This atypical feature of the book of Jonah not only sets it apart from other books, but also characterizes it as a book addressing the figure of the prophet rather than a book of 'prophecies'. Yet a prophetic book dealing with the figure of the prophet cannot but serve as commentary on, or an interpretative key for, the understanding of 'prophecy', because 'prophecy' in the prophetic books is associated with prophetic figures. In other words, the centrality given to the characterization of Jonah within the book reinforces the characterization of the book itself as a meta-prophetic book.

Jonah, of course, is not characterized as a 'typical' prophet, if the latter is defined by the standards set in the other prophetic books, or elsewhere in the Hebrew Bible for that matter. Jonah rather emerges as both the most rebellious and the most successful of the prophets. Thus, for instance, the typical scene of the prophet who raises objections to a divine com-mission[23] is defamiliarized and developed into a full-blown rejection that involves not only attempts to escape the mission, but eventually a verbal confrontation with YHWH in which the prophet's argument is based on his (i.e. the prophet's) evaluation of YHWH as one who does not deserve to be served by the prophet (see Jon. 4.2b) rather than vice versa. Whereas the usual argument was that the prophet is either unworthy of, or unable to

---

22. Cf. Jones, *Formation*, pp. 130-32.

23. To raise objections to a divine commission represents a conventional response to a divine commission (e.g. Exod. 3.11; Judg. 6.15; Jer. 1.6). This convention serves to convey a sense of humility in the person being commissioned and calls for ensuing divine reassurance. None of this is developed in the book of Jonah.

carry the divine mission assigned to him, such an argument is reversed in Jonah. Here the character Jonah does not wish to follow the divine commandment to proclaim, because he disapproves of some crucial attributes of YHWH. The logic of the argument implies that had YHWH been different, Jonah would have accepted his mission.

Further, the typical topos of the prophet whose words are rejected by the addressees[24] is also turned upside down. Everyone in Nineveh, a city that does not enjoy good reputation in the Hebrew Bible in any case, immediately recognizes the absurdly short, and even somewhat ambiguous message of a foreign prophet who just arrived in town as truthful, and repents.[25] In fact, every secondary character in the book (that is, any character other than YHWH and Jonah), whether human, animal, plant or natural force, behaves or is immediately persuaded to behave in a way that is consistent with the will of YHWH.[26] Everyone and everything except one: the prophet of YHWH. Further, since the narrator's account of YHWH's clemency in Jonah (3.10) is phrased so as to evoke YHWH's clemency towards the Israelites in Exod. 32.14, the typical expectation of a prophet behaving like Moses[27] is also turned around: a Ninevite king takes up the role of Moses and even speaks in a way reminiscent of Moses,[28] whereas the prophet stands still.

The hyperbole and drastic reversals of expectation contribute much to

---

24. E.g. 2 Kgs 17.13-18, Jer. 2.30, and passim in Jeremiah; Zech. 1.4; cf. Isa. 6.9.

25. This characterization of Nineveh is quite atypical in the prophetic books, yet its atypicality rhetorically reinforces the message of the narrative here. It comes to play also in the shaping and communication of other messages (e.g. even Nineveh is Israelitizable), see below.

26. In the case of humans, once this will is communicated either by a prophet (see the Ninevites) or by natural portents and lots (the sailors).

27. See Num. 12.6-8; Deut. 34.10; on the relation between the figure of Moses and that of the prophets see C.R. Seitz, 'The Prophet Moses and the Canonical Shape of Jeremiah', *ZAW* 101 (1989), pp. 3-27; R.E. Clements, 'Jeremiah 1–25 and the Deuteronomistic History', in A.G. Auld (ed.), *Understanding Poets and Prophets: Essays in Honour of George W. Anderson* (JSOTSup, 152; Sheffield: Sheffield Academic Press, 1993), pp. 94-113; J. Blenkinsopp, *The Pentateuch* (ABRL; New York: Doubleday, 1992), p. 235; H. McKeating, 'Ezekiel the "Prophet Like Moses"', *JSOT* 61 (1994), pp. 97-109; M. O'Kane, 'Isaiah: A Prophet in the Footsteps of Moses', *JSOT* 69 (1996), pp. 29-51.

28. See Jon. 3.9 and cf. Exod 32.12b (and see Exod 32.24). See Simon, *Jonah*, p. 29; cf. Magonet, *Form and Meaning*, pp. 71-72. On the Israelite-like characterization of pious foreigners see also Ben Zvi, 'When the Foreign Monarch Speaks'; see also Chapter 5 here.

the atypical characterization of this prophet. They surely serve as attention getters.[29] Significantly, they clearly raise the very basic question of the *necessary*, minimal attributes that a prophet of the monarchic past must have had, within the discourse/s of the postmonarchic Yehud. These atypical features draw attention to, and comment on, the character of the person fulfilling the role of prophet, and indirectly on the 'office' of prophet, on prophecy and on prophetic books—that is, books in which not only the main human character is a prophet, but also YHWH's word/s are associated directly with prophets. Hence the 'meta-prophetic' character of the book of Jonah.

The same set of features serves to engage the rereadership of the book in the rhetoric of reduction to absurdity (*reductio ad absurdum*) that characterizes so much of the theological arguments developed in this book, unlike other prophetic books. This rhetoric serves to focus the theological discourse in 'necessary' rather than 'typical' features in a prophetic character, a feature, of course, associated with the meta-prophetic rather simply prophetic character of the book of Jonah.

In addition, when one advances an argument by 'reduction to absurdity', one assumes the truth of a statement and then observes the consequences that follow and finds them absurd, unacceptable or contradictory. Jonah's understanding of God's attributes, of prophecy and its fulfillment, and of the role of the prophet are all advanced to show the unacceptable or absurd—from the perspective of the authorial voice and the intended rereadership of the book—consequences that they lead to. The authorial voice in the book rejects Jonah's positions and advances an alternative to Jonah's stances that reflects a balancing act, which places some of Jonah's positions within a much larger perspective and plainly rejects others.[30] This balancing act involves also a comment on the matter of prophetic books, the universal or contingent validity of YHWH's words as stated in these books, and on the role of prophets.[31]

To be sure, there are additional messages communicated by some of these atypical features. The characterization of the secondary characters, such as the sailors and the Ninevite king, serves to convey a construction of the 'foreign' as, to a large extent, Israelitizable,[32] that is, as having the

29. This held true for the ancient readerships on which this study is focused, but interestingly, it still holds true for many contemporary readers.

30. On these matters, see Chapters 2–5.

31. See also Chapters 7 and 8.

32. See the sailors' speech in Jon. 1.14 resonates with Deut. 21.7-8; Jer. 26.14-15;

potential to behave as an Israelite, to talk and act as a good Israelite.[33] Thus, it reflects a tendency to use 'the other' to confirm the in-group's perspective for an ideal, 'Israelitized' world.[34]

4. In Medias Res, *Constructing Historical Background—and Undermining It, Building Bridges and Setting Borders between Collections within a Repertoire of Accepted Texts*

The book of Jonah begins *in medias res*, that is, the rereaders for whom it was composed are asked to retrieve and therefore imagine a background to this story.[35] The expression X‑אל יהוה‑דבר ויהי with 'X' standing for a personal name occurs many times in the prophetic books (e.g. Isa. 38.4; Jer. 28.12; 29.30; 32.6; 33.1, 10; Zech. 7.8) and elsewhere in the Hebrew Bible (e.g. 1 Sam. 15.10; 2 Sam. 7.4; 1 Kgs 6.11; 21.17, 28), but either 'X' stands for a character that is already introduced in some preceding unit within the book, or, in the few instances in which the latter is not the case (see 1 Kgs 16.1; 2 Chron. 11.2), the expression introduces a literary sub-unit that presupposes and is clearly linked by markers of textual cohesion to a preceding text. Thus, the occurrence of the expression in Jon. 3.1 is within the expected, but the instance in Jon. 1.1 at the opening of an independent, prophetic book is atypical. This atypicality draws attention to the figure of the prophet and to a 'missing' preceding text. In other words, the book is written so as to lead its intended rereaders to expect (or even to look for) a preceding text or perhaps 'intertext' since no text is there.

The text identifies the main prophetic character as Jonah, the son of Amittay. As it is well known, a prophet with the exact same name appears in 2 Kgs 14.25. The text in the book of Jonah suggests to the rereaders that they may identify this Jonah with the one of Kings.[36] This identification serves important communicative roles discussed elsewhere in this volume.[37]

Pss. 115.3; 135.6 and the narrator's reference to them in Jon. 1.16. As for the Ninevites, in addition to hint at Exod. 34.12b see also Jon. 3.5.

33. This 'appropriation' of the pious 'other' is present in many other books in the Hebrew Bible. See Ben Zvi, 'When the Foreign Monarch Speaks'.

34. Cf., for instance, Isa. 2.3; Mic. 4.2; and discussion of the latter in Ben Zvi, *Micah*.

35. On Jonah beginning *in medias res*, see, for instance, Trible, *Jonah*, p. 129; Sasson, *Jonah*, pp. 66-68.

36. Cf. Ackerman, 'Jonah', p. 234; Sasson, *Jonah*, pp. 66-68. On related matters, see Ben Zvi, *Obadiah*, pp. 14-19; and see Chapter 4 here.

37. See Chapter 4.

The opening *in medias res*, with its connoted request to supply a background, and particularly the naming of the prophet Jonah the son of Amittay, suggests to the intended rereaders of the book that they should adopt a perspective informed by the book of Kings. Significantly, the pronounced and atypical narrative character of the book reinforces this sense of a bond between this prophetic book and the historical narrative in Kings, not only because both of them are narratives, but because the latter includes prophetic narratives.[38]

Of course, the references to the kings of Judah or Israel in the superscriptions of several prophetic books also suggest to their rereaders that the information in Kings is relevant to their reading. Moreover, the occurrence of parallel texts in Kings and prophetic literature (e.g. 2 Kgs 18.13-20.19 and Isa. 36.1-39.8; 2 Kgs 24.18-25.21, 27-30 and Jer. 52.1-34 + 40.7-9) suggests also a clear link between these two collections of books—and types of literature—within the repertoire of the rereadership. The difference, however, is that in Jonah, atypical features—such as its opening *in medias res* and the enlarged focus on the figure of the prophet—are those that connote this sense of a bridge across separate collections within the repertoire.[39]

Still, a bridge not only links two places, but assumes and to some extent calls attention to the existence of a gap. The book of Jonah was neither accepted as a historical narrative like those in Kings (and certainly not as a section of Kings) nor could it have possibly been recognized as such by the intended rereadership.[40] This is due to a number of features that are unlikely to be accidental and that on more than one occasion involve some degree of atypicality.

To begin with, the book of Jonah does not deal with 'national' history as

38. Moreover, several scholars have proposed points of connection between the Elijah (and Elisha) narratives and Jonah. See, for instance, Schneider, *Unity*, p. 111; Limburg, *Jonah*, pp. 29-30; Magonet, *Form and Meaning*, pp. 67-69, 75, 106; Allen, *Joel, Obadiah, Jonah and Micah*, p. 177.

39. It is worth mentioning that there are links between the Pentateuch and the historical books too. In fact, they together constitute the 'Primary History'. The main link between Exodus–Deuteronomy and the prophetic books as a whole is the characterization of Moses as a prophet (e.g. Num. 12.6-8; Deut. 34.10; see also Seitz, 'The Prophet Moses'; Clements, 'Jeremiah 1–25'; Blenkinsopp, *Pentateuch*, p. 235; McKeating, 'Ezekiel'; O'Kane, 'Isaiah'). On some of these issues I wrote elsewhere; see Ben Zvi, 'Looking at the Primary (Hi)Story'.

40. It goes without saying that certainly it certainly was not accepted as nor could have been imagined to be a 'missing' section of Kings. See below.

conceived in Kings, or any book in the so-called Deuteronomistic corpus, nor for that matter Chronicles, Ezra nor Nehemiah. The story itself does not explain, nor serves as a background to, any report of any event in the historical narratives, nor is it presented as the result of any event in Israel, nor does it take place in Israel's territory or its vicinity.[41] The sense of 'foreignness' is enhanced by the fact that a significant part of the narrative takes place—atypically for a biblical text—in the sea and against the background of a heterogeneous crew.[42] The recurrent occurrence of nautical terms, many of which are 'foreign' to biblical narratives, serves to underscore that 'foreignness' of the text.

Moreover, the sense of disconnection between the text itself and the fate of Israel as a nation seems to be emphasized by the lack of any reference to Assyria's relation to Israel in the book.[43] Significantly, none of the terms 'Israel', 'Judah' or even 'Jerusalem' occur in the book. Further, one may notice that when Jonah is explicitly asked about his country and his people (Jon. 1.8), he responds that he is a 'Hebrew', which is more of a socio-ethnic than a political or geographical term, such as Judah or Israel. Finally, it is worth noticing that Jonah never addresses a fellow Israelite. In fact, he is the only Israelite in the entire book; moreover, he is the only prophet in the prophetic books that is reportedly sent to a foreign land to announce a divine proclamation to a foreign people.[44]

None of this means that the book is neutral or conveys no message on theological or ideological concepts, such as 'Judah', 'Jerusalem' or 'Israel'. Quite the opposite; it has much to say about them.[45] Still the cumulative effect of all these atypical features is clear: it distances this book not only

41. Contrast, for instance, with 1 Kgs 19.11-18 or 1 Kgs 17.8-24.

42. See Jon. 1.5. The universe of discourse in which the question in Jon. 1.8 may be raised is also worth considering. The narrative world of nations that resembles the most the one in Jonah is probably that of Esther. But the *sea* still makes the book of Jonah unique.

43. To be sure, later interpreters have advanced readings in which there is a direct connection between Jonah's behavior and his knowledge of Assyria's actions against Israel. But none of this is explicit or even hinted in the text, despite the fact that there was plenty of opportunity to do so. The cumulative presence of the features discussed in this section suggests that the intended rereaders were *not* led to believe that such a lack of reference was the result of some 'strange' textual accident that they must 'overcome' in their rereading of the text.

44. To be sure, other prophets are described as proclaiming oracles about the nations, but they are not commanded to go those nations and proclaim the oracles in their midst, in their capital cities. See Limburg, *Jonah*, p. 22.

45. See Chapter 8.

from the other prophetic books, but also from the historical narratives in the so-called Deuteronomistic history. The issue addressed by the book is not the 'history of the nation' or 'YHWH's dealings with Israel (or Judah)', but those of prophecy and prophet.

Atypical features serve in this case to ensure that the book is not imagined to be part and parcel of the repertoire of the historical narratives (or even the Primary History). Had the book been considered part and parcel of collections other than that of the prophetic books, its role as a meta-prophetic book would have suffered. At the same, by raising the issue of prophecy and prophet above all others, the unexpected features contribute to the characterization of the book as meta-prophetic.

5. *Language*

The book of Jonah contains a substantial number of terms and expressions that do not occur in prophetic books set in the monarchic period. On the ground of their presence, and other considerations, the book of Jonah has often—and correctly—been dated to the Achaemenid period.[46] Yet since other prophetic texts that are dated to the Persian period (e.g. Isa. 40–66) do not contain such expressions, their presence in Jonah is not an unavoidable result of its date of composition. The cumulative evidence of the presence or absence of these expressions and terms, or in other words, lexical choices may serve to convey more than an unintentional clue to its date.

It is a truism that the language placed on the mouth of personages in a book serves to characterize them in literary works. Of course, this holds true for the Hebrew Bible texts too.[47] But the language present in a book may serve also to characterize the book itself, because it communicates socio-linguistic markers that help to classify and differentiate it from other books within the same social repertoire. In fact, to some extent, one may compare the linguistic relation between Jonah and the other prophetic books set in the monarchic period with the relationship between Samuel–Kings and Chronicles.

46. See Chapter 1.
47. Within the realm of the Hebrew Bible, one may consult the significant study advanced in M. Cheney, *Dust, Wind and Agony: Character, Speech and Genre in Job* (CB Old Testament Series, 36; Lund: Almqvist & Wiksell International, 1994), particularly pp. 203-75. For general studies, see, for instance, Sh. Rimmon-Kenan, *Narrative Fiction: Contemporary Poetics* (London: Methuen, 1983), pp. 63-65.

Significantly, Chronicles presents itself as composed later than Samuel–Kings, in dialogue with it, and it comments or advances a position on many of the issues raised in Samuel–Kings. If, as mentioned above, Jonah asks its rereadership to approach it as a meta-prophetic text, the implied author of the book must assume that its intended rereaders are aware not only of what a prophetic text is, but of the existence of prophetic texts composed prior to the book of Jonah. Language that communicates a sense of relative 'lateness' serves that purpose.

One may contrast Jonah with, for instance, Isaiah. In the book of Isaiah expressions conveying 'lateness' do not appear in a comparable manner even in its undoubtedly Persian period sections, because the book as a whole was (and was meant to be) associated with the figure of a monarchic prophet (and the same is true of the 'additions' to the text of Jeremiah).[48] Jonah too is associated in some way with the figure of a monarchic prophet. The ubiquitous presence of late language in the book of Jonah is not a 'strange' fact by itself, but derives from its appearance in a prophetic book that is clearly set in the monarchic period.[49] Here the book of Jonah contravenes the usual expectations associated with prophetic books.

This disconnection between language and setting cannot but convey meaning. It suggests to the rereaders that something strange is going on in this book. It suggests a disconnection between (a) a kind of 'historicity' whose reference is the monarchic period as understood by the community, and (b) the literary world of the text. Such a disconnection connoted to the ancient rereadership that they should approach the book as a narrative not necessarily purporting to be 'historical'. The atypical reference to the 'king of Nineveh' rather than 'king of Assyria'[50] reinforces this sense.[51]

48. On these additions see Tov, 'Literary History'; cf. *idem*, *Textual Criticism*, p. 321.

49. Both the connoted reference to the prophet mentioned in 2 Kgs 14.25 and the explicit reference to Nineveh as a flourishing city set the narrative in the monarchic period.

50. Cf. Jdt. 1.1 ('Nebuchadnezzar, who ruled over the Assyrians in the great city of Nineveh') that may serve a similar characterizing purpose. See, for instance, L. Alonso Schökel, 'Judith', in J.L Mays *et al.* (eds.), *The HarperCollins Bible Commentary* (San Francisco: HarperCollins, 2000), pp. 732-41 (733a).

51. Cf. Sasson, *Jonah*, pp. 335-37 and the bibliography mentioned there. It is worth noting that, as it is usually the case, the characterization of the text is carried out by the lexical registrar rather than syntactic choices. See Nicacci, 'Syntactic Analysis', p. 32.

6. *The Double Ending*

The ending of the book of Jonah is also atypical for a prophetic book. Rather than concluding on a note of hope, it ends with a rhetorical question whose answer, or better whose set of multilayered answers balancing each other are intrinsically related to that of the fate of Nineveh as described in the book, as viewed from the perspective of the character Jonah, and as known to the rereadership for which the book was composed. This issue is discussed at length elsewhere in this volume.[52] Thus, it will suffice here to state that the atypical ending of Jonah clearly draws the attention of the readership to basic issues about prophecy, the role of the prophet and the character of YHWH. These issues set also this book as a meta-prophetic book, and particularly as one that puts prophecy itself under examination.

7. *Space*

The narrative of the book of Jonah takes place, for the most part, in a few spaces. Most of the action in Chapter 1 takes place in the ship surrounded by water; in Chapter 2, in the belly of the fish surrounded by water; in Chapter 3, in Nineveh's urban space, which was surrounded by an inhospitable steppe; in Chapter 4, on that inhospitable steppe and partially under a precarious, failing or failed shelter.[53] There is much symbolism in these spaces,[54] but it is sufficient to note the atypical character of these spaces among the prophetic books. Specification of space is relatively uncommon within the twelve prophetic books, and when it happens space is construed differently.

---

52. See Chapter 2 and cf. Chapter 3.

53. For a discussion of space in Jonah, see J.E. Coleson, 'The Peasant Woman and the Fugitive Prophet: A Study in Biblical Narrative Settings', in J.E. Coleson and V. H. Matthews (eds.), *'Go to the Land I Will Show You': Studies in Honor of Dwight W. Young* (Winona Lake, IN: Eisenbrauns, 1996), pp. 27-44.

54. One may mention, among others, the failing 'womb' character of ship that is replaced by a better womb, namely, the fish; the shift from water to dry land; the 'oasis' character of the turned-to-be-pious urban center; and the pair of water/sea and wind as potentially life-depriving forces that are under YHWH's control. (YHWH's control of the sea is, of course, another proposition that may be studied against the background of common images of the 'sea' as a 'chaotic' place.) 'Sea' is rarely construed as a neutral place (cf. G.F. Snyder, 'Sea Monsters in Early Christian Art', *BR* 44 [1999], pp. 7-21).

The space in Jonah evokes a sense of strangeness and foreignness. It construes a gap between the rereaders' community—and their prophetic repertoire—and Jonah. But since Jonah's space is one that is full of manifestations of YHWH's presence and activity, it also sheds light on the construction of the space in which divine activity may take place.[55] Significantly, within the discourse of these communities foreign and inhospitable spaces are often associated with encounters with divine instruction, periods of didactic activity and key messages within the discourse (e.g. Sinai, the Exile, and see, for instance, Hos. 2.16; 13.5).[56]

8. *Prophet, Go to Nineveh!*

Although Nineveh is not one of the main characters in the book as a whole,[57] it contributes much to the messages created by the readings of the book within the Yehudite literati. The choice of Nineveh is clearly instrumental for the development of the double ending discussed in Chapter 2.[58] It also creates a 'foreign space', as discussed above. In addition, it introduces two other atypical elements to the book. First, within the repertoire of prophetic books, it is atypical for a prophet to be commanded by God to travel to another country to proclaim YHWH's message directly to a people other than Israel. Second, the characterization of Nineveh in this book is atypical and stands in contrast with the usual 'reputation' of the city in other prophetic books (e.g. Nahum).

These two atypical features are interlinked. To be sure, the characterization of Nineveh, as many secondary characters in biblical narratives, and as the sailors before in Jonah, serves to emphasize traits of the main character, Jonah. These are cases of characterization by contrastive analogy.[59] But as with any contrastive analogy, its direction changes if the

55. It bears note that although Jonah is a prophetic book, not Diaspora-novella, there are elements of the latter too. See R. Syrén, 'The Book of Jonah—A Reversed Diasporanovella?', *Svensk Exegetisk Årsbok* 58 (1993), pp. 7-14 and bibliography there. See also Chapter 8 here.

56. Cf. T.L. Thompson, 'Historiography in the Pentateuch: Twenty-Five Years after Historicity', *SJOT* 13 (1999), pp. 258-83 (265-71). See also Ben Zvi, 'What Is New in Yehud?'

57. See Chapter 9.

58. See Chapter 2.

59. See Rimmon-Kenan, *Narrative Fiction*, p. 70. On the role of minor characters in biblical narratives in general, see, among others, U. Simon, 'Minor Characters in Biblical Narrative', *JSOT* 46 (1990), pp. 11-19. On my contention that from the

readers focus on the secondary character, which leads us to the characterization of Nineveh and how it is emphasized by contrast with both Jonah and the commonly accepted characterization of Nineveh in prophetic literature.

The book certainly communicates to its primary readership that even Nineveh may be receptive to YHWH's words and that even that city is Israelitizable, to the extent that foreign nations can be within this discourse.[60] This position is consistent with, and supports the appeal of the narrative and *ideological* characterization of YHWH advanced in the book, which is as a deity who may decide to communicate YHWH's word to even that city and its leaders, and by implication to any non-Israelite city.

One may compare the message that Jonah carries in this respect with that of 2 Chron. 35.21-22. It is there reported that Pharaoh Neco received a divine communication. But 2 Chron. 35.21-22 goes further. Not only it is not mentioned that Neco received such a communication through an Israelite prophet, but rather it is Neco who speaks to Josiah as prophets in Chronicles do.[61]

Although not as radical as Chronicles in this matter,[62] the book of Jonah still communicates to its Yehudite (re)readership that *contrary* to the sense that they might have gathered from the other prophetic books, Israelite prophets may be sent to other nations on missions similar to those in which they engaged in and concerning Israel. Jonah enhances the rhetorical appeal for this ideological position through its sharp, emphatic characterization of the world-encompassing dominion of YHWH and the uncharacteristic image of repenting Nineveh that it vigorously draws.[63] Further, the atypical call to the prophet to go to Nineveh serves a remarkable attention getter to this particular, substantial interpretative comment that the book of Jonah makes about both the roles of prophets of old and the repertoire of prophetic books that were accepted by the literati and the community/ies in which they lived.

perspective of the book as whole, the two main characters are YHWH and Jonah, see also Chapter 9, section 6.

60. See Chapter 8.

61. I have written elsewhere about the characterization of Neco in Chronicles, in my 'When the Foreign Monarch Speaks', § 2.4 and bibliography cited there.

62. Or perhaps a 'theological bridge' towards to the position advanced in Chronicles.

63. To some extent, these two may be seen not only as consistent with, but leading to the message discussed here.

9. *Structure*

Prophetic books tend to show multiple possible structures (or outlines). Scholars are often engaged in debates about which one of these structures is the 'correct one', but in most cases, one faces a sophisticated written text that carries multiple possible structures, each one of them associated with particular meanings. These structures and meanings come alive through rereadings, inform each other, and create a web of interwoven readings that is much richer in content that any of these readings separately. In contrast, the book of Jonah shows a relatively tight and quite symmetrical structure.[64] Multiplicity of meanings is achieved here by other rhetorical methods, including the double ending situation studied in Chapter 2 (and 3) in this volume. It suffices here to restate that this double ending draws the attention of the readership to basic issues about prophecy, the role of the prophet and the character of YHWH, and that these issues identify this book as a meta-prophetic book.

10. *Conclusion*

Many of the features that differentiate Jonah from the other books of its genre (i.e. prophetic books) serve in many ways to characterize the book of Jonah as a whole as a meta-prophetic book. Rather than being accidental, they either consistently draw the attention of the intended readership to this characterization of the book, or reinforce in one way or another a call to read Jonah as a meta-prophetic book. As a whole, these atypical features provide the intended rereadership with an interpretative key to the role of the book in the repertoire of prophetic books of the Achaemenid period community for which Jonah was composed. In addition, some atypical features of Jonah serve additional purposes within the larger repertoire of communal texts, such as conveying links and developing an awareness of the differences between different types of discourse within the community, and pointing to the (partially) Israelitizable character of the 'foreign', though to be sure, the prophet remains an Israelite, and so does the Yehudite rereadership of the book, as it understands itself.

---

64. See, for instance, Simon, *Jonah*, pp. xxiv-xxx; Trible, 'Jonah', and her detailed discussion in Trible, *Rhetorical Criticism*.

Chapter 7

JONAH, THE JERUSALEMITE LITERATI AND THEIR IMAGE OF THEMSELVES

1. *Introduction*

The discussion in the previous chapter led to the conclusion that the book of Jonah set an interpretative context for the other prophetic books in the Hebrew Bible at least from the likely perspective of its intended and primary readership. In other words, that it served as a meta-prophetic book. Further, as discussed in Chapter 2, due to the double fate of Nineveh from the viewpoint and world of knowledge of the Jerusalemite literati of the Persian period (namely, that it was not destroyed, but also that it was), their reading and rereading of the book of Jonah constructed a theological and discursive space in which some divine attributes and central theological or ideological notions informed each other and thus were set in 'proper proportion'. These previous two chapters point to two different areas in which the likely reading and rereading of the book of Jonah by these literati was conducive to the creation of a space that set isolated claims in their 'due' theological proportion through interaction with other claims that were equally valid within the same space. The end result of the process is a far more nuanced net of positions than any isolated claim by itself.

In this chapter, I will focus on another aspect of the likely reading and rereading of the book by these literati, namely, on the issue of how they themselves and their image of themselves is commented upon, and to some extent construed, in the book of Jonah. Contrary to the still common idea that the book is a kind of satire that comes from a particular group or groups and is aimed at other contemporaneous groups in society, or perhaps at society as a whole,[1] this chapter argues that the book of Jonah

---

1. See, for instance, Day, 'Problems', esp. pp. 44-47; Holbert, 'Deliverance', esp. p. 75; cf. M. Smith, *Palestinian Parties and Politics That Shaped the Old Testament* (New York: Columbia University Press, 1971), pp. 160-61; LaCoque and Lacoque, *Jonah*, pp. 41-45 and bibliography; Marcus, *From Balaam to Jonah*, esp. pp. 168-70;

reflects and carries a message of inner reflection, and to some extent critical self-appraisal of the group within which and for which this book was written. This message leads to, and reflects, a nuanced self-image within the literati themselves and an awareness of the problematic character of the knowledge they possessed.

The starting point of this argument is an analysis of the potential persona with whom these literati likely identified themselves and those whom they could have associated with other groups or subgroups in their midst.

2. *With Whom Did the Primary and Intended Rereaders of the Book Identify Themselves?*

To begin with, these rereaders related to, and accepted the authority of the authorial voice or communicator of the text.[2] In other words, not only did they try to meet the communicative expectations of this communicator, but they also considered such a communicator to be one who conveys a godly and authoritative message. The communicator's voice spoke to them with the authority of an accepted prophetic book, that is, a book they were supposed to read, reread and meditate upon.[3]

However, whether consciously or unconsciously, they construed their image of that communicator through their continuous interaction with the text.[4] Given the genre of the book, the image was both authoritative and ideal. At the same time, this image could not but overlap some aspects of that of the literati themselves. In fact, it is most likely that the primary rereadership construed itself as an extension of this implied author or communicator of a prophetic book, and perhaps even as their embodiment. Just as the author of the book communicated divine knowledge, so they communicated divine knowledge to themselves and to others by reading and rereading the book. Just as the author is conceived of as a broker of

M. West, 'Irony in the Book of Jonah: Audience Identification with the Hero', *Perspectives in Religious Studies* 11 (1984), pp. 233-42; Fretheim, *Message*, pp. 34-37; Wolff, *Obadiah and Jonah*, pp. 84-88; Allen, *Joel, Obadiah, Jonah and Micah*, esp. pp. 190-91; Orth, 'Genre'.

2.   For G. Rusch, 'Understanding means to meet the interactive/communicative expectations of a communicator' (italics in the original). See Rusch, 'Comprehension', quotation from p. 115.

3.   On the genre of 'Israelite Prophetic Books' as a subcategory of 'Ancient Israelite authoritative books' and its implications, see Ben Zvi, 'Prophetic Book'.

4.   See Chapter 1.

divine knowledge, so are they. Just as the voice of the author resonates in the book, so their voices become animators of that voice as they read and reread a text that conveys—and creates—divine knowledge.

Beyond this self-characterization stood social realities: the actual authorship and the primary readership of the book were located in the same social group in Yehud—the few Jerusalemite literati of the time. They were socialized and maintained by the same mechanisms in the society as a whole. They shared similar horizons of knowledge and thought, an educational system and roles in their larger social system. In other words, the authors and their target readership belonged to the same limited social group in ancient Yehud. The basic role of the readers and rereaders of the book was to continue the communication of the divine message conveyed by the implied author of the book to the Judahite society, to activate as it were the message encoded in the text.[5]

Two observations follow. First, these literati most likely construed the communicator or implied author of the book in way that resembled its actual authorship, with whom they were directly or indirectly acquainted.[6] Second, they would not identify the implied author or communicator of an authoritative book with some group or subgroup they opposed vehemently.

Still, the communicator is not the only persona with whom the readership may identify. The usual expectation in the prophetic books is for the readership to identify itself with the prophetic character. But was the primary readership of the book of Jonah asked, or would they have been able to identify with the character Jonah? To be sure, Jonah is to a large extent ridiculed in this narrative.[7] Such a portrayal more than hints at the evaluation of Jonah's character by the implied author/communicator of the book, with whom the rereadership was supposed to identify. Far more important, the main narrative of the book is one of confrontation, and at its core of theological or ideological confrontation between the prophetic character and YHWH.[8] A most basic theological principle in their discourse/s was that YHWH was right, just, and far more knowledgeable than any

5. On these issues see Ben Zvi, 'Introduction: Writings, Speeches'.
6. To be sure, this does not hold true for the actual authorship of the sources or forerunners of the books composed by these actual authors. In these cases, the actual authors of the authoritative book would partially embody—or write 'in the spirit of'— their construction of the implied author of the source or textual forerunner, if they attached authority to it.
7. See, for instance, Marcus, *From Balaam to Jonah*, pp. 119-22.
8. Unlike any other prophetic book. See Chapter 6.

human being. In fact, from their perspective, their work as readers was essentially to learn about YHWH so they and their society could do what is right in YHWH's sight by means of studying what they considered reliable, authoritative texts. Further the principle of *imitatio dei* was certainly prominent in their discourse.[9]

All this taken into account, the question is whether it was still possible for the target readership of the book to identify with YHWH and the authorial voice of the book, and at the same time see something central of, and about themselves in the character of Jonah. If such a possibility does not exist, then the logical conclusion is that this readership was asked to and most likely closely and exclusively associated Jonah with some group different from their own, whom they strongly opposed, and whom they wanted to teach, as it were, the correct theological positions. This is, in fact, the view of several scholars.[10]

These are crucial questions for historical studies of the book of Jonah. It is impossible to understand the communicative role of satirical elements within the community of first rereaders, unless one knows whom they identified as the target of the satire. To be sure, at the level of the world of the book the target is the character Jonah, but the issue is which social group the character Jonah stood for in the minds of the intended, first readers and rereaders. A careful analysis of this matter is a precondition for any study of the communicative meanings of the book within these readerships.

3. *Turning to the Question of Whom Jonah Stood For*

A practical way in which to start a discussion of this matter is to narrow the list of potential candidates, both in terms of space and time. For instance, it is highly improbable that Jonah stood for any group of non-Israelites in this readership group. Not only does the characterization of Jonah in the book not support such an interpretation, but also satirical elements in a work rarely target people or social institutions from a different time.[11]

A still quite common position is that Jonah stands for 'exclusivist' or

---

9.   See, for instance, Lev. 19.2.

10.   See, among many others, Nogalski, *Redactional Processes*, pp. 272-73.

11.   Often they target also particular positions. On the theological or ideological aspects of the satirical elements in Jonah see Chapter 2. As it will be shown, focus here is on actual contemporaneous people.

Ezra-minded groups in Yehud,[12] and if so, the implied, and the actual author of the book represent the voices of those who opposed these groups and their ideology. This position does not have any support from the narrative itself. Moreover, as mentioned in Chapter 1, there is no evidence to support that just an Ezra-like worldview governed the Yehudite polity and its discourse for any substantial period. But had such a worldview regarding 'foreigners' been dominant in Persian Yehud, still the matter would be of little direct relevance to the understanding of the text of Jonah in its historical context. A study of the books of Ezra and Nehemiah is beyond the scope of this volume, but a few observations suffice. Unlike the case in Jonah, the rejected 'foreigners' in Ezra–Nehemiah are all inside Israel. The problem associated with their 'otherness' is an inner Israelite issue that does not necessarily involve the acceptance of the rule of YHWH. The 'foreign' women, for instance, are never accused of worshiping or leading their spouses to worship 'other gods'.[13] In fact, although Ezra–Nehemiah does not say much about foreigners outside Israel, the general tone regarding nations outside Israel, and especially Persians who do not attempt 'to marry' with members of the Golah community (e.g. the Persians) but stand outside it, is as a whole very positive. Ezra-minded individuals would not have found anything wrong with the sailors, the Ninevites or the king of Nineveh of their time, just as neither Nehemiah nor Ezra found anything wrong with their Persian rulers.[14]

There is a variant of this position, namely, that Jonah represents a xenophobic group in Israel who opposes the doctrine, or even the idea of salvation of the nations and are attacked and ridiculed by the authorship of the book. This position should be rejected from the outset since the narrative clearly does not make that claim at all. Jonah is nowhere depicted as

12. For a list of works supporting this position and a critique of it, see Trible, *Studies*, pp. 261-65.

13. Cf. Kaufman, תולדות, III, pp. 289-93.

14. The implied author of Ezra advances a positive image of the Persian monarch (e.g. Ezra 1.1-4; 5.3–6.14; 7.11-26; see also Neh. 2.1-8). The trouble may come from local leaders, but the Persian throne is construed as consistently supportive. On this matter, cf. A. Siedlecki, 'The Empire Writes Back: Diplomatic Correspondence in Ezra 4–6' (paper presented at the 2001 Annual Meeting of the PNW-SBL, held in Edmonton, AB). The exception, of course, is Neh. 9 (esp. vv. 32, 37), but one has to take into consideration the literary context, purpose and genre of the text. On Nehemiah, see T.C. Eskenazi, 'Nehemiah 9-10: Structure and Significance', *JHS* 3.9 (2001), available at www.purl.org/jhs and www.jhsonline.org, and the bibliography cited there.

stating that he opposes the survival of Nineveh because they are not Israel.[15] Further, the climax of the book in chapter four does not deal with the Ninevites or the sailors at all.[16] To be sure, this type of readings is attested much later, when readers attributed this thinking to Jonah because it was consistent with some of their main meta-narratives, and in turn allowed the book of Jonah to serve as an additional pillar on which these meta-narratives stood.[17] But later attestations do not have any bearing on our understanding of how the primary rereadership likely understood the book. For that purpose, an analysis of the text itself and of textually inscribed markers suggesting to the intended readership how to approach the book are much more valuable. In sum, the once relatively common idea that Jonah was written against the background of, and in opposition to Ezra–Nehemiah or other 'xenophobic' groups and that its main purpose in its primary setting was to address the relations between Israel and 'the nations' should be rejected.

Turning back to the text and its own claims, the character of Jonah did stand for, and embodied, multiple social and ideological or theological constructions, such as an ancient prophet from the northern kingdom in the monarchic period and a runaway slave, to mention only two discussed elsewhere in this volume. All these constructions inform each other and contribute to a multilayered characterization of the character Jonah. Moreover, as such they shape the theological or ideological message of the book as a whole.[18]

Yet, as mentioned above, it seems reasonable to narrow the focus to only those attributes that may help to characterize substantial social groups in or around the Jerusalemite community of the time of the composition and first readings and rereadings of the book. Featuring a Monarchic period prophet in the northern kingdom of Israel does not fit this description, nor is the main target of the satirical elements in Jonah the population of runaway slaves.

---

15. See, among others, Clements, 'Purpose', p. 21.

In spite of this obvious fact, the position that Jonah 'begrudged the salvation' of the nations has a long history of interpretation, because of its congruence with, or suit- ability for other meta-narratives. See, for instance, Bickerman, 'Deux erreurs', esp. pp. 44, 51-52; *idem*, *Four Strange Books*, pp. 17-18, 25-27; and Chapter 9 in this volume.

16. See, for instance, Rofé, *Prophetic Stories*, pp. 160-61 (cf. p. 163); Clements, 'Purpose', esp. pp. 17-20; Sasson, *Jonah*, pp. 25-26. On related matters see also Chapter 5 in this volume.

17. See Chapter 9.

18. See discussion in Chapter 4, and see also Chapters 2, 3 and 5.

A more promising focus is on the explicit characterization of Jonah, with an eye to particular attributes that may point to social groups that are likely to have existed in Persian Yehud. Since one of Jonah's main attributes is being a prophet, one is tempted to assume that Jonah stood primarily for contemporaneous Jerusalemite prophets. This is unlikely, because Jonah is explicitly presented as a prophet who does not interact with any other Israelite, nor prophesies in, to or about Israel (and contrast, among others with, Zech. 13.2-6).

An ideological and discursive opposition to any contemporaneous prophet wishing to claim the authority of 'classical' prophets may have, nevertheless, come to the mind of the original (re)readership. Moreover, if Jonah is understood only (or mainly) in terms of the Jonah of the book of Kings, even the stand of 'good' prophets of old to whom no book is associated within the discourse of the community is undermined.

Marcus is correct when he writes:

> if prophets are criticized for hypocrisy, foolishness, and abuse of power, then the writers, and their appreciative audiences, are expressing their views…that there has been a grievous falling away from proper standards of behavior and an implied wish that the proper standards be restored.[19]

But one has to keep in mind that the prophet Jonah was presented as a monarchic prophet. The text suggests to its rereaders, therefore, that the problems of standards existed already in ancient times. Most significantly none of the prophetic characters to whom Marcus refers (Elisha, 'the man of God' in 1 Kgs 13, Balaam) is associated with a prophetic book in the authoritative repertoire of the postmonarchic community, except Jonah. But not only is Jonah not Micah nor Isaiah nor Jeremiah, nor like any of the 'classical' prophets, but the book of Jonah is a meta-prophetic book.[20] Although the horizon of the book may include an implied wish for a future restoration of proper standards of prophecy, the book itself reflects a world in which YHWH's word was a written word, in which a meta-prophetic book that served to place claims of other authoritative books in proportion was required.

Further, not only is there little need for actual flesh and blood prophets in that world, but there are social and ideological reasons why the literati of the period would not accept the authority of contemporary prophets who claim to communicate direct messages from the deity. The authority,

19. See Marcus, *From Balaam to Jonah*, p. 170.
20. See Chapter 6.

self-identity, and raison d'être of the literati were based on their own role
as brokers of the divine instruction contained in the texts that they alone
could directly approach. These literati composed, redacted and edited
prophetic books. When they did so they identified with and expressed the
thoughts and words of authoritative prophetic voices of the past and even
that of YHWH. They also read, reread and studied these texts among
themselves, and read and explained them to others. In both cases they
'animated' these authoritative voices. They served as guardians of, and the
required path in society to, divine teachings.[21] It is very unlikely that such
a group would foster the authority of contemporaneous prophets claiming
to have direct access to communication from the divine.[22]

Given this background it is significant that one matter in which the book
of Jonah carries a clear, univocal message is its critique of positions that
grant the prophet something more than a secondary role in the administration and manifestation of the divine economy. Jonah is upset at being at
best a pawn in the chain of events initiated and controlled by YHWH that
leads to the salvation or the destruction of Nineveh. But his reaction
always remains a target of criticism within this discourse.[23] It is hardly
accidental that a similar theological, or ideological, position is expressed
elsewhere in the Hebrew Bible.[24]

To be sure, a careful study of this matter is of major importance for the
theological message conveyed by the text about prophecy and prophetic
characters. Yet, as mentioned above, the position of the book seems to
reflect the general atmosphere of the social world and the world of ideas of
the literati rather than being the main message of the book to its intended
rereadership.[25]

---

21. That is, they were necessary brokers of divine knowledge. Since I addressed
these issues elsewhere, the present remarks suffice here. See Ben Zvi, 'Introduction:
Writings, Speeches', and bibliography mentioned there.

22. See Ben Zvi, *Zephaniah*, pp. 348-53; cf. *idem*, 'What Is New in Yehud?'. One
may add that it goes almost without saying that it is very unlikely that the literati for
whom YHWH's word was mainly a written text and not an oral performance served also
prophets in the style of those in the books they compose, read and studied. They
'animated' them and wrote in their spirit, and therefore assumed a quasi-prophetic
status, but they were not they. See Ben Zvi, 'Introduction: Writings, Speeches', and
bibliography mentioned there; and my previous works.

23. See Chapter 2.

24. See Ben Zvi, 'Prophets and Prophecy'.

25. See above and Chapter 2.

4. *Jonah, the Sage*

Jonah is not described simply as a prophet who did not want to fulfill his prophetic. Nor is he described, at least in the main, as one who cared so much about what the Ninevites or anyone would say if his prophecy is not fulfilled. Above all, and when it counts the most, in the climatic confrontation between YHWH and Jonah to which the narrative leads up to, Jonah is described as a person who did not want to fulfill his role because, according to him, his job was to prophesy the destruction of Nineveh, despite the fact that the city was not about to be destroyed due to the compassionate and gracious character of the would-be destroyer, a deity slow to anger, abounding in kindness and repenting of evil (Jon. 4.2). Such a deity will never do such a thing, according to Jonah.

Certainly, Jonah—as some of the literati of the period, one may add—claims to know YHWH's attributes. But how does such knowledge function within the world created by the reading of this book by literati of Achaemenid Yehud? *Why* was Jonah convinced that he knew YHWH's attributes? The book is clear on one point: it is not because YHWH communicated them to Jonah directly, even if Jonah is a prophet. Not only is such information absent from the book, but Jonah even explicitly says to YHWH: 'Was not this *my* word when I was still in my own land?' (Jon. 4.2). Jonah is saying, 'It was *my* word, not *yours.*' Jonah does not know about these attributes of YHWH because of a particular divine disclosure to him, but rather because he knows texts that are authoritative in the Jerusalemite community. In fact, he is presented to the readers as one who quotes Joel 2.13; Pss. 86.15; 103.8; 145.8 (see Jon. 4.2).[26] This quotation, though, is not to be taken in isolation. Jonah is characterized as a person who is well acquainted with the text of many authoritative psalms. In ch. 2, his prayer is actually a pastiche of different verses from Psalms.[27] The use and combination of existing Psalms to create a new, carefully composed text to be uttered at the right occasion was considered a—or perhaps even the—correct human response to the situation. In Chronicles such a response is explicitly attributed to David (1 Chron. 18.8-36//Pss. 105.1-15

26. Cf. Neh. 9.17.

27. See Jon. 2.3 and cf. Pss. 18.7; 30.3; 118.5; 120.1; 130.1, 2; Jon. 2.4 and cf. Ps. 42.8; Jon. 2.5 and cf. Ps. 31.23; Jon. 2.6 and cf. Pss. 18.5-6; 69.2; Jon. 2.7 and cf. Pss. 30.4; 71.20; Jon. 2.8a and cf. Pss. 142.4; 143.4; Jon. 2.8b and cf. Pss. 5.8; 18.7; 88.3; Jon. 2.9 and cf. Ps. 31.7; Jon. 2.10a and cf. Pss. 42.5; 50.14, 23; 66.13; Jon. 2.10b and cf. Ps. 3.9. See Chapter 4.

+ 96.1-13 + 106.47-48), who is the paragon of righteousness in this book. To be sure, the number of quotations and references in Jon. 2.3-10 is somewhat excessive and the degree to which the prayer fits the occasion is perhaps arguable, as one may expect in a book given to exaggeration and the quasi-burlesque.[28] Yet Jonah is still described as one who knows the texts and whose speech includes crucial references to them (cf. Solomon in 2 Chron. 6.41, and see Ps. 132.8-9).[29] Further, in Jon. 4.2, the character Jonah is not only quoting authoritative texts but also aligns himself with those involved in the interpretation of equivocal passages by other passages. It is obvious that he is using Joel 2.13; Pss. 86.15; 103.8; 145.8[30] as key interpretative texts for Exod. 34.6-7 and Num. 14.18.

Although there are multiple images and perspectives on the characterizations of Jonah that likely emerged when the book was read and reread by the intended and primary audiences, one of the prominent images is of direct relevance to the issue addressed here. Jonah is described as a person who is well educated in the corpus of religious texts accepted as authoritative for the Jerusalemite community,[31] who is convinced that one can

---

28. The term 'quasi-burlesque' is meant to convey the literary use of incongruence in this book, and particularly in relation to Jonah. Such a use involves, among others, humor, parody, and ridicule. On the psalm of Jonah within the set of questions discussed in this chapter, see below.

29. Needless to state, every quotation of other texts leads to a recontextualization of the quoted text and, accordingly, it carries new meanings. See, for instance, 2 Chron. 6.41-42 and Ps. 132.8-10. A quotation of a known authoritative text in another text turns the latter into an interpretative key for at least a meaning of the former, and in any case, legitimizes or attempts to legitimize the quoting text on the grounds of the authority of the quoted text.

30. To be sure, the speakers in the other texts see YHWH's compassion as an expression of hope, whereas Jonah complains about it. Still, there is no debate that these texts share the same 'factual' information about YHWH's attributes.

31. In addition to the psalm of Jonah and Jon. 4.2, one may notice, for instance, that Jonah's first words in the narrative, namely, those to the sailors in 1.9, are a pun on and a sharp recombination of a well-known phrase that appears numerous times in Psalms. Jonah refers to the 'YHWH, the God of heavens who made [עשה] the sea [ים] and the dry land [היבשה]'. The expression is an obvious adaptation of 'YHWH who made the heavens and earth' (see Pss. 115.15; 121.2; 124.8; 134.3; 135.6; 146.6; and cf. 2 Chron. 2.11). The combination 'YHWH, the God of heavens' appears also in Gen. 24.7; Ezra 1.2; Neh. 1.5 and 2 Chron. 36.26. It serves the rhetorical purpose of explaining to the non-Israelite sailors who is YHWH, and to express YHWH's superior status (see Chapter 8 in this volume). The change from 'heaven' and 'earth' to 'sea' and 'dry land' reflects not only the spatial and narrative conditions in which Jonah and the

learn about YHWH from these texts, and who is able to recreate new prayers out of accepted texts, just like the literary David construed in the world of the book of Chronicles—and significantly, just like the Chronicler himself.[32]

The literati of Yehud among whom and for whom the book was composed shared these attributes with the character Jonah. What can we learn from this observation, from this partial convergence of attributes assigned to Jonah and of the actual literati? It is obvious that it demonstrates that the text had something to say to these literati about themselves, not only about their theology or ideology. But what did the fact that Jonah himself is a kind of 'sage' convey to them about themselves?

Given the quasi-burlesque characterization of Jonah in some portions of the book, the implied author may seem to suggest to its primary readership that they may and perhaps should take themselves with a grain of salt. More importantly, the book clearly hints at a self-recognition among the literati that to be one of the literati and to be well acquainted with the correct texts does not necessarily guarantee correct theological knowledge or attitude. The text of Jonah clearly makes the case that a person who is

---

sailors are, but evokes the mighty role of YHWH as one who may turn the sea (ים) into dry land (יבשה), if YHWH so wishes. In fact, the pair יבשה-ים appears elsewhere in the Hebrew Bible in the context of reference to the parting of sea (see Exod. 14.16, 22; 15.19; Ps. 66.6; Neh. 9.11). Jonah here cleverly combines passages and phrases, just as he does in his psalm. One may mention also that Jonah's words in 4.3 evoke the narrative in 1 Kgs 19.4, as widely recognized. See, for instance, Magonet, *Jonah*, pp. 68-69; Salters, *Jonah*, p. 20. Salters there summarizes the numerous links between the text of Jonah and other books by stating, perhaps with some humor, 'hence in only 48 verses, which is the extent of the book, there are so many connections with the Old Testament that one might begin to doubt if Jonah has anything to say'. On these links (including citations, allusions, reminiscences, and the like) see also Dell, 'Reinventing the Wheel'; Magonet, *Jonah*, pp. 65-84.

32. It is to be stressed this is not a simple case of a character to which some citation or words reminiscent of authoritative texts is attributed in another authoritative text. Many biblical characters, Israelites and non-Israelites fall into this category. See Chapter 5 in this volume. Here the point is not to construe a pious image of a Jonah who occasionally or accidentally as it were expresses himself in words of 'scripture' (cf. the sailors or the king of Nineveh), but of an Israelite whose speech and discourse is presented to the rereaders, by cumulative evidence, as based on readings—and of course, selections and interpretations—of authoritative texts. Jonah does not speak much in the book of Jonah, but much of what he says points at direct knowledge of other texts in the repertoire of the literati.

well acquainted with authoritative texts may still fail.[33]

But why would such a person fail? Is Jonah simply an individual character, in which case there is not much to learn from his misadventures? Or are some typical issues involved too? And if so, which ones? Answers to these questions depend much on the question of when, on final analysis, Jonah was right or wrong—or anywhere in that spectrum—whether in the view of the implied author, with whom the readers were supposed to identify, or from YHWH's perspective (as conceived by the literati in Persian Yehud).

This issue must be addressed within the context of the text as a whole, and as likely read and studied by these literati. The multiplicity of theological voices informing each other and creating a complex network of positions that results from the double ending mentioned above must be recognized.[34]

Let us begin with readings of Jonah heavily influenced by the survival of Nineveh in the narrative. Within these readings, YHWH was really 'a gracious YHWH, merciful, slow to anger and abounding in steadfast love, and ready to relent from punishing'. From this perspective, Jonah was not wrong in regards to what he claimed to have learnt about YHWH from the authoritative texts.

Yet it is worth stressing that Jonah grounds his opposition to the lack of coherence between YHWH's announcement of judgment[35] and actual

33. Needless to say, this position is only to be expected (cf. 'the beginning of wisdom/knowledge is the fear of the Lord', Prov. 1.7; 9.10; Pss. 111.10; Sir. 1.13—and cf. Sir. 1.11-30). Stories about literati or sages who may fail often lead to some reference, implicit or explicit, pointing to theological or social controls over assertions about divine knowledge (and cf. the mentioned phrase in Proverbs). On the surface, there is not much of that in the book of Jonah, but see below. Theological and social controls on the ability of literati to interpret authoritative texts are only expected given the social power that such interpretation may hold, and they are vastly attested.

See 'For, of course, all that has been said about the manner of interpreting Scripture is ultimately subject to the judgement of the Church which exercises the divinely conferred commission and ministry of watching over and interpreting the Word of God' (*Catechism of the Catholic Church*, §119). Although such explicit theological statements as this one are more likely to appear in some religious traditions than others, those who were accepted as legitimate, authoritative representatives of the 'Church' or the 'Klal Israel'/ the 'Synagogue' always exerted some degree of control over the teaching and interpretation of religious scripture within their own group.

34. The Persian period readers of this book were well aware of two opposites fates of Nineveh. The matter is addressed in Chapters 2 and 3.

35. As discussed in Chapter 2. See also Chapters 3 and 4.

actions not only on a particular set of divine attributes, but also in a quite clear conception of how YHWH *should* behave. Jonah's ideas on the matter are consistent with, and seem to reflect, accepted texts (Num. 23.19; 1 Sam. 15.29; Deut. 18.21-22),[36] even if they are not explicitly quoted.

One aspect of the problem of Jonah, namely, the apparent failure to reconcile different authoritative texts most likely vexed the literati too, and greatly. Jonah knew about YHWH from Psalms, prophetic and Pentateuchal books and found support in them for his positions. But he could have found support there for other positions too. How could he have squared the mentioned character of YHWH along with the proclamation he was supposed to announce in Nineveh with such texts as Num. 23.19 and 1 Sam. 15.29? It is worth stressing that even if the text does not bring Jonah to quote explicitly these verses, their words *and gist* were an integral part of the world of knowledge of the intended and the primary readership. How could *they* have squared these statements? But before addressing this question, we must deal with other readings of Jonah that informed and balanced this one.

From the perspective of readings of the book of Jonah heavily influenced by the historical destruction of Nineveh, Jonah was wrong about the divine attributes he assigned to YHWH, for the deity is certainly willing to destroy an entire city. From this perspective, Jonah was also wrong in believing that the announcement of a true prophet would not be fulfilled. He was also wrong about the time it might take for such a prediction to materialize.

From a perspective informed by both fates of Nineveh—that is, the one explicitly inscribed in the narrative and the historical one—the text indicates that YHWH is precisely

> merciful and gracious, slow to anger, and abounding in steadfast love and faithfulness, keeping steadfast love for the thousandth generation, forgiving iniquity and transgression and sin, yet by no means clearing the guilty, but visiting the iniquity of the parents upon the children and the children's children, to the third and the fourth generation (Exod. 34.6-7; NRSV; cf. Num. 14.18).

36. On these texts and the related matter of YHWH's ability to relent see Chapter 3 in this volume. It suffices here to state that there are other texts that do not square with the explicit claims and the sentiments expressed in Deut. 18.21-22, Num. 23.19 and 1 Sam. 15.29, and see, for instance, Ezek. 18.20-30. On the issue of Jonah's and the literati's assessment of seemingly contradictory texts, see below.

Thus YHWH not only saves Nineveh from judgment, but also executes judgment against it.

Likewise, repentance—another significant concept in Jonah— is surely important, but just as Jonah and the Ninevites agree, 'salvation belongs to YHWH' (Jon. 2.10; cf. Pss. 3.3; 80.3) and YHWH *may* turn back from the wrath (Jon. 3.9), but YHWH may not. Further, YHWH may have reasons other than the repentance of sinners for relenting from carrying out an announced destruction (see Jon. 4.11). Yet surely YHWH may also carry it out and on a very large scale. The postexilic community of readers was all too aware that YHWH is willing to carry out severe judgment, and has indeed done so.

The double ending, then, allows texts to be reconciled without diminishing the tension between them. As observed in Chapter 2, this situation leads to a sophisticated religious thought in which different positions are set in balance and inform each other. Yet it carries an unavoidable problem to anyone who, like the Jonah of the book and the literati themselves, knows about YHWH from the authoritative repertoire of books they have access to. How to decide among these different perspectives illuminating each other if one is to make a practical decision?

To illustrate, how could have Jonah known whether YHWH would destroy Nineveh or not? In the story he made his choice of verses, but other verses could have been used and they would have led to the very opposite conclusion. From a theological position strongly informed by the 'double ending' perspective, Jonah's mistake was to commit himself to his interpretative choice, which was evidently a narrow one. Thus he missed the point of the eventual destruction of Nineveh. He missed the point that his own words ונינוה נהפכת (and Nineveh will be overturned/turned over) (Jon. 3.4) were fulfilled not only once but thrice. The Ninevites 'turned over', that is, reformed themselves, as he unknowingly prophesied. Nineveh was eventually overturned as he prophesied. And, finally, his proclamation of YHWH's word—understood as a threatening word— caused a change of heart in the population, which may be seen as fulfilling the purpose of YHWH's word (cf. Isa. 55.6-11).[37]

Jonah was able to understand neither his triple prophetic role nor YHWH's attributes. But more importantly, from the perspective of the Yehudite literati, is the fact that Jonah, notwithstanding his personal shortcomings, could never have been able to understand his role or the

37. See Rofé, *Prophetical Stories*, pp. 169-70.

divine attributes only on the basis of the divine speeches (verbal or other-wise) explicitly mentioned in the book. He correctly set these speeches within the interpretative frame of a theology or ideology reflected in, and based on authoritative texts. He failed in his endeavor because he lacked a global, very long term, and balanced perspective.

Yet this perspective—that it was spared destruction and that it was destroyed[38]—comes at a significant price, namely, that there is no way to predict the way particular events or actions will play out, or from a theological perspective, the divine will. Had Jonah been more sophisti-cated, he still could not have known when Nineveh would be destroyed, or even if it would be destroyed. Such a Jonah would have been careful *not* to accept YHWH's theological explanations of YHWH's behavior in Jon. 4.11 as categorical,[39] rather than contingent statements that may apply directly and unequivocally to only the particular case at stake, and even there only momentarily.

It is worth stressing that these conclusions are consistent with the role of the book of Jonah as a meta-prophetic book.[40] If the book of Jonah sets other prophetic books in proportion, it cannot but set the authors and readers of these books in proportion too. If it parodies other prophetic books, it indirectly parodies authors, readers and brokers of these books. If it raises the problematic character of the communication, and understand-ing of YHWH's messages in the case of a learned figure, it cannot but raise the problematic character of the role fulfilled by the brokers of divine knowledge who wrote, read and studied prophetic books, that is, of the literati themselves.

Rereadings of the book of Jonah within its primary readerships that focus on the reasons for Jonah's most serious theological errors—that is, those that go beyond the comic or ridiculous—communicate a strong call to the literati themselves to approach the prophetic (and other) ancient Israelite authoritative literature they read, read to others, and compose, in the light of a system in which each text informs the other within the repertoire in which their world of knowledge as a whole—including, for instance knowledge of such events as the fall of Nineveh and of Jerusalem[41]—serves an interpretative key for the study of these texts. It is

---

38. See Chapter 2.

39. YHWH's words there are to be understood as a rhetorical question. See Chapter 2 n. 1.

40. On the meta-prophetic character of the book of Jonah see Chapter 6.

41. See Chapter 8 in this volume.

the implicit claim of the book of Jonah that *only* such a global, large perspective may shed true light on YHWH and YHWH's attributes.

Even so, within this discourse there is a clear and salient human predicament inextricably associated with the construction of a better understanding of YHWH from such a balanced approach. The more the literati know about YHWH through their readings and rereadings, the less they may predict or even understand particular events. The more YHWH's words become contingent, the less they can be relied upon for cases other than those in which they were uttered, even if they are phrased in the most universal language (e.g. Jon. 4.11). The more the logical *incoherence* of the truths of faith expressed in different texts becomes apparent, the more 'both-and' or 'yes, but' their approach is, the less categorical their claims about the divine must be.[42]

In sum, if the world of the producers and readers of the book of Jonah and their self-image is reflected or shaped by the reading and rereading of the book, then this prophetic text expressed and conveyed a heightened awareness of their limitations, along with the implied claim to be as writers and readers of prophetic books and indispensable brokers of this divine knowledge to Israel. One may say that the book of Jonah sets not only the prophetic books, but also the literati 'in their proper proportion'. As such, it is a book of self-reflection. The humoristic and satiric features of the book serve, as they often do,[43] to introduce a necessary self-critique. Such a critique is necessary to assure the continuance of the group, its role in society and the centrality of its literary repertoire. The flexibility and adaptability in the tradition and in the sea of positions from which the literati may choose that are implied in this trend contribute substantially to the ability of a group in society to reproduce itself through generations, that is, to its stability, and in the case of the literati to the stability of the society in which they lived.[44]

---

42. Needless to say, this holds true within a certain sub-realm of theological or ideological discourses. There is another realm in which categorical claims are not questioned. Society sets the boundaries between the two realms. For instance, positions that deny the just patronship of YHWH over Israel, never mind the YHWH's existence were well beyond anything remotely acceptable by the elite, and most likely the vast majority of the population of Jerusalem-centered Yehud.

43. Notwithstanding all the substantial differences, cf. the role of the court buffoon in medieval times.

44. Of course, this flexibility and adaptability has limits too. See note above. Yet its realm includes much of the mental, discursive space of the time. Almost anything except fundamentals was included in that realm. Among these fundamentals were

A final comment: the flexibility and adaptability of the tradition and the interpretative options for the literati is directly related to both (a) their selection of a repertoire of authoritative books and (b) their composition, editing and above all reading of particular books, as the present study of the book of Jonah demonstrates. From a social perspective, this result is not unexpected, since both processes took place in the same social location.[45] Moreover, within the theological horizon of thought of the literati, the choice of multiple voices represented nothing but an acceptance of the final arbitration of claims by YHWH, for within their discourse it is YHWH who expressed all these different positions—a YHWH as represented by the authorial voices of texts considered authoritative by the community, but these texts were, of course, deemed authoritative because they were understood to provide valid teachings of YHWH.[46]

YHWH's patronship of Israel, the role of Jerusalem/Zion in the divine economy, and the role of the literati themselves as brokers of divine knowledge. On the first two see the next chapter in this volume.

45. See also Chapter 8.

46. Had the literati agreed, for instance, that the book of Hosea misleads its readers when it claims to be YHWH's word and therefore carries no valid knowledge about YHWH for Israel, it is unlikely that it would have been studied, copied and transmitted from generation to generation.

Chapter 8

THE BOOK OF JONAH, ISRAEL AND JERUSALEM

1. *Introduction*

The book of Jonah was written within and for postmonarchic communities in Yehud. Several theological (or ideological) concepts stood at the core of their self-identification. These postmonarchic communities saw themselves as 'Israel'. They—or their elites—construed the term 'Israel' in theological terms. For them, it indicated, above all, a people with a particular relationship to YHWH—who was conceived as the High God or the God of Heaven—and with a story about themselves and about their relationship with YHWH. Both the relationship itself and its and their (hi)story—as accepted by the community—were inscribed in authoritative literature. Works included in this literature either became a source from which to learn the 'Teaching of YHWH' or were directly identified as YHWH's word or teaching. As such these works required study and a set of social practices—included worship—that either followed or were consistent with the claims of such literature, as they were understood by the literati of the time and accepted by society. This literature and its claims about Israel, Jerusalem/Zion, and thus indirectly about the province of Yehud, its capital and leadership, stood at the core of the community's[1] self-identity and of its story about itself. Accordingly, a relatively poor Yehud invested the resources necessary to develop and maintain the literati able to compose, edit, copy, read, study and read to others much of the literature that eventually ended up in the Hebrew Bible.

As for Jerusalem, it was the social, political and economic center of

---

1. Or, at very least, its intellectual elite, but given the social, historical and economic circumstances in Yehud it is highly unlikely that society was so compartmentalized that the main theological meta-narrative of its intellectual elite was not influential outside its inner circle. Moreover, had this been the case, there would have been no social reasons to allocate resources to such elite.

Yehud. Theologically, however, it was the center of Israel because of its temple. Moreover, from their perspective, the latter was the only legitimate temple for the God of all creation, and as such it turned Jerusalem, which was a minor city in the social world of the time, into a unique central place of cosmic significance. Further, Jerusalem was not only a center of worship, but also the place where literati held the true teachings of the God. Of course, these teachings promulgated the centrality of Jerusalem and its temple.

Contemporary non-Yehudite groups who worshiped YHWH and saw themselves as either belonging to Israel, or as Israel, such as the people of Achaemenid Samaria, were very unlikely to accept such Jerusalem-centered theology. It is likely that it was precisely the disputed character of this theology that contributed to its ubiquity in the accepted religious literary repertoire of Yehud, and eventually in the Hebrew Bible.[2]

The theological self-understanding of Yehudite Israel that the only legitimate temple for the only God was in its center, and that the 'God of Israel' is the 'God of Heaven' raised by necessity the question of the place of nations other than Israel, and worshipers of other gods, in the divine economy, and of their relation to Israel. One response to these matters was the notion that all nations will flow to the Jerusalemite temple when the long-term will of YHWH will be manifested on earth.[3] But there were other responses too. One of them, that which is envisaged in Isa. 19.19-21 is particularly relevant to the understanding of the book of Jonah against the background of the world of ideas of Persian period Yehud, as it will be demonstrated below.

The Israel of Yehud construed itself as historically continuous with late-monarchic Judah and its people and with exilic Israel. Accordingly, it construed itself as a social group that had suffered severe judgment at the hands of YHWH (i.e. the fall of monarchic Jerusalem, its temple, the monarchic polity and the Davidic dynasty). Yet the Yehudite community was not itself conceived, in its own discourses, as 'restored' Israel, but rather as a post-judgment but not-yet-restored Israel. It was an Israel that looked much at the monarchic past—as construed by the community—to understand the reasons for the harsh divine punishment, and to find ways to avoid its repetition. It was also an Israel that looked much forward to an

---

2. In addition to the obvious dissonance between the actual status of Jerusalem in the actual world and in the divine economy, as advanced by the literati and their theological discourses.

3. See, for instance, Isa. 2.3; Mic. 4.2.

ideal future in which the glory of its temple and Jerusalem would be manifested to all. Further, it was an Israel that showed a very ambiguous attitude towards the monarchic period. It related to it as a 'classical' period and associated with it much of the constitutive divine communications, but also understood it as a period that eventually led to grievous sin and destruction.[4]

The book of Jonah reflects this theological setting, as it is expected from the social location of the book's authorship and the target, primary readership of the book (i.e. Yehudite and most likely Jerusalemite literati). This chapter deals with the ways in which the book reflects this theological setting and constructs it through its reading and rereading by Yehudite literati.

2. *The Fate of Monarchic Jerusalem and Postmonarchic Readings of the Book of Jonah*

The fate of monarchic Jerusalem looms large over the book of Jonah. To be sure, in the minds of the Achaemenid period Jerusalemites, Nineveh was neither the only nor the first great city that most likely came to mind when the thought of a mighty city overturned by YHWH because of its sins. But in which way did the all-present knowledge of the fate of Jerusalem most likely inform the reading and rereading of Jonah at that time?

These readings seem to bifurcate again according to the assumed fate of Nineveh. Let us first focus on readings of Jonah that were strongly informed by the eventual destruction of Nineveh. These readings were framed within an ideological expectation that all the divine pronouncements of judgment against sinful cities would be fulfilled, if only given time. From this perspective, the book of Jonah advances a strong claim that the argument advanced by YHWH in 4.11, and the divine acceptance of Nineveh's repentance, were of much relevance to the people who lived at the time, but irrelevant in the long term. Within this approach, the sins of the Ninevites, before their repentance, would bring assured destruction to their descendants at some future point. Significantly, this theological

---

4.   This summary reconstruction of core aspects of the period suffices for the purposes of this chapter. I have dealt with these matters in detail in a series of works, and there is no need to repeat here the arguments advanced there. See, especially Ben Zvi, 'Inclusion in and Exclusion from', *idem*, 'Urban Center', 'Introduction: Writings, Speeches', 'What Is New in Yehud?'

approach is well known from the book of Kings.[5] This being so, the Ninevite king's response to YHWH's call through Jonah becomes somewhat parallel to Josiah's reform: neither saved their city and kingdom, for neither repentance nor reform can annul the divine decree (see 2 Kgs 23.26-27). Thus, this approach to the book of Jonah deals not only with the overwhelming awareness of the destruction of monarchic Jerusalem in the discourse of Achaemenid Yehud, but provides an explanation to the event that was consonant with and supported explanations that already existed within the discourses and authoritative literature of the period.

Further, this reading contributed to the ideological resolution of the dissonance created by the self-evident underdog status of Jerusalem in the world. As Jerusalem was punished for its sins, so will other sinful nations be judged, including those who oppressed Israel, as explicitly proclaimed in other prophetic books. The only difference is that Jerusalem has already being punished, whereas other cities, such as Babylon—the destroyer of Jerusalem—have not yet suffered retribution for its deeds. If the presence of descriptions of or references to the future judgment of the nations in prophetic literature is any indication, then this ideological motif was certainly not marginal within the discourse of postmonarchic Israel.[6] Yet

5. See 2 Kgs 24.3; cf. 2 Kgs 20.16-19. It bears note that the last king of northern Israel is not really responsible for the destruction of the kingdom. In fact, he is even better evaluated than most of the others (see 2 Kgs 17.2). Similarly, the worst king of Judah, Manasseh, died in peace, whereas Jerusalem was destroyed several kings later. To be sure, the same idea is expressed in Jer 15.4, which raises the issue of multiple theological discourses interacting with each other in that book (and cf. Jer. 18.7-10). A study of the book of Jeremiah is obviously beyond the scope of this work, but such a presence of multiple voices is worth mentioning given that similar features are ubiquitous in Jonah as most likely read in ancient Yehud.

6. Cf. Ben Zvi, *Zephaniah*, pp. 325-37. One may contrast this position with that in Sweeney, *Twelve Prophets*, p. 306. Sweeney maintains that Jonah advances a response to a question that many Yehudites had during the early Persian period, namely, despite the prophecies in Isa. 13–14; 21 and Jer. 50–51 Babylon survived as a main administrative center. His interpretation of the text is based only on a reading informed by the salvation of Nineveh through YHWH's mercy—but not by its actual fate as known to Yehudites. Thus he correctly points out that the book may explain to this historical readership why Babylon has not been destroyed, but he does not seem to recognize that at the same time, the book carries a second meaning, Babylon, like Nineveh (and Jerusalem, one may add), will be destroyed at some point in the future. The double ending of the book of Jonah (see Chapter 2) is of paramount importance in this regard. I agree, however, with Sweeney (p. 307) that the book of Jonah provides hope to the Yehudite community, but, as it becomes clear in this monograph, I

as prophetic literature also shows, such destruction is often associated with the creation of a new world order. In that order, the worldly status of Zion will correspond to its place in the divine economy, according to the inner discourses of Yehud.[7] Given the status of Achaemenid Yehud in the actual world, these images may be considered among these dreams of reversal that are often advanced by those who consider themselves oppressed. These dreams, and the literature expressing them, are a common feature in many societies through the ages. They seem to serve some social and psychological needs.

The book of Jonah, if read in this way, becomes an interpretative key for still unfulfilled prophetic announcements in the other prophetic books. From the perspective of its readers, it points to hope because it reaffirms unequivocally the future fulfillment of divine announcements—explicitly those of judgment, but implicitly also those of future salvation.[8] From the viewpoint of post-judgment but not yet restored Israel, such an affirmation carried hope.

Even if all this is taken into account, the mentioned 'story' was likely to face many objections in postmonarchic Israel. The reason is that such 'story' undercuts the value (in the sight of YHWH) of repentance, religious reform and socially authorized behavior and practices. This approach may help to explain a disaster in the past, but may not be the most helpful for community building and community socialization according to the norms advanced by its center. It is not an 'accident' that (a) Chronicles directly rejects the approach of Kings in this respect and tends to emphasize the role of repentance and personal accountability, and (b) that multiple references to repentance and individual responsibility are also present in the prophetic books composed in the postmonarchic period.[9] This second voice in the theological world of the literati comes to the forefront in the other readings of Jonah, namely, those readings that emphasized that Nineveh was spared destruction initally—at least—because of its repentance (cf. Amos 5.15; Zeph. 2.3), or due to YHWH's mercy, or both (cf. Joel 2.12-14).

associate such hope with a multivocal set of images and messages informing each other rather than with a restatement of the merciful character of YHWH per se.

7.   Cf. Isa. 2.2-4; 14.1-2 (and cf. its context in the book); 19.22-25; Mic. 4.1-5; Hag. 2.6-9; cf. Jer. 4.1-2.

8.   See also Chapters 2 and 6.

9.   See, for instance, Jer. 3.12–4.2; 18.7-11; Ezek. 18; 33.11; Hos. 14.2-4; Joel 2.12-14; Zeph. 2.3.

These voices complement each other. Moreover, together they reflect some basic components of the Yehudites' understanding of their own world. For instance, for them just as Nineveh was spared destruction but also destroyed, Jerusalem was destroyed, but also spared destruction, as its place at the core of Persian period Israel and its housing of YHWH's temple showed to them. Just as personal and communal behavior (and repentance) are important, so is the eventual fulfillment of YHWH's pronouncements, and the hope they provide regarding the establishment of a future, ideal world.

Seemingly opposite claims expressed in different books or clearly de-marcated subunits within a single book[10] balance each other and together better reflect and shape the general worldview of the literati. Likewise, seemingly opposite readings of Jonah perform the same task.

3. *The Fate of Monarchic Jerusalem and the Characterization of the Prophet Jonah*

The acute awareness of the fate of Jerusalem among postmonarchic literati most likely influenced also their understanding of the character of Jonah, at least in some rereadings of the book. How would Jonah have reacted if his mission had been to announce the destruction of Jerusalem—as actually was the case for many cherished prophetic characters within the dis-course/s of the literati—and YHWH relented from destroying Jerusalem? Would Jonah complain? Since the identity of the city is at best peripheral to the main theological discussion between YHWH and Jonah in Chapter 4, it is likely that the intended readers were asked at the very least to imagine the possibility of an affirmative answer. In fact, this understanding of Jonah seems to be supported by the fact that his behavior is implicitly, but quite obviously given the choice of language, sharply contrasted with main intercessors within the discourse of these literati (i.e. Abraham and Moses).[11]

The characterization evoked by the text, according to this reading, is

10. Cf., for instance, Kings and Chronicles; Jer. 15.4 and Jer. 3.12–4.2; 18.7-11; 1 Sam. 15.29 and Jer. 18.8. Significantly, Chronicles itself sets many of its claims in 'proportion' as I have shown elsewhere. See Ben Zvi, 'Sense of Proportion'. See also Chapter 7.

11. See Chapters 2 and 5 in this volume regarding Abraham and 4, 5 and 6 regarding Moses. Jonah is also contrasted with other prophets, for instance, Jeremiah, and see, for instance, Jer. 7.16; 12.14.

thus one that includes a combination of an anti-Moses or anti-Abraham with a prophet (and literati) who would have been angered had monarchic Jerusalem been spared destruction, even if it repented from its sins. This combination serves as rhetorically potent and emotionally charged reminder to the literati of their self-limitations. It points at the dangers associated with taking *some* true divine teachings as absolutely categorical, rather than contingent and open to be balanced with others.[12] In other words, the figure of Jonah serves to make a theological point by means of a negative image of a prophet who may have been considered as 'strange', if not plainly absurd.

4. *The Jerusalemite Temple in the Book of Jonah*

To be sure, within the main theological discourse of Yehud, some divine teachings were considered unequivocal and, accordingly, texts dealing with them were univocal. They included some claims concerning Israel's past, YHWH's relation to Israel and the Jerusalemite temple.

The book of Jonah conveys a clear message about the central role of the Temple. The psalm in chapter 2 reflected and conveyed a theological understanding of the Temple as a house of prayer and sacrifices. As for the former, Jonah is described as far away from the Temple as the literati could imagine—he is not even at the mouth of Sheol, but already in its belly (see 2.3). From the most foreign 'land' to which he is sent because of his refusal to obey YHWH, he sends his prayer towards the Temple (see 2.8). The book of Jonah not only reflects and communicates an understanding of the Temple similar to that associated with Solomon in 1 Kgs 8.12-53// 2 Chron. 6.1-40 in its general terms, but takes the message of a text like 1 Kgs 8.44-50 and exemplifies its validity against the most extreme circumstances.

As for sacrifices, the text reflects and construes an image of the Temple as the only place in which an Israelite may offer sacrifices to YHWH. Unlike the story of Noah (see Gen. 8.20), Jonah does not and cannot offer sacrifices once he reaches dry land. Instead, he hopes to fulfill his vows at the temple of YHWH (2.10). The non-Israelite sailors, however, are allowed to offer sacrifices to YHWH wherever they are, and implicitly praised for that behavior (cf. Isa. 19.19-21). I will return to this matter in the next section.

12. On these matters see Chapter 7. As mentioned there, this holds true for many of these teaching, but not for all. See below.

It bears particular note that the world of the book sets these constructions of the Jerusalemite Temple in the monarchic period. To be sure,
there is no explicit reference to Jerusalem or Zion in the book of Jonah,
but it is unlikely that the literati of Yehud would have associated the
temple referred to in the book of Jonah with any cultic place other than the
Jerusalem Temple. Moreover, the thematic links between the psalm of
Jonah and 1 Kgs 8, along with the numerous citations from Psalms (see
Chapter 4 in this volume) make such a proposal extremely unlikely. The
readership is asked to construe Jonah—and most likely did construe him—
as a person well versed in the religious textual repertoire of Yehudite
Jerusalem. If so, when this Jonah is read in terms of the Jonah in 2 Kgs
14.23-29,[13] then the book advances the claim that a prophet of YHWH from
the northern kingdom accepted basic theological tenets of the postmonarchic community around Jerusalem. In other words, the text of Jonah
reflects and conveys a message of continuity.[14] Not only were these basic
tenets of postmonarchic Yehud those of monarchic Judah, but also they
were those held by northern Israelites who had 'true knowledge' about
YHWH and YHWH's ways, and who in some cases interacted with YHWH.
A similar claim is advanced in 2 Chron. 21.12-14 (Elijah's letter),[15] and in
other places in Chronicles (e.g. 2 Chron. 11.13-16). It goes almost without
saying that all these claims not only legitimize the Jerusalemite-centered
community, but de-legitimize any other community of worshipers of YHWH
that did not accept the basic ideology or theology and the authoritative
texts of that community.[16]

5. *Israel and the Nations in the Book of Jonah*

The non-Israelite sailors and the Ninevites and their elite are depicted in
unmistakably positive terms in the book of Jonah. Further, there is a clear
tendency to partially Israelitize them. They are characterized as people
who speak, behave and assume knowledge that is associated with 'pious
Israelites', as I have explained in several places already. This characteriza-

13. See Chapter 4.
14. The setting of the book in the 'classical' monarchic period, and its association
with a known prophet from the past also contributed to its claim for authority.
15. Jonah here goes beyond the claims of Kings. Elijah is still allowed to sacrifice
to YHWH outside Jerusalem. But cf. the Elijah of Chronicles.
16. On these matters see Ben Zvi, 'Inclusion in and Exclusion from', esp. pp. 137-
45.

tion makes use of the 'other' to discursively show the potential universal acceptance of theological positions, attitudes and social behaviors considered divinely ordained within the main discourse of the Yehudite community. As such they comfort the readership and serve to adumbrate a future world in which all nations will consist of pious people who will follow many of the divine teachings held now by the Israelites, including, for instance, Deut. 23.16-17, which stood against all common practice in the ancient Near East (see Chapter 5).

When the Yehudites imagined the nations as bearing Israelite-like characteristics, they blurred by necessity some of the theological differences between Israel and the nations. Yet the maintenance of a separate identity was important for the small Jerusalemite-centered community, and most likely also to its imperial overlords.[17] Separate identity calls for boundaries, and boundaries call for identification of what is central to self-identification.

Jonah is surely not the only text dealing with this matter in postmonarchic Israel. In fact, one may recognize a significant variation in the theological discourse of postmonarchic communities on the question of the possible extent of the Israelitization of non-Israelites. Apart from Isa. 56.3-7, there are many other texts that envisage a different future for the nations. As it will be shown below, the book of Jonah construes limits to the extent of the Israelite character of the non-Israelites, and boundaries between Israel and the nations that construe a sense of core of Israelite–Yehudite identity.

For instance, the sailors are presented in some ways as Israelite-like. Such a characterization has substantial bearings for the understanding of the messages of the text within ancient communities of readers (see ch. 5). But the sailors remain non-Israelites. They are not bound to the Jerusalemite Temple, nor do they long for it. They can offer sacrifices elsewhere to YHWH; further, they can cry to their gods without incurring in any sin. None of these applies to Israelites within the discourse of Yehud.

Temple, worship and absolute trust in YHWH to exclusion of any other deity, along with the teachings of YHWH on which these matters were theologically grounded differentiate between the sailors and the Israelites.[18] The same holds true for the Ninevites. They are not described as

---

17. See Ben Zvi, 'Inclusion in and Exclusion from', esp. pp. 125-29, 137-48.

18. Even the utterances of the sailors may hint at discursive and ideological reservations regarding the extent of the possible overlap between the sailors and the Israelites. For instance, the language of shedding innocent blood in association with the

embracing the 'torah' held by Yehudite Israel, nor as undergoing circumcision, nor as sending prayers towards the Jerusalemite Temple, nor as offering sacrifices only at that temple, nor even as rejecting their gods and considering YHWH alone to be their deity and worshipping YHWH only.[19]

Thus the book implies and communicates a discourse in which there is a profound difference in YHWH's requirements from Israel and the nations. This difference is expressed and grounded in the divine teachings or 'YHWH's torah' held by the Yehudites, or from their theological perspective, by Israel. Thus the difference itself calls attention to the matter on which it stands, namely, YHWH's torah. These divine teachings, and because of them the Temple and particular norms of religious behavior are presented as boundaries that set Israel apart from pious non-Israelites who developed even *some* Israelite-like features. If the main boundary is grounded in the full extent of the divine teachings, then the latter take a central role in the self-understanding of postmonarchic Israel.[20]

In turn, YHWH's teachings, as held by the Yehudites and within their discourse, derive their authority from YHWH. This deity is presented as universal in power and dominion in the book of Jonah, but also as a deity whose sole rule is not universally accepted. To be sure, this reflects the historical reality of the time. Within the horizons of the world known to Yehudites, a minuscule percentage of humanity accepted their theology. This situation creates theological tensions and a constant rhetorical need to emphasize the incomparable character of YHWH vis-à-vis other deities. But these other deities do not come alone, they are the deities of nations other than Israel. In the world of Jonah, non-Israelites may acknowledge

treatment of the powerless (in this case Jonah, who was a running away slave—see Chapter 5 in this volume) could have both brought the theological underpinning of the actions of the sailors closer to those advanced in such texts as Jer. 7.6; 22.3, but also accentuated the different identities of both, given the context in which the latter appear (see Jer. 7.1-7; 22.1-5). Similarly, a portion of Ps. 115.3 reverberates in the language of the sailors (1.14), but the literati would have known the immediate context of the verse, namely, Ps. 115.1-8. Similarly, the sailors' words, and their gist, could have evoked Ps. 135.6 (or 6-7), but see Ps. 135.1-21. Needless to say, the literati, just as the Jonah of the book, knew 'scripture'.

19. It follows from these considerations that the book of Jonah in its primary setting surely did not address the question of proselytizing. On these matters and for many of the examples mentioned above, see Clements, 'Purpose', esp. p. 18.

20. To be sure, this conception of Israel is ubiquitous in the Hebrew Bible. The point advanced here is that it is implied, reflected and communicated also by the book of Jonah.

the power of YHWH and occasionally worship YHWH, but they still have their own gods. The sailors cried each to his god. The Ninevites believed in 'god', a term that within the context of the book points at YHWH, and the words of YHWH's prophet. They cried to YHWH, who was the deity about to destroy them for their iniquities. They renounced their חמס ('violence in the realm of social, interpersonal interaction'),[21] but not their gods. There is a substantial amount of polemic against gods other than YHWH in postmonarchic literature. Given that in this theological discourse there is an association between Israel and YHWH to the exclusion of other deities, on the one hand, and the nations with the other deities, on the other, the polemic against other gods bears relevance to the question of Israel's discursive self-identity vis-à-vis the other nations.

Readings of the book of Jonah within their primary context include such polemics. YHWH is characterized to non-Israelites as the God of Heaven, the creator and master of the entire world. In other words, by implication, YHWH is as a deity that cannot be compared to any of their deities. Rereadings of Jon. 2.9 informed by, for instance, Deut. 32.21 most likely raise at the very least a sense of stern polemic against deities other than YHWH.

It bears note that in Jonah, Nineveh needed to hear the word of YHWH from the mouth of an Israelite prophet. In fact, the image of a non-Israelite (Ninevite?) prophet of YHWH coming to Nineveh, or of a true prophet of a deity other than YHWH, are simply beyond the theological and discursive horizon of the book of Jonah, its authorship and primary readership. Again, the book reflects and communicates boundaries between Israel and the other nations.

A final consideration: all the mentioned boundaries and polemics, including those against the gods of other nations, are part of the inner discourses of Yehud and its literati. The expected readership of Jonah did not include Ninevites, nor sailors of a variety of nations. The target readership and rereadership of the book were Yehudite literati, and those Yehudites to whom they may read the book. Jonah, in the book, may tell the sailors that YHWH is the supreme deity, but readers of the book told that to themselves. This is a self-asserting exercise, within a minute group that had to wrestle with cognitive dissonance, with the tension between the theological claims that stood at its core and the world in which they lived.

21. See Chapter 4.

6. *The Exile and Exilic Features in the Book of Jonah*

The book of Jonah cannot address the exile directly because of its monarchic setting, well before the exile of northern Israel and Judah. Yet it seems that some exilic dimensions are present too.

Jonah is outside the land; in his distress he prays towards the (Jerusalemite) Temple, and longs to see its temple. In all these actions, the characterization of Jonah is directly comparable to that of readership's image of a good Israelite in exile, at any point after the construction of the Second Temple, and with minor variations, before it as well.

P. Ackroyd suggested an allegorical reading of Jonah, in which Jonah stands for Israel and the fish for Babylon. [22] Although there are problems with this allegorical reading (e.g. the role of the fish is not easily identifiable with Babylon as construed during the postmonarchic period), it is still possible that when ancient literati read and reread the book, at times they could have played with potential allegorical readings. But it is unlikely that allegorical understandings would have replaced the wealth of non-allegorical readings, and became the main reading of the book. Moreover, there are no textual inscribed markers suggesting to the intended readers of the book that they should approach the book as an allegory; in fact, the opposite seems to be true.[23]

Turning back to the story, Jonah lives and interacts with non-Israelites, and probably—though not explicitly stated—eats their food. In this regard,

22. See P. Ackroyd, *Exile and Restoration: A Study of Hebrew Thought of the Sixth Century B.C.* (Philadelphia: Westminster Press, 1975 [1968]), pp. 244-45.

23. See Trible, *Studies*, pp. 153-58; cf. Sasson, *Jonah*, pp. 337-38. As a rule of thumb one may safely assume that the intended readership was not worlds apart from the actual primary readership of the book. See Chapter 1.

To be sure, other readerships in their own times and within their own discourses read the book of Jonah as an allegory or according to allegorical tendencies. This phenomenon is well attested in both Christian and Jewish traditions of readings. Instances in the former are well known. So, for instance, Bede wrote: 'Jonah should be interpreted either as the dove or as the man of sorrows; he signifies Christ, on whom the Holy Ghost descends in the form of a dove; or because He bought our sorrows with his body on the cross. Nineveh should be interpreted as the splendid; it signifies the Church ornate with the glory of all virtue' (cited from Bowers, *Legend of Jonah*, p. 40). For allegorical interpretations within Jewish reading traditions, see, for instance, H. Shy, *Tanhum HaYerushalmi's Commentary*, pp. 109-39; and A. Shusman, 'קווים אלגוריים, תאולוגיים ופולמוסיים פירוש לספר' יונה מאת ר תנחום הירושלמי', *Pa'amim* 59 (1994), pp. 85-104. See also Chapter 9.

Jonah is no different from Esther or Joseph.[24] Moreover, like these two narratives, the book maintains that Jonah's presence in Nineveh brought much benefit to the foreign city—and its royal court. The story of an Israelite who brings blessings to the nations is present again in the Joseph narrative and in Esther.[25] In fact, Jonah pushes the common motif beyond its usual boundaries. Even if the Israelite is only like Jonah, still he or she may bring a blessing to a foreign nation. This is so because this ability is not grounded on the character of the Israelite, but rather in YHWH's behavior. The book of Jonah clearly advances such a claim.[26]

Finally, one may notice that within the postmonarchic discourses of Yehud, 'torah' comes from outside the land. To be sure, it becomes part of the knowledge of the literati and one day will spread out of Jerusalem, but it comes from outside. The book of Jonah that serves as an interpretative key for the other prophetic books, that is, as a metaprophetic book, is set outside the land. The knowledge that it imparts is, however, inside, within the Yehudite literati.

The book of Jonah was not written in the exile; it does not have to be understood in terms of an association with an experience of the exile, nor is a *Diasporanovelle*. Yet, it reflects and contributes to the creation of a discourse or discourses in which images of exile, and of Israel being outside the land are significant.[27]

24. One may note also that the use of a particular vocabulary in Esther—including Persianisms—contributes to the literary characterization of the 'foreign world' in which the narrative develops; cf. Jon. 1. See Chapter 6.

25. It does not follow from the presence of these similarities that the book of Jonah was *Diasporanovelle*—even if, for the sake of the case, one were to agree that there was a recognizable genre of *Disaporanovelle*. The book of Jonah is a meta-prophetic book composed in narrative form (see Chapter 6). Some of its ideological messages and literary features are comparable to those in the Joseph story and the book of Esther. But there are substantial differences. For instance, the royal court is not as important in Jonah; Joseph and Esther dwell in Egypt and Persia respectively, whereas Jonah is 'in transit', and references to the Temple are nowhere to be found in Esther (without the additions). On these matters and the claim that the book of Jonah might be a 'reversed diaspora-novella' see Syrén, 'Book of Jonah'.

26. Significantly, the blessing motif stands even if the readers approached the book in way fully informed by the eventual destruction of Nineveh. Postponement of judgment was seen as a blessing (see 2 Kgs 20.19//Isa. 39.8).

27. In other words, it is a book written within and for a postmonarchic Persian period community. See my partial portraits of the period and its discourse in Ben Zvi, 'What Is New in Yehud?' and 'Inclusion in and Exclusion from'. Also cf. 'Introduction: Writings and Speeches'.

Chapter 9

INFINITE BUT LIMITED DIVERSITY: A HEURISTIC, THEORETICAL FRAME
FOR ANALYZING DIFFERENT INTERPRETATIONS OF THE BOOK OF JONAH

1. *Introduction*

The goal of this chapter is to suggest a theoretical frame for the study of
the bewildering variety of readings of the book of Jonah developed by
different interpretative communities.

It is well-known that diverse interpretative communities of readers have
understood the book of Jonah, and construed its message in different and,
at times, quite opposite ways. The diversity is clearly documented in
scholarly works[1] and is supported by even a cursory, comparative reading
of the plethora of contemporary treatments of the book both in the academic world and popular culture. To be sure, this feature holds true for all
biblical literature, and for literature in general for that matter. However, it
is worth stressing that interpretative communities within which the biblical
tradition has held—and continues to hold—a dominant discursive and
theological role have much more at stake in the interpretation of biblical
books than in other works of literature.

This diversity in interpretation is not surprising. Readers do not approach
any biblical book in a vacuum, but within a particular, historically bound
location and discourse. Thus, some degree of correspondence between
diversity of locations and discourses on the one hand, and of interpretations, on the other, is inevitable. Moreover, at least to some extent, one
may outline the process involved in the production of multiple interpretations by multiple communities. Understanding the biblical text is often
equated with understanding the *message* of the text. The 'message' is
usually thought of what the author, and at times some of the main characters in the book, wished to convey. In other words, the entire process is

---

1. See, for instance, Bickerman , *Four Strange Books*; Bowers, *Legend of Jonah*;
Sherwood, *Biblical Text*; *idem*, 'Cross-Currents'; *idem*, 'Rocking the Boat'.

construed as involving communication. As such, and from the viewpoint of the interpretative community, it involves a communicator/s (i.e. the author or the main characters), a recipient of the communication (i.e. themselves) and a message.[2]

To be sure, the interpretative community deals with its own construction of the (implied) author of the book, as well as its own characterization and evaluation of the main characters. Since constructions of implied author and characters are culturally and socially dependent, so are the communicators. Since the latter may communicate only what is plausible for them to communicate within the world of knowledge and discourse of each community of interpretation, then the communicators' message is also culturally and socially dependent (see below).

Further, since the book of Jonah (and other biblical books) held a 'canonical' and to a large extent normative position within most of its interpretative communities in history, there was something of importance at stake in the production of the meaning of a biblical book. This being the case, the production and control of the meaning of biblical books tended to be shaped—directly or indirectly—according to the prevalent positions of the authorities of the interpretative community. The 'text' was expected to be at least coherent with these positions.[3] Given the diversity of authorities and their theological, social and political agendas, the number of potential and actual readings of the book of Jonah may well be considered infinite for all practical purposes.[4]

---

2. For G. Rusch '*Understanding* means to *meet the interactive/communicative expectations of a communicator*' (italics in the original). ('Comprehension', quotation from p. 115; cf. Introduction to this volume).

3. To be sure, and because of the considerations mentioned above, this tendency is alive in contemporary communities of faith for whom the Bible is sacred scripture. Cf., among others, *Catechism of the Catholic Church* (1994), §101-41. The relatively common position in Protestant groups that 'the criterion by which the Bible is to be interpreted is Jesus Christ' (quotation from *The Baptist Faith and Message* as adopted by the Southern Baptist Convention, 9 May 1963) serves in historical and sociological terms the same purpose, as the image of Jesus Christ that is upheld by the community is most often consistent with the prescribed, prevalent positions of the religious and theological authorities. Similar observations can be made concerning traditional or orthodox Jewish commentators. For instance, the series דעת מקרא explicitly stated that it would take into account modern studies in the areas of interpretation, philology, history, geography, archaeology and the like in so far as their results do not contradict מסורת ישראל (i.e. the [accepted] Tradition of Israel).

4. There are constraints to this diversity too. One would not find, for instance, a

Yet it must be stressed, however, that 'infinite' does not mean uncon-strained or unlimited. Despite all the differences among the interpretative communities, and their diverse theological or ideological agendas, all of their readings of Jonah share at the very least the fact that they have to relate in one way or another to the text of the book of Jonah.[5] But what follows from that? In which way and to what extent does the textually bound nature of interpretations of Jonah regulate the interpretive process and its end results?

On the surface, there are two ways of approaching this question. One may (a) study one particular interpretation after another, then look at common trends and finally attempt to advance an explanatory hypothesis; or (b) one may advance a working hypothesis about the process/es through which the text of Jonah regulates to some extent actual interpretations, and then begin to assess the explanatory value of this hypothesis against the evidence. Practical considerations clearly favor the second option.

2. *A Working Hypothesis*

The working hypothesis advanced here is that three factors play a sub-stantial role, regulating, and to some extent delimiting, the range of potential interpretations and social uses of the book or portions thereof as a narrative. These three factors are (a) *the horizon of pertinence* claimed by the text, and as perceived by a most substantial number of interpretive communities in history; (b) *basic global, semantic contents* (or macro-structures) that can be attributed to either the narrative of the book or selected sections thereof, which include already clear limits on the number and nature of the characters and accordingly, on the possible permutations of their relationships; and (c) *the degree of perceived coherence or inte-gration between the global content of a selected section of the narrative (or the book as a whole) and central meta-narratives* of the interpretative community.

To be sure, the situation is far more complex when substantial portions, or the entire narrative of Jonah, is brought into the discussion. In these cases, the three factors mentioned above seem to play major, and inter-dependent roles. The rest of this discussion aims at an analyzing these factors and their interactions with the text of Jonah, and among themselves

christological interpretation of Jonah in rabbinic sources. On these issues see below.

5.   Needless to say, the text of the book of Jonah, or any other text for that matter, is far more than a simple sequence of arbitrary graphemes.

in the process of developing readings of the book. Some examples will illustrate these interrelationships.

It must be stressed that the examples discussed in this chapter, although relatively numerous, are brought *only* for the purpose of *illustrating* the relation between the theoretical frame suggested here and actual inter-pretations held by particular interpretative communities. This chapter is not meant to serve as a survey of the history of interpretation, nor does it attempt to reach any degree of comprehensiveness. These examples are intentionally taken from a great variety of periods, and from very diverse interpretative communities so as to indicate that the viability of the heuristic hypothesis advanced here does not depend on the individual character of a particular community, set of communities or on a particular historical time frame. To facilitate a fluent reading of the chapter, many of the examples and most of the material associated with them is incorpo-rated in the footnotes. But these examples should not be understood as constituting an implicit survey of the history of interpretation. No attempt is made here to provide even a partially comprehensive overview of such history.[6]

Another important caveat: This hypothesis excludes certain modes of reading the book; for instance, as a source of proof-texts. To illustrate, against the background of the efforts by the crown of England to forbid non-authorized fasts, George Abbot argued in 1600 that Jon. 3.6-7 (but see Jon. 3.5) shows that a fast is only permitted if declared or authorized by the king and his nobles.[7] In these cases, the text is required to show

---

6.   There are several good surveys and some full-length studies on the matter, each with its own particular characteristics and emphases. See Bickerman, *Four Strange Books*, and 'Les deux erreurs'; Bowers, *Legend of Jonah*; Steffen, *Die Jona-Geschichte*; Sherwood, *Biblical Text*; see also Limburg, *Jonah*, pp. 99-123; and Magonet, 'Book of Jonah', I, pp. 620-22. For a comprehensive study of the influence of Jerome's commentary on Jonah in Greek and Latin literature, see Duval, *Le livre de Jonas*.

7.   See C. Hill, *The English Bible and the Seventeenth Century Revolution* (Lon-don: Penguin Books, 1994), p. 80. On the surface at least, the attribution of the fast to the king and his nobles rather than to the 'people' seems to contradict v. 5. Sig-nificantly, J. Calvin, who also understood the text here as stating that 'the edict respect-ing the fast had proceeded from the king' is aware of, and attacks alternative interpre-tations of the text (*Commentary on Jonah*, in *Commentaries on the Minor Prophets* [Grand Rapids, MI: Baker Book House, 1989], p. 101). Fasting (accompanied by preaching) had important political dimensions in England at that time and in the first half of the seventeenth century.

a reference that if decoded according to the rules of interpretation accepted in the interpretative community either communicates or may communicate the 'right message'.[8] Allegorical and mystical readings represent another mode of reading that will not be addressed here,[9] though the present study may show some aspects of the 'grammar' of the text that contributed to the development of later readings of Jonah, such as those in which the prophet is conceived as a pre-figuration of Jesus,[10] or identified with future Messiah-son-of-Joseph.[11]

First of all, the book's claims about its own genre and about its main characters, along with book's authoritative and canonical status, and even its basic structure delimit a set of horizons of pertinence for the interpretation of the book. So it is not surprising that no one interpreted Jonah as a cooking book, a phonebook, or the like. Although this statement

8. For an example of this approach within the rabbinic tradition, see, for instance:

'R. Ammi said: Rain is withheld only because of the sin of גזל [which may be translated as 'violent robbery'], as it is said, "He covers his hands with אור" [i.e. 'lightning/light', Job 36.32]; that is to say, because of the sin of "hands", he covers אור. And "hands" certainly stands for גזל [some mss. חמס], as it is said, "and from the חמס that is in their hands" [Jonah 3.8.] and אור certainly stands for rain, as it is said, "he spreads out the clouds of his אור" [Job 37.11, as most likely understood in this context]' (*b. Ta'an.* 7b).

It bears note that in this case, even such a proof-text using of Jonah serves to illuminate the 'plain' readings of the texts accepted by the community. It clearly assumes that חמס in Jon. 3.8 was understood as גזל.

9. For instance, Tanhum b. Yosef HaYerushalmi (died in 1291 CE) includes in his commentary not only the expected commentary according to the *peshat* (pp. 112/13-128/29 in H. Shy's critical edition, that is, *Tanhum HaYerushalmi's Commentary*) but a substantial section devoted to an allegorical reading (pp. 130/31-135/36 in Shy's critical edition). In this section, for instance, Jonah stands for the human soul, the ship for the body in which the soul dwells temporarily to allow its perfection, the sea points at the world of physical senses that threatens to swallow the soul; 'the three days walk' to the three sources of the forces in the body, namely, mind, heart and liver. See Shy, *Tan-um HaYerushalmi's Commentary*, and Shusman, 'קווים אלגוריים'. The presence of neo-platonic elements in this allegorical reading is clear.

10. See Mt. 12.40. This motif is common in early Christianity; see below.

11. Jonah was identified with the son of the widow of Zare̤phath (1 Kgs 17) and the latter with the Messiah-son-of-Joseph (e.g., *Seder Eliahu Rabba*, ch. 18, *siman* 19). On eschatological and messianic constructions of Jonah in some Jewish sources see A.J. Seltzer, 'Jonah in the Belly of the Great Fish: The Birth of Messiah Ben Joseph', *JNSL* 25 (1999), pp. 187-203, and A. Wineman, 'The Zohar on Jonah: Radical Retelling or Tradition?', *HS* 31 (1990), pp. 57-69.

may sound about as revolutionary as claiming that winters are cold in Antarctica, it does make the point that the structure of the text and its own claims about genre do regulate the activity of interpretative communities across different historical circumstances. Numerous genres and genre expectations are fully incompatible with the claims of the book and its structure.

The book of Jonah claims to be a prophetic book and, as such, it was included in the Twelve, and in the Hebrew and Christian Bibles.[12] For most Christian and Jewish communities of interpretation through history, the inclusion of the Jonah in theological, authoritative canons provides an interpretative context that regulates its range of possible interpretations, in theological/ideological, literary and social terms.

This perceived horizon of pertinence most often leads to (a) the position that the book imparts to the interpretative community some 'true' theological knowledge, and (b) a tendency to adopt the point of view of the implied author; in other words, a tendency *not* to read against the grain.[13] If (a) is accepted, then there is a severe restriction on the genres that are likely to be assigned to the book, since genre by definition is associated with communicative expectations.

Furthermore, since these interpretative communities tend to adopt a reading stance that accepts (at least) the theological reliability of the book, they tend to accept the characterization of God and God's actions advanced in the book as reliable not only in the world of the book, but outside that world too. In fact, they tend to consider this characterization as a valuable key for an understanding of a transcendental God. Given that the latter is conceived of as the most positive figure in their discourse, the character God in the book is viewed likewise. These considerations strongly disfavor any reading of the book in which the character God is evaluated in clearly negative terms, and in which acts of defiance of God are considered in an uncompromisingly positive light. Needless to say, such a positive character will never be identified with the theological or

---

12. Cf. Chapter 6 and also Ben Zvi, 'Prophetic Book'.

13. To be sure a significant number of contemporary exegetes the reading of biblical texts against 'its grain'. These readers are aware of the traditional horizon of pertinence of biblical books, but argue that it necessary to go beyond that theological horizon, to develop an hermeneutics of suspicion, on ethical, moral, theological or ideological grounds. See, for instance, D.J.A. Clines, *Interested Parties: The Ideology of Writers and Readers of the Hebrew Bible* (JSOTSup, 205; Sheffield: Sheffield Academic Press, 1995). See also below.

political opponents of the interpretative community. These regulating conditions for the production of meaning explain why a reading similar to 'Jonah is enraged because God is simply using him as a fall guy to let himself off the hook of his own soft-bellied liberalism'[14] was not likely to gain acceptance (nor develop) in the interpretative communities considered here, even if one allows, of course, for the replacement of 'liberalism' by an equivalent discursive term that is appropriate to the historical circumstances of the particular community.

In sum, a perceived horizon of pertinence creates a set of features that are shared by many interpretative communities when they approach the text. It also directly leads to diversity of interpretation. This is because these communities raise the stakes of the interpretation by assigning to the text authoritative, theological value. This value leads to a second constraint in the selection process, namely, that the interpretation be consistent with the theological worldview of the community of interpreters. After all, these communities are unlikely to believe that a godly text promulgates ideas and positions that are 'obviously' theologically misleading and even ungodly.[15]

To be sure, a perceived horizon of pertinence is not universally relevant. It does not hold true for roughly half of the world's population whose tradition is other than Christianity, Judaism or Islam. This horizon also does not hold true for contemporary Christian or Jewish thinkers for whom the text is not authoritative to begin with, or who 'consecrate' it for certain contemporaneous interpretative communities by deconstructing or subverting it or its narratorial claims. Still, these considerations contribute to an understanding of similarities and differences among interpretations of the book of Jonah in a wide variety of historical communities for whom a hermeneutics of adoption rather than suspicion was rule. For these

14. Eagleton, 'J.L. Austin', esp. p. 232.

15. This basic rule is comparable to those associated with theological discussions about the omnipotence of God. There is a long Jewish and Christian theological tradition that does not understand God's omnipotence as God's capability to do anything at any time. Instead, it claims that God is omnipotent because God is able to do what is reasonable (or 'logically possible') for God to do (e.g. Anselm, Aquinas, Saadia Gaon, Maimonides/Rambam). For instance, God need not be able to die, to produce one like God, to bring back the past and, many would add, to behave in ways incompatible with morality in order to be considered omnipotent. These considerations apply not only to God, but also to God's words. For a discussion of divine omnipotence, see E.R. Wierenga, *The Nature of God: An Inquiry into Divine Attributes* (Ithaca, NY: Cornell University Press, 1989), pp. 12-35.

communities, the book of Jonah was, and is, authoritative Scripture.

The second factor mentioned above concerns global, semantic contents or semantic macrostructures that can be attributed to either the entire narrative or significant portions of it.[16] That macrostructures play a role in the interpretative process seems plausible from the outset, since they represent the most basic summaries that people produce and remember after reading or hearing a story.

The hypothesis advanced here states that during the process of production and adoption of interpretations semantic macrostructures or basic, mental summaries of the text activate and strongly interact with a third regulating factor. This third factor is the degree of perceived correspondence or even integration between the global meaning of a selected section of the narrative (or the book as a whole) and central meta-narratives of the interpretative community. In other words, the process is controlled by a double system of constraints that involves (a) basic macrostructures that may show substantial similarities among different interpretative communities and (b) the relationship, or lack of thereof, between these basic macrostructures and meta-narratives that are particular to certain communities or sets of interpretative communities.

For the purpose of this discussion it suffices to focus our attention on four substantial narratives in the book of Jonah: (a) Jonah 1–2; (b) Jonah 3; (c) Jonah 1–3; and (d) Jonah 1–4. Other selected narratives are possible. For instance, one may focus on Jon. 1.4-16 and accordingly turn the

---

16. For the concept of macrostructure in discourse analysis see, among others, T.A. van Dijk and W. Kintsch, *Strategies of Discourse Comprehension* (New York: Academic Press, 1983); T.A. van Dijk, *Macrostructures* (Hillsdale, NJ: Erlbaum, 1980); and for its use in biblical narrative, see R.E. Longacre, 'Interpreting Biblical Stories', in T.A. van Dijk (ed.), *Discourse and Discourse Literature* (Amsterdam: John Benjamins, 1985), pp. 169-85.

Macrostructures may be deduced by three macrorules: '(a) Deletion Rule. This rule eliminates propositions that are not relevant to the interpretation of other propositions in discourse... (b) Generalization Rule. With the help of this rule a series of specific propositions are converted in a more general proposition... (c) Construction Rule. By means of this rule one proposition can be constructed from a number of propositions.' See J. Renkema, *Discourse Studies* (Amsterdam: John Benjamins, 1993), pp. 56-60 (quotation from pp. 57-58).

It is to be stressed that 'macrorules are not rules which can be used to trace *the* meaning structure of discourse. The rules only describe the procedures with which *a* meaning structure can be assigned' (emphasis in the original; Renkema, *Discourse Studies*, p. 60).

sailors into the main rather than secondary characters in the narrative. The four narratives have, however, received much more attention in interpretative communities than Jon. 1.4-16. This selective attention is probably due to (a) the central role played by Jonah in the book, which makes him less likely to be considered a secondary character, and (b) the prominent role of Nineveh in the book, which turns the behavior of the sailors into a kind of forerunner of that of the Ninevites.

3. *The Case of Jonah 1–2*

The following seems a reasonable rendering of the global content of Jonah 1–2 as a whole:

> Jonah failed to heed YHWH. He fled from YHWH in a ship. YHWH brought a mighty storm that led the sailors to throw Jonah into the sea. YHWH provided a fish that at his command (a) swallowed Jonah and (b) brought him safely to dry land, once Jonah prayed and acknowledged YHWH.[17]

If one accepts this summary, which is a particular instance of the general theme of a person failing to heed a divine call,[18] the story may be interpreted as communicating that defiance of YHWH brings one to a status that is symbolically akin to death,[19] whereas praise of YHWH may remove

---

17. This macrostructure reflects the sequence in Jon. 1–2. It was proposed already in antiquity that the praise of YHWH may follow rather than precede the deliverance from the fish. See Josephus, *Ant.* 9.208-14. Ibn Ezra was aware of, and argued against the altering of the sequence of the narrative.

18. Cf. Bickerman, *Four Strange Books*, pp. 9-10. One of the main messages of this theme is that the divine plan will prevail no matter what the individual may do to avoid it. Cf. *Exod. R.* 4.3; and see, for instance, note 4128 to Sura 37.148, in *The Holy Qur'an* (trans. Abdullah Yusuf Ali; Beirut: Dar Al Arabia). All quotations from the Qur'an in this chapter will be from Yusuf Ali's translation.

It is worth stressing that the inevitability of God's decision may serve to enhance hope. Cf. 'Jonah, that headstrong prophet, once fled from me, yet in the depths of the sea he was still mine. If you really believed your daughter to be alive, you would not grieve that she had passed to a better world' (Jerome, *Ep.* 39.3). (All quotations from Jerome's letters in this chapter are according to the translation in P. Schaff and H. Wace [eds.], *The Nicene and Post-Nicene Fathers of the Christian Church. Second Series*, vol. 6—*The Principle Works of Jerome* [Grand Rapids: Eerdmans, 1989]).

19. Notice the choice of words in Jonah 2.3, 7, and see, for instance, *b. 'Erub* 18b. 'R. Joshua b. Levi said: Gehenom (Heb. גיהנם) has seven names, and they are: Sheol... Abaddon (Heb. אבדון)...Sheol since it is written: "out of the belly of Sheol I cried, and you heard my voice" [Jonah 2.3]; Abaddon as it is written...'

one from that status. This being the case, it is reasonable to assume that interpretative communities whose meta-narratives give a prominent role to a motif of death and resurrection would tend to adopt a reading of Jonah 1–2 that is consistent with that motif. Thus, for instance, it is not surprising that Jonah's being for three days in the belly of the sea monster was considered as a pre-figuration of Jesus' being three days in the heart of the earth (Mt. 12.40).[20] Against this background, it is easy to understand the common comparisons between Jesus and Jonah within Christian interpretative communities at different times and under different circumstances.[21]

20. Cf. the following texts from Cyril of Jerusalem: 'They further object: A dead man recently deceased was raised by the living; but show us that it is possible for a man dead and buried for three days to rise again. The testimony we seek is supplied by the Lord Jesus Himself in the Gospels, when He says: "For even as Jona (sic) was in the belly of the fish three days and three nights, so will the Son of Man be three days and three nights in the heart of the earth" ' (*Cathechesis* 14.17). 'Jona fulfilled a type of our Savior when he prayed from the belly of the fish and said: "I cried for help from the midst of the nether world." He was in fact in the fish, yet he says that he is in the nether world. In a later verse he manifestly prophesies in the person of Christ: "My head went down into the chasms of the mountains." Yet he was still in the belly of the fish. What mountains encompass you? But I know, he says, that I am a type of Him who is to be laid in the sepulchre hewn out of the rock. While he was in the sea Jona says: "I went down into the earth"; for he typified Christ, who went down into the heart of the earth…' (*Cathechesis* 14.20).

All quotations from Cyril of Jerusalem's words in this chapter are according to *The Works of Saint Cyril of Jerusalem* (trans. L.P. McCauley and A.A. Stephenson; The Fathers of the Church. A New Translation, 61, 64; 2 vols.; Washington, DC: Catholic University of America, 1969, 1970).

See also, among others, Jerome, *Ep.* 53.9.

21. Comparisons between Jesus and Jonah are relatively frequent in patristic literature. See, for instance: 'Now when we study the story of Jona (sic) the force of the resemblance becomes striking. Jesus was sent to preach repentance; so was Jona. Though Jona fled, not knowing what was to come, Jesus came willingly, to grant repentance for salvation. Jona slumbered in the ship and was fast asleep amid the stormy sea; while Jesus by God's will was sleeping, the sea was stirred up, for the purpose of manifesting thereafter the power of Him who slept. They said to Jona: "What are you doing asleep? Rise up, call upon your God! that God may save us"; but the Apostles say: "Lord, save us!" In the first instance they said: Call upon your God, and in the second, Save us. In the first Jona said to them: "Pick me up and throw me into the sea, that it may quiet down for you" in the other Christ Himself "rebuked the wind and the sea, and there came a great calm". Jona was cast into the belly of a great fish, but Christ of His own will descended to the abode of the invisible fish of death.

Since Jonah went into the deep, but was returned to the surface, to life, he could and was taken as a symbol of resurrection. In fact, there is a very large corpus of evidence pointing to the understanding of Jon. 1–2 in terms of triumph over death.[22]

Further, since Jonah was in water before his return to life, and this action can be associated symbolically with being born again (notice the explicit reference to being in the *belly* of the fish). This macrostructure may lead some Christian interpretative communities to consider the story of Jonah as a hint, at least, at the sacrament of baptism, a key component of Christian meta-narratives.[23]

He went down of His own will to make death disgorge those it had swallowed up, according to the Scripture: "I shall deliver them from the power of the nether world, and I shall redeem them from death" ' (Cyril of Jerusalem, *Cathechesis* 14.17). '…like Jonah when he was in the belly of the fish I [Jesus] prayed to You…' (Ambrose, *The Prayer of Job and David* §6.25, in *Saint Ambrose: Seven Exegetical Works* [trans. M.P. McHugh; The Fathers of the Church. A New Translation, 65; Washington, DC: Catholic University of America, 1972], p. 408).

Comparisons are also attested in contemporaneous literature: 'Dios salvó al profeta del peligro mortal para salvar por el un pueblo gentil. Dios salvó a Cristo, no apartando el cáliz de la pasión, sino resucitándolo de la muerte, para salvar con esta muerte y resurrección de su Hijo a todos los pueblos de la tierra' (L. Alonso Schökel and J. Mateos [eds.], 'Introducción a Jonás', *Nueva Biblia Española* [Madrid: Ediciones Cristiandad, 1976], p. 1043). This quotation may be translated in English as follows: 'God saved the prophet from the mortal danger so as to save through him a Gentile people. God saved Christ, but not by removing the chalice of the passion but by resurrecting him from death, to save with this death and resurrection of his Son all the peoples of the earth.'

22. See, for instance, Jerome, *Ep.* 39.3; 60.2-3; M. Luther, 'Lectures on Jonah', the Latin Text (1525) in *Luther's Works*, XIX (St Louis: Concordia Publishing House, 1974), pp. 1-31 (15, 20). This motif is well attested in early Christian iconography (including catacombs and sarcophaguses). In these works Jonah stands mainly as symbol of deliverance from death, rather than as a prophet (at times representations of Jonah remind of those of Endymion in classical art). See, for instance, J. Lowden, *Early Christian and Byzantine Art* (London: Phaidon Press, 1997), pp. 27-32, and esp. pl. 13; pl. 22 in A. Gabar, *Christian Iconography* (Princeton, NJ: Princeton University Press, 1968); T.F. Mathews, *The Clash of Gods: A Reinterpretation of Christian Art* (Princeton, NJ: Princeton University Press, 1993), esp. p. 32, pls. 13 and 14; J. Engemann, 'Biblische Themen im Bereich der frühchristlichen Kunst', *Jahrbuch für Antike und Christentum* 23 (1996), pp. 543-56, and esp. pp. 553-56; Snyder, 'Sea Monsters', esp. pp. 19-20. For a summary of the evidence and bibliography, see Bowers, *Legend of Jonah*, pp. 20-32 and Steffen, *Die Jona-Geschichte*, pp. 56-83.

23. Steffen, *Die Jona-Geschichte*, pp. 68-70.

Jewish interpretative communities, for their part, could not and did not adopt understandings of the proposed macrostructure of Jonah 1–2 in terms of the most central meta-narrative motifs in Christian communities. Against this background, it is not surprising that the Targum tries to discourage the interpretative move from 'near death' to 'death', from 'Jonah in the fish', to 'Jonah in the grave'. Thus the Targum renders the Hebrew word שאול in v. 2 as 'from the bottom of the deep' (מארעית תהומא) rather than 'hell' or the like.[24] Likewise, Midrash Jonah seems to stress the bodily rather than symbolic character of the fish, or better two fishes in this source.[25]

It is worth noticing that, however, שאול in Jon. 2.2 is rendered גיהנם (Gehenna) in other rabbinic sources (*b. 'Erub.* 19a). Interpretative concerns, even within theologically similar communities, are also a function of the particular discourse within which they are expressed. In other words, interpretation takes place within a textual world and is influenced by this world. The context of the discussion in *b. 'Erub.* 19a is certainly a substantial factor in the understanding of שאול as גיהנם.[26]

Finally, the possible association of Jonah with a miraculous triumph over death could lead and has led to the attachment of messianic or eschatological characteristics to Jonah also within Jewish traditions.[27] Since Jonah served as a prefiguration of Jesus in Christian meta-narratives, such characterizations of Jonah within Judaism were consistent with Jewish metanarratives that counteracted the Christian ones, and particularly around the question of Jesus' messianic status.[28]

24. The Targum understands שחת in v. 7 as 'destruction' (חבלא). See Levine, *Aramaic Version*, pp. 72-73, 77.

25. See B.H. Mehlman and D.F. Polish, 'Midrash Jonah', *CCARJ* 24.1 (1977), pp. 30-41 (33-34).

26. The text reads: R. Jeremiah b. Eleazar said Gehennom (Heb. גיהנם) has three gates; one in the wilderness (Heb. מדבר), one in the sea (Heb. ים) and one in Jerusalem. 'In the wilderness', since it is written 'they and all that was theirs went down alive 'to *sheol*' (Heb. שאלה; Num. 16.33); 'in the sea', since it is written from the belly of *sheol* I cried out and (and) you heard my voice' (Jon. 2.3); in Jerusalem, since it is written 'Utterance of the Lord, who has a fire (Heb. אור) in Jerusalem and a furnace (Heb. תנור) in Jerusalem' (Isa. 31.9). The school of R. Ishmael taught, 'who has a fire is in Zion', this is (or refers to) Gehenom (Heb. גיהנם); 'and a furnace in Jerusalem' this is (or refers to) the gate of Gehenom.

27. See Seltzer, 'Jonah' and Wineman, 'The Zohar on Jonah', and bibliography there.

28. This holds true even if the association between Jonah and resurrection preceded

It should be noticed that the macrostructure in question led also to motifs that could be, and have been, easily shared by Jewish and Christian interpretative communities. The basic content of Jonah 1–2 stresses that Jonah, in his distress, prays to God, who in turn responds to his prayer by saving him. The figure of Jonah may therefore be integrated into general meta-narratives that see humans, including worthy prophets, as people who are liable to sin and do sin, [29] but who may also acknowledge and proclaim the greatness of God and be forgiven by a gracious God. In this role Jonah not only serves as a reminder of God's willingness to forgive, but also may be seen as representative of both human frailty and greatness. These messages also resonate within basic meta-narratives of Islam.[30] Thus, for instance, one reads in the Qur'an:

> but he [Jonah] cried through the depths of darkness, 'There is no god but thou: glory to thee: I was indeed wrong!' So We listened to him: and delivered him from distress: and thus do We deliver those who have faith. (Sura 21.87-88).

Christianity, as Wineman suggests, following Goodenough's lead. See Wineman, 'The Zohar on Jonah', esp. pp. 66-67. On these issues see also, Shusman, 'קווים אלגוריים', esp. pp. 86-87 and the bibliography mentioned there.

29. Some commentators pointed to some positive features of Jonah, even when he was in defiance of God. See, for instance, 'Beside the disgrace, there was the flight from the prison. For the self-styled "Advocate" and champion of the truth [i.e. Mani] ran away. He was no successor of Jesus who went eagerly to the cross, but the very opposite, a runaway. Then the king of the Persians ordered the guards of the prison to be executed… Should he not have imitated Jesus and said: "If, therefore, you seek me, let these go their way." Should he not have said, like Jonah: "Pick me up and throw me into the sea," for "it is because of me that this violent storm has come upon you"' (Cyril of Jerusalem, *Catechesis* 6.25).

To be sure, other interpreters tended to emphasize the sin of Jonah. Such a stress leads usually to an exaltation of the merciful character of God, and of the sinful nature of humanity, including pious individuals, such as prophets. See M. Luther, 'Lectures on Jonah', the German Text (1526), *Luther's Works*, XIX (St Louis: Concordia Publishing House, 1974), pp. 32-104 (45-47), but notice also his words: 'It is also a source of great comfort to us to see that even the greatest and best of the saints sin grievously against God and that we are not the only poor, miserable sinners…' (p. 47), and see also pp. 42-43.

30. It is worth mentioning that Jonah is the only one among the 15 prophets associated with prophetic books in the Hebrew Bible that is mentioned explicitly in the Qur'an. He is mentioned in 4.163; 6.86; 10.98-99; 21.87-88; 37.139-48; 68.48-50. Moreover, Sura 10 is named Yunus (i.e. Jonah).

Significantly, Jonah's prayer is represented here also in terms of another overarching Muslim concept, the Shahadah (i.e. 'the declaration of faith', which begins with 'there is no god except God').[31]

Al-Ṭabarī (839–923) a few centuries later wrote:

> According to Ibn Ḥumayd—Salama—Ibn Isḥāq—one who told him—'Abdallāh b. Rāfi', the mawlā of the Prophet's spouse Umm Salamah—Abū Hurayah: The Prophet said '…Then Jonah, in the whale's belly, glorified God. The angels heard his glorification of God, and exclaimed, "Oh Lord, we hear a faint voice in a strange land." God said, "That is my servant Jonah. He disobeyed Me, so I detained him in the whale's belly at sea." They exclaimed, "The righteous servant from whom every day and night a righteous deed rose to Thee?" God replied, "Yes." At this, they interceded for Jonah. The whale was thus ordered to cast him upon the shore.'[32]

The latter example also gives expression to another element in this macrostructure: Jonah is and remains a servant of God, a prophet, though to be sure a somewhat strange one, because of his obvious human frailty.[33] The shortcomings of Jonah and the fact that he was still a prophet then become proof of God's merciful character (cf. Sura 68.48-50).[34] Despite this, the image of a prophet bearing substantial negative characterization

---

31. Cf. also *The History of al-Ṭabarī (Ta'arīkh al-rusul wa'l mulūk)* (trans. and annotated by M. Perlmann; Bibliotheca Persica, 4; Albany, NY: State University of New York Press, 1987), p. 160 §783. All references to this work in this chapter will be to this edition.

32. *The History of al-Ṭabarī*, IV, p. 165, §788. It is worth mentioning that Muslim traditions about Jonah do not necessarily agree in all details with the biblical narrative. The sequence of events may appear in a different manner. Additional characterizing features may also appear, for instance, 'He [Jonah] is said to have been from a town in the region of Mosul, called Nineveh.' See *The History of al-Ṭabarī*, IV; the quotation is from p. 160, §782, and the full, and very interesting, summary of various retellings of story of Jonah is on pp. 160-66, §782-89.

Still, even here the basic elements of the mentioned macrostructure, namely, a prophet who defies God, is swallowed by a big fish, prays to God in his distress and is saved by God remain. The same holds true for the topic of Nineveh's repentance and of God's relenting from executing judgment against the city, following its repentance. See below.

33. Muhammad is explicitly asked not to follow Jonah's example in Sura 68.49.

34. It bears note that in the Hadith, Jonah is numerous times compared with Muhammad, as in 'None should say that I am better than Yunus,' and similar sayings are attributed by a number of sources to Muhammad. Quotation from Sahih Bukhari 4.55.624. See also Sahih Bukhari 4.55.608, 625, 626, 627; 6.60.127, 128, 154, 155, 328, 329; 9.93.630; and cf. Sahih Muslim 1.318.

was bound to cause some theological unease. Thus, it is not surprising to find literature in both Jewish and Muslim traditions that tends to minimize the negative image of Jonah.[35]

A variant on these interpretations originates when this macrostructure encounters a combination of an evaluation of Jonah as a righteous person even when he attempts to flee—on this issue see below—and a basic meta-narrative according to which God desires the prayers of the righteous and certainly wishes to save them. In this case, God is characterized as one who does everything to save Jonah, beginning with the creation of the fish prior to the six days of creation and culminating with consistent pressure aimed at bringing Jonah not only to pray, to proclaim that God is the one who causes death and revives and ask that God 'revive' him, but also to accept his expected role in God's economy.[36]

4. *The Case of Jonah 3*

The next macrostructure will enhance some of the meanings mentioned above. It brings forward the themes of repentance and salvation, this time involving more than one individual. A reasonable rendering of the global content of Jonah 3 may be as follows:

> Nineveh is a sinful city about to be punished, but when a prophet of YHWH proclaims its imminent doom Nineveh repents and changes its ways. YHWH relents from bringing calamity upon the city.

The dominant theme here concerns the actions of Nineveh and YHWH, namely repentance and relenting from punishment, respectively. As for Jonah, from the perspective of Jonah 3, he is only a helper, a secondary figure.

The theme of human sin, repentance and hope for God's mercy appears in common meta-narratives of many communities. When the proposed macrostructure is approached from the viewpoint of these meta-narratives, those who evaluate themselves as sinners and worthy of divine judgment identify with the Ninevites, and hope that their fate will be like theirs. The Nineveh of Jonah 3 and its repentance are then transformed into objects worthy of emulation. To a large extent, they also become a symbolic code

35. See, Shusman, 'קווים אלגוריים', esp. pp. 96-100 and bibliography cited there.
36. See Mehlman and Polish, 'Midrash Jonah', pp. 33-36. And one may add also, to accept YHWH's position and reject his own in his theological dispute with YHWH in ch. 4.

for desired behavior and, accordingly, the fullness of the repentance of Nineveh tends to be emphasized.[37]

These developments are well attested in Christian,[38] Muslim[39] and Jewish traditions. The liturgy of Yom Kippur in which the book of Jonah is read is a typical example of the interweaving of the book with this type of meta-narrative within Jewish traditions. But this example only points at a rich Jewish tradition on that matter. Thus, for instance, *m. Ta'an* 2.1— a text written probably much earlier than the final composition of the synagogal liturgy of Yom Kippur—states:

> What is the order of the ceremony for days of fast [תענית]: The ark is taken out to the open place of the city. Burnt ashes are placed on the ark, on the head of the *nasi* and on the head of the *ab-beit-din*; and each person places burnt ashes on his head. The elder among them says before them words of admonition [דברי כבושין], 'Our brothers, it is not said regarding the people

37. See, for instance, *b. Ta'an* 16a. To be sure, within discourses that strongly emphasize the theological topos (and meta-narrative) of the 'unmerited grace of God', one may encounter interpretations of the repentance of the Ninevites as less than full and, accordingly, as clearly undeserved of their salvation. Still, within those discourses their repentance is considered a worthy deed, even if it does not or cannot merit divine grace. Cf. J.W. Walton, 'The Object Lesson of Jonah 4:5-7 and the Purpose of the book of Jonah', *BBR* 2 (1992), pp. 47-57.

38. See, for instance, 'O happy penitence which has drawn down upon itself the eyes of God, and which has by confessing its error changed the sentence of God's anger! The same conduct is in the Chronicles attributed to Manasseh, and in the book of the prophet Jonah to Nineveh, and in the gospel to the publican' (Jerome, *Ep.* 77.4).

39. In the Qur'an, Nineveh is the example of a city that believes in Allah as opposed to the many cities to which signs were brought to and never believed:

> (96) 'Those against whom the word of thy Lord hath been verified would not believe—
> (97) Even if every Sign was brought unto them,—until they see (for themselves) the penalty grievous.
> (98) Why was there not a single township (among those We warned), which believed,—so its Faith should have profited it,—except the People of Jonah? When they believed, We removed from them the Penalty of Ignominy in the life of the Present, and permitted them to enjoy (their life) for a while' (Sura 10.96-98).

The expression 'for a while' brings to the forefront the awareness of the eventual fate of Nineveh. See also Sura 37.148. See also, 'how…the Message disbelieved until is too late for repentance; and how, in the case of Yūnus (Jonah) and his people, even the rejection (when repentance supervenes) does not prevent God's grace and mercy from working, and how far that working is beyond man's comprehension' (Introduction to Sura 10, in the translation mentioned above).

of Nineveh "God saw their sackcloth and their fasting [תעניתם]", but rather "God saw their deeds, that they turned from their evil ways..." "[40]

Of course, there is the matter of characterization here. The Ninevites, no matter their previous deeds, represent the potential in human beings—including severe sinners—to behave in a clearly godly way. YHWH is construed as a God who relents from implementing what is presented as just punishment. This characterization of God is, of course, consistent with meta-narratives that emphasize the attribute of mercy in God, and God's ability, because of that attribute, to relent from punishment even in the case of grievous sinners, and even if such judgment was already announced by a true prophet.[41]

5. *The Case of Jonah 1–3*

A reasonable rendering of the global content of Jonah 1–3 as a whole may be as follows:

> Nineveh is a sinful city about to be punished. YHWH sends a reluctant prophet to proclaim its doom. The prophet eventually does so. Then Nineveh turns around, repents and is saved.

If this macrostructure is adopted, then two issues and plots are immediately raised. The first, and the dominant one, is still that of Jonah 3. Yet a second issue is clearly present in this macrostructure, and it concerns the tension between YHWH and Jonah, and the related opposition between Jonah and Nineveh. It is possible (and particularly from the perspective of Jonah 1–4, see below) to focus on the tension between YHWH and the prophet and explain that the opposition between Jonah and Nineveh is simply accidental. If this is the case, then Jonah's reluctance may be interpreted in terms of his character or 'profession' (i.e. being a prophet). But given that the climax of the story of Jonah 1–3 is the salvation of Nineveh, the general tendency is to explain the tension between YHWH and Jonah in terms of the opposition between Jonah and Nineveh; or, in other words, to give the largest interpretative weight to the main plot.

---

40. See Jon. 3.6-10; the quotation is from Jon. 3.10.

See also *b. Roš. Haš.* 16b; *b. Ta'an* 15a; *Qoh. R.* 5.6.1; and cf. Rambam, *Mishneh Torah, Zmanim, Ta'aniot* 4.2. Cf. E. Urbach, 'תשובת אנשי נינוה והויכוח יהודי־נוצרי', *Tarbiz* 20 (1949–50), pp. 118-22.

41. See, for instance, Radak on Jon. 3.10.

If this is the case, then a key interpretative question emerges: Why is Jonah so reluctant to proclaim the divine announcement to the Ninevites? This question is 'built-in' within a global meaning that is shared by those who recognize it and accordingly engage in this type of readings. But the likelihood that they will give a certain answer to that shared question depends on the answer's suitability to common meta-narratives already adopted by particular interpretative communities.

A common way of dealing with the tension between Jonah and Nineveh has been to rephrase it in terms of a tension between Jonah, the Israelite or Jew, and Nineveh, the non-Jewish city. If the difference between non-Israel (Nineveh) and Israel is brought to the forefront, then an additional set of readings of Jon. 1.3 may easily cohere or support common meta-narratives in both Judaism and Christianity.

Nineveh's repentance may be seen as the example that Jerusalem/Israel ought to have followed in Jewish theological explanations of the fall of the First Temple. This response is consistent with the construction of the Ninevites of Jonah 3 as an object of emulation and identification for Jews and Jewish communities, which were called and expected to follow these Ninevites' footsteps.[42] If this approach is taken, then the reluctance of Jonah may be interpreted as resulting from his prophetic knowledge that monarchic Israel will not behave as Nineveh,[43] and therefore of his fear that the example of Nineveh will be used by God against monarchic Israel. Thus one reads that Jonah 'insisted upon the honor of the son [Israel], but did not insist on the honor of the Father [God]' (*Mek. Pisha* 1.100-101).[44]

---

42. E.g. *m. Ta'an* 2.1. See also Radak who maintained that the book of Jonah was written for didactic purposes ('נכתבה להיות מוסר לישראל', see Radak on Jon. 1.1), namely, to encourage repentance in Israel by pointing at the complete repentance of the Ninevites ('שבו תשובה שלמה מרעתם') the first time that a prophet admonished them.

43. Of course, in spite of their ability to do so. The implicit notion here is that the Israelites of the monarchic period were potentially able to behave as well as the Ninevites. According to this reading, Jonah knew that monarchic Israel/Judah will be able to repent, even at the last moment, but they will not do so, and therefore condemn themselves for divine judgment.

44. See, for instance, ' "Oppressing (yonah) city": ought she not have learnt from the city of Jonah, viz. Nineveh? One prophet I sent to Nineveh and she turned in penitence; to Israel in Jerusalem I sent many prophets' *Lam. R.*, proem XXXI; ET according to *Midrash Rabbah, Lamentations* (trans. A. Cohen; Hindhead, Surrey: Soncino Press, 3rd edn, 1993), p. 57. This approach is well attested much earlier and much later than *Lam. R.* For the former, see, for instance, *Mek. Pisha* 1.70-85, 100-94 (see *Mekilta de-Rabbi Ishmael* [ed. J.Z. Lauterbach; Philadelphia: Jewish Publication

Early Christian interpretative communities could, and some did, adopt the explanation that Jonah was worried that his own people will not behave as the Ninevites, but they tended to interweave this reading with meta-narratives explaining the Jews' rejection of Jesus. Thus the story about the monarchic Israelites who declined to follow the path of the Ninevites (i.e. the Gentiles) becomes a prefiguration of their rejection of Jesus (cf. Mt. 12.41-42; Lk. 11.31-32) and, accordingly, of their demise.[45] Conversely, within this interpretative frame, the response of the Ninevites may be seen as a prefiguration of the Gentiles' reception of the gospel and Christianity in general.[46]

Society of America, 1933], I, pp. 6-9) and for the latter see, for instance, Radak on Jon. 1.3.

45. See, for instance, Jerome's commentary on Jonah (1.3; 4.1). It is worth noting that both Jerome and Ephraem the Syrian clearly based their comments on Jewish sources, though they certainly transformed their communicative message. See Urbach, 'תשובת אנשי נינוה והויכוח יהודי-נוצרי', pp. 119-21.

Cf. Augustin's words: 'In the next place, as to Jonah's building for himself a booth, and sitting down over against Nineveh, waiting to see what would befall the city, the prophet was here in his own person the symbol of another fact. He prefigured the carnal people of Israel. For he also was grieved at the salvation of the Ninevites, that is, at the redemption and deliverance of the Gentiles, from among whom Christ came to call, not righteous men, but sinners to repentance. Wherefore the shadow of that gourd over his head prefigured the promises of the Old Testament, or rather the privileges already enjoyed in it, in which there was, as the apostle says, "a shadow of things to come", is furnishing, as it were, a refuge from the heat of temporal calamities in the land of promise. Moreover, in that morning-worm? which by its gnawing tooth made the gourd wither away, Christ Himself is again prefigured, forasmuch as, by the publication of the gospel from His mouth, all those things which flourished among the Israelites for a time, or with a shadowy symbolical meaning in that earlier dispensation, are now deprived of their significance, and have withered away. And now that nation, having lost the kingdom, the priesthood, and the sacrifices formerly established in Jerusalem, all which privileges were a shadow of things to come, is burned with grievous heat of tribulation in its condition of dispersion and captivity, as Jonah was, according to the history, scorched with the heat of the sun, and is overwhelmed with sorrow; and notwithstanding, the salvation of the Gentiles and of the penitent is of more importance in the sight of God than this sorrow of Israel and the "shadow" of which the Jewish nation was so glad' (*Ep.* 102.35; quotations from Augustin's letters are according to the translation in *Nicene and Post-Nicene Fathers, Series I*, vol. I).

46. So, for instance, Maxine. See Duval, *Le livre de Jonas*, I, p. 37. Cf. 'While he [Jonah] preaches to Nineveh, announces salvation to all the heathen' (Jerome, *Ep.* 53.8). Also cf. Augustin's position: 'As, therefore, Jonah passed from the ship to the belly of the whale, so Christ passed from the cross to the sepulchre, or into the abyss of

The latter example brings to the forefront another constraint to the adoption of readings of the book of Jonah, namely, that created by the reading adopted by 'the other' within a more or less common discourse. If the excellence of the Ninevites' repentance is widely communicated by Christians as a major symbol pointing to the obstinacy, shame and eventual demise of their contemporaneous Jews, then within that social context, Jews may tend to de-emphasize that excellence. Thus, whereas the Babylonian Jewish sources remain faithful to the glorious interpretation of the Ninevites' response already present in the Mishnah since they did not live within 'Christendom', later Palestinian Jewish sources written against the background of (theological and otherwise) tensions between Christianity and Judaism (e.g. *y. Talmud*) became more critical of Nineveh's response.[47]

It is worth noting that alternative versions of the understanding of Jonah's reluctance in terms of his concern for Israel's fate may be interwoven in significantly different meta-narratives and worldviews. For

---

death. And as Jonah suffered this for the sake of those who were endangered by the storm, so Christ suffered for the sake of those who are tossed on the waves of this world. And as the command was given at first that the word of God should be preached to the Ninevites by Jonah, but the preaching of Jonah did not come to them until after the whale had vomited him forth, so prophetic teaching was addressed early to the Gentiles, but did not actually come to the Gentiles until after the resurrection of Christ from the grave' (*Ep.* 102.34).

Calvin's position on these matters is worth noting. He agrees that Israelites stand accused by the comparison of their reaction to the prophets and that of the Ninevites, but he does not claim that this is the reason for Jonah's reluctance. Moreover, he diminishes the value and nature of the Ninevites' repentance (it is only temporary), and argues against the position that the proclamation to the Ninevites is a token of the (Christian) call to the Gentiles—though he compares the call to go to Nineveh with the call to Peter to teach Cornelius (Acts 10; see p. 26). It seems that Calvin wants to emphasize the great break with the past that the coming of Jesus represents [cf. Augustin] and accordingly the similarities between pre- and post-Jesus events tend to decrease. On the emphasis on the mentioned break within Calvin's commentary on Jonah, see, for instance, 'It was... God's will that the adoption of the race of Abraham should continue unaltered to the coming of Christ, so that the Jews might excel all other nations, and differ from them through a gratuitous privilege, as the holy and elect people of God' (J. Calvin, 'Commentaries on the Prophet Jonah', in *Commentaries on the Minor Prophets* [Grand Rapids, MI: Baker Book House, 1989], p. 26, and see his commentary on Jonah 1.1-2).

47. See E. Urbach, 'תשובת אנשי נינוה והויכוח יהודי־נוצרי'. For a somewhat similar reduction on the greatness of the repentance of the Ninevites, but for a very different set of reasons see Calvin. See above.

instance, within a rationalistic and 'historically/factually' oriented frame, the story turns into Jonah's strategic understanding of the situation of Israel and the might of Assyria. According to this alternative, Jonah knew that if Assyria were not to be destroyed soon—during his mission—it would conquer and devastate Israel in the future. In other words, the reason for Israel's calamity moves from the realm of sin to that of a strategic lack of power.[48] To be sure, some interpreters and some basic narratives will relate the two realms (see already Chronicles).

If the story is read against a meta-narrative about the contrast between Christian (or Enlightenment) universalism and Jewish particularism, then Jonah, now construed as a 'paradigmatic Jew', does not need any particular reason to oppose the salvation of Nineveh in terms of its effect on Israel. He would be described as narrow-minded, particularist, national-ist Jew who opposes the salvation of Nineveh because the inhabitants are Gentiles. The book of Jonah, as opposed to the character of Jonah, would carry a divine message that stresses God's strong opposition to this position.[49] The obvious point that if this is so, an ancient Jewish author identified with God's opposition to Jonah and, more importantly, Jewish communities that accepted this book identified with God and not with the character of Jonah was most often ignored or circumvented, because such characterizations of Judaism and Jewishness would have contradicted central meta-narratives of the proponents of these reading.

Modern theological approaches influenced by aspects of Pauline

48. See, for instance, the entry for 'Jonah, the Book of' in H.S. Gehman (ed.), *The New Westminster Dictionary of the Bible* (Philadelphia: Westminster Press, 1970), pp. 508-10, esp. p. 508. Cf. the characterization of Jonah proposed in Gitay, 'Jonah'.

49. 'We might infer that he disobeyed God's command because of his dislike for the city of Nineveh, that he still had a Jewish, a carnal, idea of God, regarding Him as the exclusive God of the Jews and not also of the Gentiles. Therefore Jonah's heart inclined to the view that the people of Nineveh were not deserving God's grace and Word because they were not God's people, that is not Jews, or of the people of Israel' (Luther, 'Lectures on Jonah', the German Text, p. 50). (Cf. Luther's words here with the previously quoted passage from Augustine.) Although Luther's image of Jonah is far more complex than this quotation suggests, still the main point about the likelihood that Jonah's reluctance was based on the Gentile nature of the Ninevites remains. The anti-Judaic (and anti-Jewish) tendency is also clear.

On these matters, see Bickerman, *Four Strange Books*, pp. 17-28. For some con-siderations regarding Enlightenment, Judaism and Pauline theology, see, for instance, the recent work by B. Harrison, 'The Strangeness of Leviticus', *Jud* 48 (1999), pp. 208-28.

theology may also partake of meta-narratives that stress the opposition between nationalism or narrow particularism, on the one hand, and universalism, on the other,[50] whether they associate one or both aspects of the opposition with ancient Israelites.[51]

Certainly, an emphasis on 'universalism' is likely to be developed if a central feature of the self-perception of the interpretative community is to have a mission to the world. This is true for contemporaneous Christian communities,[52] but also in some streams of Judaism. This is so because this type of reading of the Jonah sits very well with some prominent meta-narratives about Israel's role as a 'light to the nations' and servant of YHWH within certain liberal streams in modern Judaism.[53] Needless to say,

50. See, for instance, A. Bentzen who wrote that 'he [the author] will led his hearers to see and refrain from their narrow particularism' and he quotes Engnell who wrote: 'He [Jonah] represents consciously universalism, he makes front against Judaic particularism.' See A. Bentzen, *Introduction to the Old Testament* (2 vols.; Copenhagen: G.E.C. Gads Forlag, 1949), II, p. 147. See also, among others, Allen, *Joel, Obadiah, Jonah, and Micah*, p. 194.

These interpretations have, of course, to explain Jon. 1.12. It may be explained in terms of Jonah's wish to die, which will serve the purpose of avoiding God's commission, but in other manners too, according to particular meta-narratives. See, for instance, W. Scarlett's exposition: 'Like many others, he [Jonah] hated en masse. He hated Gentiles, Assyrians, Nineveh. He is the type who would hate Russians, Germans, Negroes, Jews, en masse. He would indict a whole people. In his hatred he is like Harry A. Overstreet's "gentle people of prejudice", who are courteous, kindly, but who draw a line against a whole class of their fellow citizens. It is this spirit that gives rise to anti-Semitism and racialism' (W. Scarlett, 'The Book of Jonah—Exposition', *IB*, VI, pp. 883-84).

51. 'The preservation and survival of this book among the sacred scriptures of the Hebrew Bible indicates that the Jews themselves saw in Jonah's actions and attitudes a universal human figure rather than a representative of Jewish particularism' (J. Krašovec, 'Salvation of the Rebellious Prophet Jonah and of the Penitent Heathen Sinners', *SEÅ* 61 [1996], pp. 53-75 [75]).

52. See, for instance, '*Yahweh's compassion extends to all the nations of the earth, and Israel is under responsibility to be the vehicle by which that compassion is made known*... Yahweh loves the Ninevehs of this world, and so should those within the community of faith' (J.D. Newsome Jr, *The Hebrew Prophets* [Atlanta: John Knox Press, 1984], p. 200; italic in the original).

53. See, for instance, the following quotations from Rabbi S.D. Schwartzman and Rabbi J.D. Spiro, *The Living Bible: A Topical Approach to the Jewish Scriptures* (New York: Union of American Hebrew Congregations, 1962): '...the book of Jonah was written as a reminder to the people of their wider mission to all mankind. In this interesting tale built upon the experience of a reluctant prophet, the Jewish people is taken to task for neglecting its role as servant of the Lord' (p. 55). 'This story, of

within this approach the writer of the book is extolled as a symbol of the spirit of Judaism, whereas the character Jonah is strongly criticized.

It is also possible to interweave the same basic macrostructure (or global narrative meaning) with significantly different meta-narratives. The moment the Nineveh of the book of Jonah is associated the city of other biblical sources (e.g. Isaiah, Nahum), it is easily seen as a symbolic archetypal enemy of Israel and of YHWH.[54] If this is the case, then Jonah may be interpreted as a unselfish person who is willing to sacrifice himself to avoid calamity from his own people, and perhaps within this discourse YHWH's dishonor.

Since Nineveh becomes the archetypal enemy, it is not surprising that some contemporaneous readers may compare it to Hitler, and Assyrian actions against Jerusalem (and Samaria) to the Holocaust. If the book of Jonah is read in this light, then Jonah's actions resonate with the voice of Jewish struggle against Nazism,[55] and from a larger perspective to any kind of human resistance to persecution and oppression.[56]

6. *The Case of Jonah 1–4*

Jonah 1–4, as a whole, has at its forefront the confrontation between YHWH and Jonah, the two main characters in the book. The Ninevites—

course, is a parable; that is, fiction which tries to teach a moral lesson. In the mind of the author, Jonah represents the people of Israel. Like the prophet, their viewpoint has become narrow; they think only of themselves. But must they also not bear in mind the welfare of the other peoples of the world? Their existence and conduct must be such as to remind the non-Jews of their own moral responsibilities... In their concern only for themselves, the people of Israel have been shirking their wider responsibilities. But, as the Servant of the Lord, they, like Jonah, cannot escape them' (p. 56).

54. To be sure, this is not the only way to relate the texts. Other relations may and were construed and ways that are consistent with other main meta-narratives. See, for instance, Nahum 1.1 in the Targum: 'Previously Jonah the son of Amittai, the prophet from Gath-hepher, prophesied against her [Nineveh] and she repented from her sins; and when she sinned again there prophesied once more against her Nahum of Beth Koshi, as is recorded in this book' (ET according to K.J. Cathcart and R.P. Gordon, *The Targum of the Minor Prophets* [Aramaic Bible, 14; Wilmington: Michael Glazier, 1989], p. 131). The text there reaffirms the theological position that when Nineveh repents from its sins, YHWH relents; but when it sins again, a new prophecy against her is proclaimed (so Jer. 18.7-10; cf. Ezek. 18).

55. See LaCocque and Lacoque, *Jonah*, p. xxiv; cf. N. Rosen, 'Jonah'.

56. To be sure, this interpretative approach to Jonah raises the question of the characterization of God. See below.

just as the sailors before, in Jonah 1—become secondary characters that move the plot ahead and whose presence serves to characterize Jonah.[57] The repentance of Nineveh becomes secondary too, and it is not mentioned in Jon. 4.11 at all. Against this background, perhaps a reasonable macrostructure of Jon. 1–4 may be as follows:

> YHWH tries to persuade a reluctant Jonah to accept some aspects of YHWH's behavior as godly, that is, as worthy of God.

If this macrostructure is accepted then a key issue is: Which are aspect/s of God's behavior (or attributes) that YHWH tries to convince Jonah that are worthy of God? The answer to this question is usually framed in terms of 'the (main) message of the book is…' Among the possible answers to this question one usually finds mercy (as opposed to strict justice),[58] grace, universalism, obedience to God,[59] the radical freedom of decision of God,[60] or that God's ways cannot be contained in human categories (linguistic or otherwise),[61] or often different combinations of more than one of these motifs.[62]

---

57. Secondary chapters often serve to characterize main characters in biblical narratives. See, for instance, the case of Orpah in the book of Ruth.

58. E.g. A. Heschel, *The Prophets* (2 vols.; New York: Harper & Row, 1975 [1962]), II, p. 67; Fretheim, *Message*, esp. pp. 128-36; Kaufmann, תולדות, II, p. 282, and Calvin.

See also Midrash Jonah, which concludes as follows: 'At that moment [immediately after YHWH asks the final question in Jon. 4.11] he [Jonah] fell upon his face and said: "Guide Your worlds by the attribute of Mercy", as it is written: "To the Lord our God belong mercy and forgiveness" [Dan 9.9].' See Mehlman and Polish, 'Midrash Jonah', p. 40.

59. See, for instance, 'the disobedience of Israel would prevent them from effectively "declaring God's glory among the heathen" (Ps. 96.3)' (C. J. Collins, 'From Literary Analysis to Theological Exposition: The Book of Jonah', *Journal of Translation and Textlinguistics* 7 [1995], pp. 28-44 [40]).

60. See, for instance, Bolin, *Freedom Beyond Forgiveness*.

61. E.g. G. Elata-Alster and R. Salmon, 'The Deconstruction of Genre in the Book of Jonah', *Journal of Literature and Theology* 3 (1989), pp. 40-60.

62. See, for instance, 'The book of Jonah expresses the fundamental rules of divine government: on the one hand, God is not obliged to punish sinners, on the other hand, bestowal of divine mercy may be motivated by repentance, but it can never be considered as something owed to human merit… The guiding concern of the book of Jonah is the manifestation of the supremacy of divine grace and mercy over the requirements of strict justice' (Krašovec, 'Salvation'; see also Golka, 'Jonah', pp. 125-28).

Further, whereas traditional interpretative communities tend to adopt the position of the character YHWH in the story and evaluate positively his attempt to convince Jonah,[63] some contemporary readers may identify with Jonah and his reluctance to accept that message. New sets of communicative meanings emerge from this attitude to the text.

There is no need to review, at this point, the basis of these responses in macrostructures of the text. It is important, however, to realize that as a whole the popularity of these answers in most interpretative communities through history does not seem to be based on their superior ability to deal with the details of the narrative, or the most likely historical background of the writing of the book.[64] Their popularity within the discourse of most communities, and through time, seems to rest more on the degree to which the reading may be integrated within accepted meta-narratives.[65] This result is consistent with (a) the fact that shared meta-narratives play an important role in social cohesion, and (b) the importance given to the interpretation of Scripture in most interpretative communities through history.

7. Summary

Although the number of possible interpretations of the book of Jonah seems infinite, these interpretations are still constrained by a number of factors. The horizon of pertinence of the text within interpretative frames that consider the book authoritative, propositional macrostructures and the ability of an interpretation to integrate itself within an adopted meta-narrative have all been proposed as important factors. But there are others.

---

63. Midrash Jonah and Yalkut Shimoni include an explicit statement by Jonah following YHWH's words in Jon. 4.11. According to these sources, 'at that moment, he fell on his face and said, "Guide your world by the attribute of mercy, as it is written: To the Lord, our God, belongs mercy and forgiveness"'. See Mehlman and Polish, *Midrash Jonah*, p. 40; P. Kahn, 'The Epilogue to Jonah', *JBQ* 28 [2000], pp. 146-55 [155]).

64. In fact, it is often the case that the history of the period is reconstructed on the basis of an already adopted reading of the book rather than vice versa.

65. To some extent, one may approach the popularity of interpretations within particular groups as a question of suitability of the 'product' (i.e. the interpretation) to a particular market. The 'product' should be consistent with the expectations of the market (cf. horizon of pertinence and consistency with already adopted meta-narratives). If the product is of much social importance, then it is likely to be controlled by the relevant authorities (notice discussion in section 2 above).

Since the interpretation of Scripture may have vast implications in many societies and communities, relevant authorities may also have a say in these matters. Moreover, in historical situations, such as when two interpretative communities involve themselves in a significant social and theological confrontation over the interpretation of the book, the interpretation of the one is bound to affect that of the other. Additional factors may include the textual environment in which the interpretation is produced.

Whereas many of these constraining factors tend to create much diversity, still, not only the 'rules of the game', but also basic macrostructures, and in most cases through history, the horizon of pertinence of the book contributed to some extent of shared interpretative elements, which in fact go back to claims and basic propositional meanings of the text itself.

Although it is true that each listener may hear a different voice in the midst of silence, the readers (and rereaders) of Jonah were never completely in the midst of silence. There was the book of Jonah saying to them, as it were, something that most of them held to be godly and worthy of being godly. There were always other listeners too, for the readers were never alone, but were members of an interpretative community, with expectations and shared meta-narratives, for above all, the interpretation of text, and particularly scriptural texts, is a social phenomenon.

BIBLIOGRAPHY

Abrabanel, I., פירוש על נביאים וכתובים (Jerusalem: Abrabanel Press, 1960).

Ackerman, J.S., 'Satire and Symbolism in the Song of Jonah', in B. Halpern and J.D. Levenson, (eds.), *Traditions in Transformation: Turning Points in Biblical Faith* (Winona Lake, IN: Eisenbrauns, 1981).

—'Jonah', in R. Alter and F. Kermode (eds.), *The Literary Guide to the Bible* (Cambridge: Belknap Press, 1987), pp. 235-43.

Ackroyd, P.R., *Exile and Restoration: A Study of Hebrew Thought of the Sixth Century B.C.* (Philadelphia: Westminster Press, 1975 [1968]).

Albertz, R., *A History of the Israelite Religion in the Old Testament Period* (2 vols.; Louisville, KY: Westminster/John Knox Press, 1994 [German, 1992]).

Alexander, T.D., 'Jonah and Genre', *TynBul* 36 (1985), pp. 35-59.

Allen, L.C., *The Books of Joel, Obadiah, Jonah, and Micah* (Grand Rapids, MN: Eerdmans, 1976).

Almbladh, K., *Studies in the Book of Jonah* (Studia Semitica Upsaliensia, 7; Uppsala: Uppsala University; Stockholm: Distributed by Almqvist & Wiksell International, 1986).

Alonso Schökel, L., 'Judith', in J.L Mays *et al.* (eds.), *The HarperCollins Bible Commentary* (San Francisco: HarperCollins, 2000), pp. 732-41.

Amit, Y., ' "The Glory of Israel Does Not Deceive or Change his Mind": On the Reliability of Narrator and Speakers in Biblical Narrative', *Prooftexts* 12 (1992), pp. 201-12.

Anderson, B.A., 'When God Repents', *BR* 12.3 (1996), pp. 21, 44.

Andrew, M.E., 'Gattung and Intention of the Book of Jonah', *ORITA* (1967), pp. 13-18, 78-85.

Band, A.J., 'Swallowing Jonah: The Eclipse of Parody', *Prooftexts* 10 (1990), pp. 177-95.

Barré, M.L., 'Jonah 2,9 and the Structure of Jonah's Prayer', *Bib* 72 (1991), pp. 237-48

Barthélemy, D., *et al.*, *Critique textuelle de l'Ancien Testament tome 3* (OBO, 50.3; Fribourg: Éditions Universitaires; Göttingen: Vandenhoeck & Rupprecht, 1992).

Begg, C.T., 'Josephus and Nahum Revisited', *REJ* 154 (1995), pp. 5-22.

Ben-Yosef, I.A., 'Jonah and the Fish as a Folk Motif', *Semitics* 7 (1980), pp. 102-17.

Ben Zvi, E., *A Historical-Critical Study of the Book of Zephaniah* (BZAW, 198; Berlin: W. de Gruyter, 1991).

—'Prophets and Prophecy in the Compositional and Redactional Notes in I–II Kings', *ZAW* 105 (1993), pp. 331-51.

—'A Sense of Proportion: An Aspect of the Theology of the Chronicler', *SJOT* 9 (1995), pp. 37-51.

—'Inclusion in and Exclusion from Israel as Conveyed by the Use of the Term "Israel" in Postmonarchic Biblical Texts', in S.W. Holloway and L.K. Handy (eds.), *The Pitcher is Broken: Memorial Essays for Gosta. W. Ahlstrom* (JSOTSup, 190; Sheffield: JSOT Press, 1995), pp. 95-149.

—'Twelve Prophetic Books or "The Twelve" ', in Watts and House (eds.), *Forming Prophetic Literature*, pp. 125-56.

—*A Historical-Critical Study of the Book of Obadiah* (BZAW, 242; Berlin: W. de Gruyter, 1996).

—'The Urban Center of Jerusalem and the Development of the Literature of the Hebrew Bible', in W.G. Aufrecht, N.A. Mirau and S.W. Gauley (eds.), *Aspects of Urbanism in Antiquity* (JSOTSup, 244; Sheffield: Sheffield Academic Press, 1997), pp. 194-209.

—'Micah 1.2-16. Observations and Possible Implications', *JSOT* 77 (1998), pp. 103-20.

—'Looking at the Primary (Hi)Story and the Prophetic Books as Literary/Theological Units within the frame of the Early Second Temple: Some Considerations', *SJOT* 12 (1998), pp. 26-43.

—'When the Foreign Monarch Speaks', in M.P. Graham and S.L. McKenzie (eds.), *The Chronicler as Author: Studies in Text and Texture* (JSOTSup, 263; Sheffield: Sheffield Academic Press, 1999), pp. 209-28.

—*Micah* (FOTL, 21B; Grand Rapids: Eerdmans, 2000).

—'Introduction: Writings, Speeches, and the Prophetic Books—Setting an Agenda', in Ben Zvi and Floyd (eds.), *Writings and Speech*, pp. 1-29.

—'What is New in Yehud? Some Considerations', in Rainer Albertz and Bob Becking (eds.), *Yahwism after the Exile. Perspectives on Israelite Religion in the Persian Period* (STAR, 5; Assen: Van Gorcum, 2003), pp. 32-48.

—'The Prophetic Book: A Key Form of Prophetic Literature', in M.A. Sweeney and E. Ben Zvi (eds.), *The Changing Face of Form Criticism for the Twenty-First Century* (Grand Rapids: Eerdmans, 2003).

Ben Zvi, E., and M.H. Floyd (eds.), *Writings and Speech in Israelite and Ancient Near Eastern Prophecy* (Symposium, 10; Atlanta: Society of Biblical Literature, 2000).

Bentzen, A., *Introduction to the Old Testament* (2 vols.; Copenhagen: G.E.C. Gads Forlag, 1949).

Berlin, A., 'A Rejoinder to John A. Miles Jr, with some Observations on the Nature of Prophecy', *JQR* 66 (1976), pp. 227-35.

Bickerman E., *Four Strange Books in the Bible: Jonah, Daniel, Kohelet, Esther* (New York: Schocken Books, 1967).

—'Les deux erreurs du prophète Jonas', in E. Bickerman (ed.), *Studies in Jewish and Christian History Part One* (Leiden: E.J. Brill, 1976), pp. 33-71 (originally published in *RHPR* 45 [1965], pp. 232-64; a partial ET of the article appears in Bickerman, *Four Strange Books*, pp. 3-49).

Blenkinsopp, J., *The Pentateuch* (ABRL; New York: Doubleday, 1992).

Bolin, T.M., ' "Should I Not Also Pity Nineveh?" Divine Freedom in the Book of Jonah', *JSOT* 67 (1995), pp. 109-20.

—*Freedom Beyond Forgiveness: The Book of Jonah Re-examined* (JSOTSup, 236; Sheffield: Sheffield Academic Press, 1997).

Bowers, R.H., *The Legend of Jonah* (The Hague: Martinus Nijhoff, 1971).

Brenner, A., 'לשנו של ספר יונה כמדד לקביעת זמן חיבורו', *Beit Miqra* 24 (1979), pp. 396-405.

—'Jonah's Poem out of and within its Context', in Davies and Clines (eds.), *Among the Prophets*, pp. 183-92.

Brichto, H.C., *Toward a Grammar of Biblical Poetics* (Oxford: Oxford University Press, 1992).

Calvin, J., *Commentaries on the Minor Prophets* (Grand Rapids, MI: Baker Book House, 1989).

Carroll, R.P., 'Jonah as a Book of Ritual Responses', in K.-D. Schunck and M. Augustin (eds.), *Lasset uns Brücken bauen...*' (BEATA, 42; Bern: Peter Lang, 1998), pp. 261-68.

Cathcart, K.J., and R.P. Gordon, *The Targum of the Minor Prophets* (Aramaic Bible, 14; Wilmington, DE: Michael Glazier, 1989).

Cheney, M., *Dust, Wind and Agony: Character, Speech and Genre in Job* (CB Old Testament Series, 36; Lund: Almqvist & Wiksell International, 1994).

Christensen, D.L., 'The Song of Jonah: A Metrical Analysis', *JBL* 104 (1985), pp. 217-31.

—'Narrative Poetics and the Interpretation of the Book of Jonah', in E.R. Follis (ed.), *Directions in Biblical Hebrew Poetry* (JSOTSup, 40; Sheffield: Sheffield Academic Press, 1987), pp. 29-48.

—'Jonah and the Sabbath Rest in the Pentateuch', in G. Braulik, W. Gross and S. McEvenue (eds.), *Biblische Theologie und gesellschaftlicher Wandel: für Norbert Lohfink SJ* (Freiburg: Herder, 1993), pp. 48-60.

Clark, D.J., *et al.*, *A Handbook on the Books of Obadiah, Jonah, and Micah* (UBS Handbook Series; New York: UBS, 1993)

Clements, R.E., 'The Purpose of the Book of Jonah', in J.A. Emerton *et al.* (eds.), *Congress Volume Edinburgh 1974* (VTSup, 28; Leiden: E.J. Brill, 1975), pp. 16-28.

—'Jeremiah 1–25 and the Deuteronomistic History', in A.G. Auld (ed.), *Understanding Poets and Prophets: Essays in Honour of George W. Anderson* (JSOTSup, 152; Sheffield: Sheffield Academic Press, 1993), pp. 94-113.

Clines, D.J.A., *Interested Parties: The Ideology of Writers and Readers of the Hebrew Bible* (JSOTSup, 205; Sheffield: Sheffield University Press, 1995).

Cohen, A.D., 'The Tragedy of Jonah', *Judaism* 21 (1972), pp. 164-75.

Coleson, J.E., 'The Peasant Woman and the Fugitive Prophet: A Study in Biblical Narrative Settings', in J.E. Coleson and V.H. Matthews (eds.), *'Go to the Land I Will Show You': Studies in Honor of Dwight W. Young* (Winona Lake, IN: Eisenbrauns, 1996), pp. 27-44.

Collins, C.J., 'From Literary Analysis to Theological Exposition: The Book of Jonah', *Journal of Translation and Textlinguistics* 7 (1995), pp. 28-44.

Cook, S.L., and Winter, W.C. (eds.), *On the Way to Nineveh: Studies in Honor of George M. Landes* (ASOR Books, 4; Atlanta: Scholars Press, 1999).

Cooper, A., 'In Praise of Divine Caprice: The Significance of the Book of Jonah', in Davies and Clines (eds.), *Among the Prophets*, pp. 144-63.

Couffignal, R., 'Le Psaume de Jonas (Jonas 2,2-10). Une catabase biblique, sa structure et sa function', *Bib* 71 (1990), pp. 542-52.

Craig, K.M., 'Jonah and the Reading Process', *JSOT* 47 (1990), pp. 103-14.

—*A Poetics of Jonah: Art in the Service of Ideology* (Columbia: University of South Carolina Press, 1993).

Cross, F.M., 'Studies in the Structure of Hebrew Verse: The Prosody of the Psalm of Jonah', in H.B. Huffmon *et al.* (eds.), *The Quest for the Kingdom of God. Studies in Honor of G.E. Mendenhall* (Winona Lake, IN: Eisenbrauns, 1983), pp. 159-67.

Crouch, W.B., 'The Question of an End, to End a Question: Opening and Closure of the Book of Jonah', *JSOT* 62 (1994), pp. 101-12.

Crüsemann, F., *The Torah: Theology and Social History of Old Testament Law* (trans. A.W. Mahnke; Philadelphia: Fortress Press, 1996).

Dahood, M., 'The Independent Personal Pronoun in the Oblique case in Hebrew', *CBQ* 32 (1970), pp. 86-90.

Dan, B., 'לשון ספר יונה בספרות מחקר עיון והערכה נוספים', *Beit Mikra* 41 (1996), pp. 344-68.

Dandamaev, M.A., *Slavery in Babylonia: From Nabopolassar to Alexander the Great (626–331 BC)* (ed. M.A. Powell and D.B. Weisberg; trans. V.A. Powell; Dekalb, IN: Northern Illinois University Press, rev. edn, 1984).

Daube, D., 'Jonah: A Reminiscence', *JJS* 35 (1984), pp. 36-43.

Davies, P.R. *In Search of 'Ancient Israel'* (JSOTSup, 148; Sheffield: Sheffield Academic Press, 1992).

Davies, P.R., and D.J.A. Clines (eds.), *Among the Prophets* (JSOTSup, 144; Sheffield: Sheffield Academic Press, 1993).

Day, John, 'Problems in the Interpretation of the Book of Jonah', in A.S. van der Woude (ed.), *In Quest for the Past: Studies on Israelite Religion, Literature and Prophets. Papers Read at the Joint British-Dutch Old Testament Conference, Held at Elspeet, 1988* (OTS, 26; Leiden: E.J. Brill, 1990), pp. 32-47.

Dell, K.J., 'Reinventing the Wheel: The Shaping of the Book of Jonah', J. Barton and D.J. Reimer, *After the Exile: Essays in Honour of Rex Mason* (Macon, GA: Mercer University Press, 1996), pp. 85-101.

Deurlo, K.A., 'YHWH in den Büchern Ruth und Jona', in K.A. Deurlo and J. Diebner (eds.), *YHWH–Kyrios–Antitheism or the Power of the Word* (Festschrift R. Zuurmond; DBAT, 14; Heidelberg: DBAT, 1996), pp. 105-16.

Dozeman, T.B., 'Inner-biblical Interpretation of Yahweh's Gracious and Compassionate Character', *JBL* 108 (1989), pp. 207-23.

Duval, Y.M., *Le livre de Jonas dans la littérature chrétienne grecque et látine* (2 vols.; Paris: Etudes Augustiniennes, 1973).

Dyck, E., 'Jonah among the Prophets: A Study in Canonical Context', *JETS* 33 (1990), pp. 63-73.

Eagleton, T., 'J.L. Austin and the Book of Jonah', in R. Schwartz (ed.), *The Book and the Text: The Bible and Literary Theory* (Cambridge, MA: Basil Blackwell, 1990), pp. 231-36.

Ebach, J., *Kassandra und Jona: Gegen die Macht des Schicksals* (Frankfurt: Athenäum, 1987).

Elata-Alster, G., and R. Salmon, 'The Deconstruction of Genre in the Book of Jonah', *Journal of Literature and Theology* 3 (1989), pp. 40-60.

Engemann, J., 'Biblische Themen im Bereich der frühchristlichen Kunst', *Jahrbuch für Antike und Christentum* 23 (1996), pp. 543-56.

Eskenazi, T.C., 'Nehemiah 9–10: Structure and Significance', *JHS* 3.9 (2001) (available at www.purl.org/jhs and www.jhsonline.org).

Feldman, L., 'Josephus' Interpretation of Jonah', *AJSRev* 17 (1992), pp. 1-29.

Feuillet, A., 'Les sources du livre de Jonas', *RB* 54 (1947), pp. 161-86.

Fishbane, M., *Biblical Interpretation in Ancient Israel* (Oxford: Clarendon Press, 1985).

Fretheim, T.E., *The Message of Jonah* (Minneapolis, MN: Augsburg, 1977).

—'Jonah and Theodicy', *ZAW* 90 (1978), pp. 227-37.

—'Divine Foreknowledge, Divine Constancy, and the Rejections of Saul's Kingship (1 Sam 15)', *CBQ* 47 (1985), pp. 595-602.

—'The Repentance of God. A Key to Evaluating Old Testament God-Talk', *HBT* 10 (1988), pp. 47-70.

Fuller, R.E., 'The Form and Formation of the Book of The Twelve: The Evidence from the Judean Desert', in Watts and House (eds.), *Forming Prophetic Literature*, pp. 86-101.

—'4QXII[a], 4QXII[f], and 4QXII[g]', *DJD*, XV, pp. 221-32, 267-70, 271-318.

Gabar, A., *Christian Iconography* (Princeton, NJ: Princeton University Press, 1968).

Galil, G., *The Chronology of the Kings of Israel and Judah* (Leiden: E.J. Brill, 1996).

Gehman, H.S. (ed.), *The New Westminster Dictionary of the Bible* (Philadelphia: Westminster Press, 1970).

Gese, H., 'Jona ben Amittai und das Jonabuch', *Tbei* 16 (1985), pp. 256-72.

Gibson, J.C., *Textbook of Syrian Semitic Inscriptions*. II. *Aramaic Inscriptions Including Inscriptions in the Dialect of Zenjirli* (Oxford: Clarendon Press, 1975).

Gitay, Y., 'Jonah: The Prophet of Antirhetoric', in A.B. Beck *et al.* (eds.), *Fortunate the Eyes That See: Essays in Honor of D.N. Freedman* (Grand Rapids, MI: Eerdmans, 1995), pp. 197-206.

Glancy, J.A., 'The Mistress–Slave Dialectic: Paradoxes of Slavery in Three LXX Narratives', *JSOT* 72 (1996), pp. 71-87.

Golka, F.W., 'Jonaexegese und Antijudaismus', *Zeitschrift für Kirche und Israel* 1 (1986), pp. 51-61.

—'Jonah', in G.A.F. Knight and F.W. Golka, *Revelation of God: The Song of Songs and Jonah* (ITC; Grand Rapids, MI: Eerdmans, 1988), pp. 65-136.

Good, E.M., *Irony in the Old Testament* (Sheffield: Almond Press, 2nd edn, 1981 [1965]).

Goodhart, S., ' "Out of the Fish's Belly": Prophecy, Sacrifice and Repentance in the Book of Jonah', in S. Goodhart, *Sacrificing Commentary: Reading the End of Literature* (Baltimore: The John Hopkins University Press, 1996), pp. 139-67.

Gordon, C.H., ' "This Time" (Genesis 2.23)', in M. Fishbane and E. Tov, *'Sha'arei Talmon': Studies in the Bible, Qumran, and the Ancient Near East Presented to Shemaryahu Talmon* (Winona Lake, IN: Eisenbrauns, 1992).

Grabbe, L.L., *Judaic Religion in the Second Temple Period: Belief and Practice from the Exile to Yavneh* (London: Routledge, 2000).

Group from Rennes, 'An Approach to the Book of Jonah: Suggestions and Questions', *Semeia* 15 (1979), pp. 85-96 (translation of 'Approahe du livre de Jonas: propositions et questions', *Sémiotique et bible* 7 [1977], pp. 30-38).

Gruber, M.I., 'The Motherhood of God in Second Isaiah', in *The Motherhood of God and Other Studies* (Atlanta, GA: Scholars Press, 1992), pp. 3-15.

Gunn, D.M., and D.N. Fewell, *Narrative in the Hebrew Bible* (Oxford: Oxford University Press, 1993), pp. 129-46.

Halpern, B., and R.E. Friedman, 'Composition and Paronomasia in Jonah', *HAR* 4 (1980), pp. 79-92.

Hamel, G., 'Taking the Argo to Nineveh: Jonah and Jason in a Mediterranean Context', *Jud* 44 (1995), pp. 341-59.

Hamiel, Ch.Y., 'דין רחמים בספר יונה', *Beit Mikra* 36 (1990–91), pp. 323-34.

Hanks, W.F., 'Discourse Genres in a Theory of Practice', *American Ethnologist* 14 (1987), pp. 668-92.

Harrison, B., 'The Strangeness of Leviticus', *Jud* 48 (1999), pp. 208-228.

Hauser, A.J., 'Jonah: In Pursuit of the Dove', *JBL* 104 (1985), pp. 21-37.

Heschel, A., *The Prophets* (2 vols.; New York: Harper & Row, 1975 [1962]).

Hill, C., *The English Bible and the Seventeenth Century Revolution* (London: Penguin Books, 1994).

Holbert, J.C., ' "Deliverance Belongs to YAHWEH!" Satire in the Book of Jonah', *JSOT* 21 (1981), pp. 59-81.

Holgrem, F.C., 'Israel, the Prophets and the Book of Jonah', *CurrTM* 21 (1994), pp. 127-32.

Hoop, R. de, 'The Book of Jonah as Poetry: An Analysis of Jonah 1:1-16', in W. van der Meer and H.C. de Moor (eds.), *Structural Analysis of Biblical and Canaanite Poetry* (JSOTSup, 74; Sheffield: JSOT Press, 1988), pp. 156-71.

Howell, M., 'A Prophet Who Pouts', *Bible Today* 33 (1995), pp. 75-78.

Hurvitz, A., 'The History of a Legal Formula כל אשר חפץ עשה (Psalms cxv 3, cxxxv 6)', *VT* 32 (1982), pp. 257-67.

Ibn Ezra, A., *Commentary: According to Miqraot Gedolot with Malbim's Commentary* (ed. R.J. Buch and A. Buch; Jerusalem: Re'em, 1964).

Jones, B.A., *The Formation of the Book of the Twelve: A Study in Text and Canon* (SBLDS, 149; Atlanta: Scholars Press, 1995).

—'The Book of the Twelve as a Witness to Ancient Biblical Interpretation', in J.D. Nogalski and Sweeney (eds.), *Book of the Twelve*, pp. 65-74.

Joüon, P. and T. Muraoka, *A Grammar of Biblical Hebrew* (originally by P. Joüon and translated and revised by T. Muraoka (Rome: Editrice Pontificio Biblico, 1991).

Kahn, Paul, 'An Analysis of the Book of Jonah', *Jud* 43 (1994), pp. 87-100.

Kahn, Pinchas, 'The Epilogue to Jonah', *JBQ* 28 (2000), pp. 146-55.

Kaufmann, Y., תולדות האמונה הישראלית (4 vols.; Tel Aviv: Mosad Bialik, 1938–56).

Kidner, F.W., 'The Distribution of the Divine Names in Jonah', *TynBul* 21 (1970), pp. 126-28.

Knoppers, G.N., ' "Great among His Brothers" but Who Is He? Heterogeneity in the Composition of Judah', *JHS* 3.4 (2000) (available at www.purl.org/jhs and www.jhsonline.org).

—'Intermarriage, Social Complexity, and Ethnic Diversity in the Genealogy of Judah', *JBL* 120 (2001), pp. 15-30.

Kraeling, E.G., 'The Evolution of the Story of Jonah', in *Hommages à Andre Dupont-Sommer* (Paris: Adrien-Maisonneuve, 1971), pp. 305-18.

Kraemer, D., 'The Intended Reader as a Key to Interpreting the Bavli', *Prooftexts* 13 (1993), pp. 125-40.

Krašovec, J., 'Salvation of the Rebellious Prophet Jonah and of the Penitent Heathen Sinners', *SEÅ* 61 (1996), pp. 53-75.

Krüger, T., 'Literarisches Wachstum und theologische Diskussion im Jona-Buch', *BN* 59 (1991), pp. 57-88.

LaCoque, A., and Lacocque, P.-E., *Jonah: A Psycho-Religious Approach to the Prophet* (Columbia, SC: University of South Carolina Press, 1990).

Landes, G., 'Jonah: A Masal?', in J.G. Gammie *et al.* (eds.) *Israelite Wisdom: Theological and Literary Essays in Honor of Samuel Terrien* (Missoula, MT: Scholars Press, 1978).

—'Linguistic Criteria and the Date of the Book of Jonah', *Eretz Israel* 16 (Orlinsky Volume, 1982), pp. 147*-70.*

—'A Case for the Sixth-Century BCE Dating for the Book of Jonah', in P.H. Williams Jr and T. Hiebert (eds.), *Realia Dei: Essays in Archaeology and Biblical Interpretation in Honor of Edward F. Campbell, Jr. at his Retirement* (Atlanta: Scholars Press, 1999), pp. 100-116.

—'Textual "Information Gaps" and "Dissonances" in the Interpretation of the Book of Jonah', in R. Chazan, W.W. Hallo and L.H. Schiffman (eds.), *Ki Baruch Hu : Ancient Near Eastern, Biblical, and Judaic Studies in Honor of Baruch A. Levine* (Winona Lake, IN: Eisenbrauns, 1999), pp. 273-93.

Lehmann, M.R. 'הרקע להתנהגותו של יונה נביא על־פי מקורות מקראיים', *Beit Mikra* 35 (1999), pp. 348-50.

Levine, B.A., 'The Place of Jonah in the History of Biblical Ideas', in Cook and Winter (eds.), *Nineveh*, pp. 201-17.

Levine, E., *The Aramaic Version of Jonah* (New York: Sepher-Hermon Press, 3rd edn, 1981).

—'Jonah as a Philosophical Book', *ZAW* 96 (1984), pp. 235-45.

Lewis, Ch., 'Jonah—A Parable for our Time', *Jud* 21 (1972), pp. 159-63.

Lillegard, D., 'Narrative and Paradox in Jonah', *Kerux* 8.3 (1993), pp. 19-30.

Limburg, J., *Jonah* (OTL; Louisville, KY: Westminster/John Knox Press, 1993).

Linafelt, T., and T.K. Beal (eds.), *God in the Fray: A Tribute to Walter Brueggemann* (Philadelphia: Fortress Press, 1998).

Lohfink, N., 'Jonah ging zur Stadt hinaus (Jon. 4,5)', *BZ* 5 (1961), pp. 185-203.

Longacre, R.E., 'Interpreting Biblical Stories', in T.A. van Dijk (ed.), *Discourse and Discourse Literature* (Amsterdam: John Benjamins Publishing Co., 1985), pp. 169-85.

Longacre, R.E., and Shin Ja J. Hwang, 'A Textlinguistic Approach to the Biblical Hebrew Narrative of Jonah', in R.D. Bergen (ed.), *Biblical Hebrew and Discourse Linguistics* (Summer Institute of Linguistics: Dallas, 1994).

Lowden, J., *Early Christian and Byzantine Art* (London: Phaidon Press, 1997).

Luther, M., 'Lectures on Jonah', the German Text (1526), in *Luther's Works*, XIX (St Louis: Concordia Publishing House, 1974), pp. 32-104.

—'Lectures on Jonah', the Latin Text (1525), in *Luther's Works*, XIX (St Louis: Concordia Publishing House, 1974), pp. 1-31.

Magonet, J.D., *Form and Meaning: Studies in Literary Techniques in the Book of Jonah* (Sheffield: Almond Press, 1983).

—'The Names of God in Biblical Narratives', in Jon Davies, Graham Harvey and Wilfred G.E. Watson (eds.), *Words Remembered, Texts Renewed: Essays in Honour of John F.A. Sawyer* (JSOTSup, 196; Sheffield: Sheffield Academic Press, 1995), pp. 80-96.

—'Book of Jonah', in J.H. Hayes (ed.), *Dictionary of Biblical Interpretation* (Nashville: Abingdon Press, 1999), pp. 620-22.

Marcus, D., *From Balaam to Jonah: Anti-prophetic Satire in the Hebrew Bible* (BJS, 301; Atlanta: Scholars Press, 1995).

—'Nineveh's "Three Days' Walk" (Jonah 3:3): Another Interpretation', in Cook and Winter (eds.), *Nineveh*, pp. 42-53.

Mather, J., 'The Comic Art of the Book of Jonah', *Soundings* 65 (1982), pp. 280-91.

Mathews, T.F., *The Clash of Gods. A Reinterpretation of Christian Art* (Princeton, NJ: Princeton University Press, 1993).

McKeating, H., 'Ezekiel the "Prophet Like Moses"', *JSOT* 61 (1994), pp. 97-109.

McKenzie, S.L., *The Trouble with Kings: The Composition of the Book of Kings in the Deuteronomistic History* (VTSup, 42; Leiden: E.J. Brill, 1991).

Mehlman, B.H., and D.F. Polish (trans.), 'Midrash Jonah', *CCARJ* 24.1 (1977), pp. 30-41.

Mekilta de-Rabbi Ishmael, I (ed. J.Z. Lauterbach; Philadelphia: Jewish Publication Society of America, 1933).

Michaels, L., 'Jonah', in Rosenberg (ed.), *Congregation*, pp. 232-37.

Midrash Rabbah, Lamentations (trans. A. Cohen; Hindhead, Surrey: Soncino Press, 3rd edn, 1993).

Miles, J.A., 'Laughing at the Bible: Jonah as Parody', *JQR* 65 (1975), pp. 168-81 (reprinted in Y.T. Radday and A. Brenner [eds.], *On Humour and the Comic in the Hebrew Bible* [JSOTSup, 92; Sheffield: Almond Press, 1990], pp. 203-15).

Miller, C.L., K.M. Craig and R.F. Person, 'Conversation Analysis and the Book of Jonah: A Conversation', *JHS* 1 (1996–97) (available at www.purl.org/jhs and www.jhsonline.org).

Moberly, R.W.L., ' "God Is Not Human That He Should Repent' (Numbers 23:19 and 1 Samuel 15:29)', in Linafelt and Beal (eds.), *God in the Fray*, pp. 112-23.

Moore, C.A., *Tobit* (AB 40A; New York, NY: Doubleday, 1996).

Muffs, Y., *Love and Joy: Law, Language and Religion in Ancient Israel* (New York: Jewish Theological Seminary of America, 1992).

Mulzer, M., 'ספינה (Jona 1,5) "(gedeckter) Laderaum"', *BN* 104 (2000), pp. 83-94.

Mutius, Hans-Georg von, 'Eine nichtmasoretische Lesung in Jona 1,5 bei Abraham Bar Chijja von Barcelona (11./12.Jrh.)', *BN* 105 (2000), pp. 12-15.

Na'aman, N., 'Habiru and Hebrews: The Transfer of a Social Term to the Literary Sphere', *JNES* 45 (1986), pp. 271-88.

—'The Contribution of Royal Inscriptions for a Re-evaluation of the Book of Kings as a Historical Source', *JSOT* 82 (1999), pp. 3-17.

Newsome, J.D., Jr, *The Hebrew Prophets* (Atlanta: John Knox Press, 1984).

Nicacci, A., 'Syntactic Analysis of Jonah', *LA* 46 (1996), pp. 9-32.

Niclós, J.-V., 'Comentario al profeta Jonás de Abraham Ibn Ezra y la liturgia del perdón', *EstBíb* 53 (1999), pp. 483-515.

Nielsen, E., 'Le message primitif du livre de Jonas', *RHPR* 59 (1979), pp. 499-507.

Nogalski, J., *Redactional Processes in the Book of the Twelve* (BZAW, 218; Berlin: W. de Gruyter, 1993)

Nogalski, J.D., and M.A. Sweeney (eds.), *Reading and Hearing the Book of the Twelve* (Symposium, 15; Atlanta: Society of Biblical Literature, 2000).

O'Kane, M., 'Isaiah: A Prophet in the Footsteps of Moses', *JSOT* 69 (1996), pp. 29-51.

Orth, M., 'Genre in Jonah: The Effects of Parody in the Book of Jonah', in W.W. Hallo *et al.* (eds.), *The Bible in the Light of Cuneiform Literature: Scripture in Context III* (Lewiston, NY: Edward Mellen Press, 1990), pp. 257-81.

Payne, D.F., 'Jonah from the Perspective of its Audience', *JSOT* 13 (1979), pp. 3-12.

Pearson, R.F., *In Conversation with Jonah: Conversation Analysis, Literary Criticism and the Book of Jonah* (JSOTSup, 220; Sheffield: Sheffield Academic Press, 1996).

Peleg, Y., 'עוד ארבעים יום נינוה נהפכת' (יונה ג' 4) (שתי קריאות—בספר יונה)', *Beit Mikra* 44 (1999), pp. 226-43.

Peli, M., 'The Literary Art of Jonah', *HS* 20-21 (1979–80), pp. 18-29.

—'יונה כסיפור אומנותי', *Beit Mikra* 39 (1994), pp. 210-21.

Perdue, L.G., 'The Israelite and Early Jewish Family: Summary and Conclusions', in Perdue *et al.* (eds.), *Families in Ancient Israel*, pp. 163-222.

—'The Household, Old Testament Theology, and Contemporary Hermeneutics', in Perdue *et al.* (eds.), *Families in Ancient Israel* (Louisville, KY: Westminster Knox Press, 1997), pp. 223-57.

Perdue, L.G., J. Blenkinsopp, J.J. Collins and C. Meyers (eds.), *Families in Ancient Israel* (Louisville, KY: Westminster/John Knox Press, 1997).

Pesch, R., 'Zur konzentrischen Struktur von Jona 1', *Bib* 47 (1966), pp. 577-81.

Porten, B., 'Baalshamem and the Date of the Book of Jonah', in M. Carrez *et al.* (eds.), *De la Tôrah au Messie: Etudes d'exégèse et d'herméneutique bibliques offertes à Henri Cazelles pour ses 25 années d'enseignement à l'Institut Catholique de Paris, octobre 1979* (Paris: Desclée, 1981), pp. 237-44.

Qimron, E., 'לשנו של ספר יונה כמדד לקביעת זמן חיבורו', *Beit Mikra* 25 (1980), pp. 181-82.

Radak, *Commentary*. Miqraot Gedolot (*see* Ibn Ezra).

Rashi, *Commentary*. Miqraot Gedolot (*see* Ibn Ezra).

Ratner, R.J., 'Jonah, the Runaway Servant', *Maarav* 5–6 (1990), pp. 281-305.

Redditt, P.L., 'The Production and Reading of the Book of the Twelve', in Nogalski and Sweeney (eds.), *Book of the Twelve*, pp. 11-33.

Redford, D.B., 'Scribe and Speaker', in Ben Zvi and M.H. Floyd (eds.), *Writings and Speech*, pp. 145-218.

Renkema, J., *Discourse Studies* (Amsterdam: John Benjamins, 1993).

Rimmon-Kenan, Sh., *Narrative Fiction: Contemporary Poetics* (London: Methuen, 1983).

Rofé, A., *The Prophetic Stories* (Jerusalem: Magnes Press, 1988).

Roffey, J.H., 'God's Truth, Jonah's Fish: Structure and Existence in the Book of Jonah', *AusBR* 36 (1988), pp. 1-18.

Rosen, N., 'Jonah. Justice for Jonah, or a Bible Bartleby', in Rosenberg (ed.), *Congregation*, pp. 222-31.

Rosenberg, D. (ed.), *Congregation: Contemporary Writers Read the Jewish Bible* (New York: Harcourt Brace Jovanovich, 1987).

Rüdiger, L., *Jona: Prophet zwischen Verweigerung und Gehorsam. Eine erzählanalytische Studie* (FRLANT, 162; Göttingen: Vandenhoeck & Ruprecht, 1994).

Rusch, G., 'Comprehension vs. Understanding of Literature', in S. Tötösy de Zepetnek and I. Sywenky (eds.), *The Systemic and Empirical Approach to Literature and Culture as Theory and Application* (Siegen: Siegen University Press, 1997), pp. 107-19.

Salters, R.B., *Jonah and Lamentations* (OTG; Sheffield: Sheffield Academic Press, 1994).

Sasson, J.M., *Jonah* (AB, 24B; New York: Doubleday, 1990).

Scarlett, W., 'The Book of Jonah—Exposition', *IB*, VI, pp. 869-94.

Schart, A., 'Reconstructing the Redaction History of the Twelve Prophets: Problems and Models', in Nogalski and Sweeney (eds.), *Book of the Twelve*, pp. 34-48.

Schmidt, L., *'De Deo': Studien zur Literakritik und Theologie des Buches Jona, des Gespraches zwischen Abraham und Jahwe in Gen 18.22ff. und von Hi 1* (BZAW, 143, Berlin: W. de Gruyter, 1976).

Schneider, D., 'The Unity of the Book of the Twelve' (PhD diss., Yale University, 1979, UMI order no. 7926847).

Schniedewind W.M., 'Qumran Hebrew as an Antilanguage', *JBL* 118 (1999), pp. 235-52.

Schökel, A.L., and J. Mateos (eds.), *Nueva Biblia Española* (Madrid: Ediciones Cristiandad, 1976).

Schöpflin, K., 'Notschrei, Dank und Disput: Beten im Jonahbuch', *Bib* 78 (1997), pp. 389-404.

Schumann, S., 'Jona und die Weishet: Das prophetische Wort in einer zwedeutigen Wirklichkeit', *TZ* 45 (1989), pp. 73-80.

Schwartzman S.D., and J.D. Spiro, *The Living Bible: A Topical Approach to the Jewish Scriptures* (New York: Union of American Hebrew Congregations, 1962).

Seitz, C.R., 'The Prophet Moses and the Canonical Shape of Jeremiah', *ZAW* 101 (1989), pp. 3-27.

Seltzer, A.J., 'Jonah in the Belly of the Great Fish: The Birth of Messiah Ben Joseph', *JNSL* 25 (1999), pp. 187-203.

Sherwood, Y., 'Rocking the Boat: Jonah and New Historicism', *Bib Int* 5 (1997), pp. 364-402.

—'Cross-Currents in the Book of Jonah: Some Jewish and Cultural Midrashim on a Traditional Text', *Bib Int* 6 (1998), pp. 49-79.

—*A Biblical Text and its Afterlives: The Survival of Jonah in Western Culture* (Cambridge: Cambridge University Press, 2000)

Shusman, A., ‚קווים אלגוריים, תאולוגיים ופולמוסיים בפירוש לספר יונה מאת ר' תנחום הירושלמי', *Pa'amim* 59 (1994), pp. 85-104.

Shy, H., *Tanhum HaYerushalmi's Commentary on the Minor Prophets: A Critical Edition with an Introduction* (Jerusalem: Magnes Press, 1991).

Siedlecki, A., 'The Empire Writes Back: Diplomatic Correspondence in Ezra 4–6' (paper presented at the 2001 Annual Meeting of the PNW-SBL held in Edmonton, AB).

Simon, U., 'Minor Characters in Biblical Narrative', *JSOT* 46 (1990), pp. 11-19.

—מקרא לישראל) יונה עם מבוא ופירוש; Tel Aviv: Am Oved, 1992).

—*Jonah* (JPS Bible Commentary; Philadelphia: The Jewish Publication Society of America, 1999).

Simpson, W., *The Jonah Legend* (London: Grant Richards, 1971 [1899]).

Skehan, P.W., and A.D. Di Lella, *The Wisdom of Ben Sira* (AB, 39; New York: Doubleday, 1987).

Smart, J.D., 'The Book of Jonah—Introduction and Exegesis', *IB*, VI, pp. 689-94.

Smelik, K.A.D., 'The Literary Function of Poetical Passages in Biblical Narrative: The Case of Jonah 2:3-10', in W. Dijk. (ed.), *Give Ear to my Words: Psalms and Other Poetry in and around the Hebrew Bible. Essays in Honour of Professor N.A. van Uchelen* (Amsterdam: Kamp Societas Hebraica, 1996), pp. 147-51.

Smith, M., *Palestinian Parties and Politics That Shaped the Old Testament* (New York: Columbia University Press, 1971).

Snyder, G.F., 'Sea Monsters in Early Christian Art', *BR* 44 (1999), pp. 7-21.

Spangenberg, I.J.J., 'Jonah and Qohelet: Satire Versus Irony', *OTE* 9 (1996), pp. 495-511.

Steffen, U., *Die Jona-Geschichte: Ihre Auslegung und Darstellung im Judentum, Christentum und Islam* (Neukirchen–Vluyn: Neukirchener Verlag, 1994).

Sternberg, M., *The Poetics of Biblical Narrative* (Bloomington: Indiana University Press, 1987).

Stoebe, H.J., 'חמס', *TLOT*, I, pp. 437-39.

Stuart, D., *Hosea–Jonah* (WBC, 31; Waco, TX: Word Books, 1987).

Sweeney, M.A., *The Twelve Prophets* (2 vols.; Collegeville, MN: Liturgical Press, 2000).

—'Sequence and Interpretation in the Book of the Twelve', in Nogalski and Sweeney (eds.), *Book of the Twelve*, pp. 49-64.

Syrén, R., 'The Book of Jonah—A Reversed Diasporanovella?', *SEÅ* 58 (1993), pp. 7-14.

Szarmach, P.E., 'Three Versions of the Jonah Story: An Investigation of Narrative Technique in Old English Homilies', *Anglo-Saxon England* 1 (1972), pp. 183-92.

Talmon, S., 'דגים ובתולות־ים בספר יונה', *'Et HaDaat* 3 (1999), pp. 8-20.

Thompson, T.L., 'How Yahweh Became God: Exodus 3 and 6 and the Heart of the Pentateuch', *JSOT* 68 (1995), pp. 57-74.

—'Historiography in the Pentateuch: Twenty-five Years after Historicity', *SJOT* 13 (1999), pp. 258-83.

Tigay, J.H., *Deuteronomy* (JPS Commentary; Philadelphia: Jewish Publication Society of America, 1996).

Tov, E., 'The Literary History of the Book of Jeremiah in the Light of its Textual History', in J.H. Tigay (ed.), *Empirical Models for Biblical Criticism* (Philadelphia: University of Pennsylvania Press; 1985), pp. 211-37.

—*Textual Criticism of the Hebrew Bible* (Philadelphia: Fortress Press, 2nd edn, 2001).

Trible, P., 'Studies in the Book of Jonah' (PhD dissertation, Columbia University, 1963).

—*Rhetorical Criticism: Context Method and the Book of Jonah* (Guides to Biblical Scholarship; Philadelphia: Fortress Press, 1994).

—'The Book of Jonah', in L.E. Keck, D.L. Peterson *et al.* (eds.), *The New Interpreter's Bible* (Nashville, TN: Abingdon Press, 1996), pp. 463-529.

—'Divine Incongruities in the Book of Jonah', in Linafelt and Beal (eds.), *God in the Fray*, pp. 198-208.

—'A Tempest in a Text: Ecological Soundings in the Book of Jonah', in Cook and Winter (eds.), *Nineveh*, pp. 187-200.

Tucker, G.M., *Form Criticism of the Old Testament* (Guides to Biblical Scholarship; Philadelphia: Fortress Press, 1988).

Ulrich, E. *et al.* (eds.), *Qumran Cave 4: The Prophets* (DJD, 15; Oxford: Oxford University Press, 1997).

Urbach, E., 'תשובת אנשי נינוה והויכוח יהודי־נוצרי', *Tarbiz* 20 (1949–50), pp. 118-22.

van Dijk, T.A., *Macrostructures* (Hillsdale, NJ: Erlbaum, 1980).

van Dijk, T.A., and W. Kintsch, *Strategies of Discourse Comprehension* (New York: Academic Press, 1983).

Van Heerden, W., 'Humour and the Interpretation of the Book of Jonah', *OTE* 5 (1992), pp. 389-401.

Van Wijk-Bos, J.W.H., 'No Small Thing: The "Overturning" of Nineveh in the Third Chapter of Jonah', in Cook and Winter (eds.), *Nineveh*, pp. 218-37.

von Rad, G., 'The Deuteronomistic Theology of History in the Book of Kings', in *Studies in Deuteronomy* (SBT, 9; London: ACM Press, 1953), pp. 74-91.

Walsh, J., 'Jonah 2, 3-10: A Rhetorical Critical Study', *Bib* 63 (1982), pp. 219-29.

Waltke, B., and M. O'Connor, *An Introduction to Biblical Hebrew Syntax* (Winona Lake, IN: Eisenbrauns, 1990).

Walton, J.H., 'The Object Lesson of Jonah 4:5-7 and the Purpose of the Book of Jonah', *BBR* 2 (1992), pp. 47-57.

Watts, J.W., *Psalm and Story: Inset Hymns in Hebrew Poetry* (JSOTSup, 139; Sheffield: Sheffield Academic Press, 1992).

—'Song and Ancient Reader', *Perspectives in Religious Studies* 22 (1995), pp. 135-47.

Watts, J.W., and P.R. House (eds.), *Forming Prophetic Literature: Essays on Isaiah and the Twelve in Honor of John D.W. Watts* (JSOTSup, 235; Sheffield: Sheffield Academic Press, 1996).

Weimar, P., 'Beobachtungen zur Enstehung der Jonaerzälung', *BN* 18 (1982), pp. 86-109.

—'Literarische Kritik und Literarkritik: Unzeitgemässe Beobachtungen zu Jon 1:4-16', in L. Ruppert *et al.* (eds.) *Künder des Wortes: Beiträge zur Theologie der Propheten, Josef Schreiner zum 60ten Geburtstag* (Würzburg: Echter Verlag, 1982), pp. 217-35.

—'Jon 2, 1-11: Jonapsalm and Jonaerzählung', *BZ* 28 (1984), pp. 43-68.

Wellhausen, J., *Skizzen und Vorarbeiten.* V. *Die Kleinen Propheten* (Berlin: Georg Reimer, 1892).

Wendland, E.R., 'Text Analysis and the Genre of Jonah', *JETS* 39 (1996), pp. 191-206.

—'Text Analysis and the Genre of Jonah (part 2)', *JETS* 39 (1996), pp. 373-95.

—'Recursion and Variation in the "Prophecy" of Jonah: On the Rhetorical Impact of Stylistic Technique in Hebrew Narrative Discourse, with Special Reference to Irony and Enigma', *AUSS* 35 (1997), pp. 67-98.

—'Recursion and Variation in the 'Prophecy' of Jonah: On the Rhetorical Impact of Stylistic Technique in Hebrew Narrative Discourse, with Special Reference to Irony and Enigma (Part Two)', *AUSS* 35 (1997), pp. 189-209.

West, M., 'Irony in the Book of Jonah: Audience Identification with the Hero', *Perspectives in Religious Studies* 11 (1984), pp. 233-42.

Westermann, C., 'עבד Servant', *TLOT*, II, pp. 819-32.

Whedbee, J.W., *The Bible and the Comic Vision* (Cambridge: Cambridge University Press, 1998).

Wierenga, E.R., *The Nature of God: An Inquiry into Divine Attributes* (Ithaca, NY: Cornell University Press, 1989).

Willis, J.T., 'The "Repentance" of God in the Books of Samuel, Jeremiah and Jonah', *HBT* 16 (1994), pp. 156-75.

Wilt, T.L, 'Lexical Repetition in Jonah', *Journal of Translation and Textlinguistics* 5 (1992), pp. 252-64.

—'Jonah: A Battle of Shifting Alliances', in Davies and Clines (eds.), *Among the Prophets*, pp. 164-82.

Wineman, A., 'The Zohar on Jonah: Radical Retelling or Tradition?', *HS* 31 (1990), pp. 57-69.

Winslow, K.S., 'Ethnicity and Exogamy in the Bible' (paper presented at the 2000 annual meeting of the PNW-SBL, held in Spokane, WA).

Winter, S.C., 'A Fifth Century Christian Commentary on Jonah', in Cook and Winter (eds.), *Nineveh*, pp. 238-56.

Wolff, H.W., *Obadiah and Jonah: A Commentary* (Minneapolis, MN: Augsburg, 1986 [German, 1977]).

Woodward, B.L., 'Death in Life: The Book of Jonah and Biblical Tragedy', *GTJ* 11 (1990), pp. 3-16.

The Works of Saint Cyril of Jerusalem (trans. L.P. McCauley and A.A. Stephenson; Fathers of the Church. A New Translation, 61, 64; 2 vols.; Washington, DC: Catholic University of America, 1969, 1970).

Zapff, B.M, 'Die Völkerperspektive des Michabuches als "Systematisierung" der divergierenden Sicht der Völker in den Büchern Joël, Jona und Nahum? Überlegungen zu einer buchübergreifenden Exegese im Dodekapropheton', *BN* 98 (1999), pp. 86-99 (German version of preceding article).

—'The Perspective of the Nations in the Book of Micah as a "Systematization" of the Nations' role in Joel, Jonah and Nahum? Reflections on a Context-Oriented Exegesis in the Book of the Twelve', *SBLSP* 38 (1999), pp. 596-616.

Zlotowitz, M., *Yonah/Jonah: A New Translation with a Commentary Anthologized from Talmudic, Midrashic and Rabbinic Sources* (Brooklyn, NY: Mesorah Publications, 2nd edn, 1980).

INDEXES

INDEX OF REFERENCES

BIBLE

Genesis		34.6-7	21, 28,	29.22	21
4.16	73		108, 111	31.16-21	18, 36
5	46	34.6	56	32.21	126
6.7	36	34.12	90	32.30	68
6.11	53			34.10	88, 91
6.13	53	*Leviticus*			
8.11-12	41	5.7	41	*Joshua*	
8.20	122	5.11	41	1.8	10
16	69	19.2	102	24.29	66
16.5	70	25.35-43	68		
16.9	69	25.42	66, 72	*Judges*	
16.11	69, 70	25.55	66	2.14	68
18–19	17, 42			3.8	68
18.20-33	78, 79	*Numbers*		4.2	68
18.20	17, 21	11.10-15	72	6.15	87
18.23-33	42	11.15	72	10.7	68
24.7	108	12.6-8	88, 91		
24.14	66	14.18	21, 28,	*Ruth*	
25.24	66		108, 111	4.18-22	86
39	69	14.24	66		
		16.33	140	*1 Samuel*	
Exodus		23.19	29, 58, 60,	2.1-10	83
3.11	87		111	12.9	68
14.16	109			15.10	90
14.22	109	*Deuteronomy*		15.11	36
14.31	66	10.14	68	15.29	29, 58,
15.11	12	15.12-18	68		111, 121
15.19	109	18.21-22	62, 111	25.10	70
21.2-11	68	21.7-8	89	25.17	34
21.20	68	21.8	75		
32.7-14	78	21.10-14	9, 68	*2 Samuel*	
32.12	75, 88	23.16-17	71, 75-77,	3.18	66
32.14	60, 75, 88		124	7.4	90
32.24	88	24.15	68		

INDEX OF AUTHORS

This JSOTS book forms part of the *Journal for the Study of the Old Testament* series

We also publish

Journal for the Study of the Old Testament
Edited by
John Jarick, *University of Oxford, UK*
Keith Whitelam, *University of Sheffield, UK*

You can read about the most up-to-date scholarship and research on the Old Testament by subscribing to the *Journal for the Study of the Old Testament*, which is published five times a year. The fifth issue comprises of the *Society for Old Testament Study Book List*, a book containing reviews of the most important works being published on the Old Testament from authors and publishers world-wide.

The *Journal for the Study of the Old Testament* is published by Sheffield Academic Press, a Continuum imprint and you can find out more including current subscription prices by visiting:

www.continuumjournals.com/jsot

FREE Sample Copy
Please request a no obligation sample copy by contacting:

Orca Journals
FREEPOST (SWB 20951)
3 Fleets Lane, Stanley House
Poole, Dorset BH15 3ZZ
United Kingdom

Tel: +44 (0)1202 785712
Fax: +44 (0)1202 666219
Email: journals@orcabookservices.co.uk

OR

Visit **www.continuumjournals.com/jsot** and request a FREE sample copy from our website

SHEFFIELD ACADEMIC PRESS
A Continuum imprint
www.continuumjournals.com